Data Engineering for Beginners

Chisom Nwokwu

WILEY

To my parents, Mr. Osita & Dr. Mrs. Ngozi Nwokwu

Acknowledgments

First and foremost, I would like to thank God, the ultimate source of my wisdom and strength, for guiding me through every stage of my career and providing me with the clarity and direction I needed. He sustained and continually renewed my passion for teaching and writing through every chapter of this book and moments of self-doubt. I am grateful to him!

To my incredible managing editor, Navin Vijayakumar; my project manager, Connor O'Brien; and my technical editor, Arthur Augustus: thank you for being the steady hands behind this project. Your structure, feedback, and unwavering belief in this book's mission helped shape it into something I am proud of. You steadily ensured nothing fell through the cracks, making this work exceptional. Also, special thanks to Kenyon Brown for giving me an opportunity to work with Wiley on this project; it was truly an honor. I've learned so much through this experience as an author, and I look forward to future collaborations with Wiley.

To my amazing family, thank you for believing in me long before I believed in myself. Your love, sacrifices, and endless prayers laid the foundation for everything I do. You instilled in me the value of hard work, the discipline to follow through, and the courage to take bold steps. You have always been my greatest cheerleaders! And to my friends, my incredible support system, thank you for your never-ending encouragement toward all my endeavors and for being there to celebrate every small victory.

Finally, to every reader holding this book, thank you for trusting me to be part of your learning journey. I wrote this book with you in mind, hoping to make data engineering a little more accessible and a little less intimidating. I hope you find clarity in its pages.

About the Author

Chisom Nwokwu is a multitalented software engineer, published author, and digital creator. She's passionate about big data and artificial intelligence, and her expertise cuts across leveraging big data and cloud technologies to designing and developing scalable data platforms for organizations. She is currently contributing to the development of the next generation of systems that redefine how data powers large-scale AI model training.

Chisom holds a bachelor's degree in computer science and is currently pursuing a master's in computer science at the Georgia Institute of Technology. She has worked with some of the biggest international firms, such as Microsoft, where she was a Big Data Engineer on the Windows Engineering Team, and Bank of America, where she was a Technology Analyst on the Robotics and Automation Team.

As someone who has made tremendous progress in her career in a short period, she was nominated as a Rising Star of the Year by the Women Tech Network, Author of the Year by Women Business Awards, and a finalist for the Young Digital Woman of the Year Award by Digital Women UK.

In addition to her professional achievements, Chisom is an accomplished public speaker and technology thought-leader, playing a pivotal role in the global tech scene.

About the Technical Editor

Arthur Augustus is a distinguished software engineer and technical leader with a proven track record of designing and deploying high-impact systems at scale. With over a decade of experience spanning fintech, logistics, consulting, and sustainability, Arthur has consistently delivered engineering solutions that drive business value and technological innovation. He has led end-to-end architecture and implementation of real-time logistics systems and intelligent matchmaking engines to large-scale data experimentation frameworks powered by generative AI.

At Microsoft, Arthur was part of the Sustainability team, where he collaborated closely with OEM partners to embed energy efficiency directly into Windows. He also led the development of orchestration tooling that now underpins data pipelines processing telemetry from millions of devices globally.

Arthur's contributions extend beyond the industry. He teaches systems design to undergraduate students and mentors aspiring engineers. When he isn't writing code, you can find him enjoying a Netflix classic!

Contents at a Glance

Contents

Foreword

Over the past decade, I've worked across the spectrum of data-driven organizations—from nimble startups to global tech leaders. In that time, I've collaborated with data engineers, leaders, product managers, and countless others who rely on data to make decisions. Through both professional experience and online engagement with aspiring data engineers, I've noticed one recurring theme: confusion. Again and again, the same question surfaces: Who exactly is a data engineer, and what do they do?

I only wish this book had existed when I was starting out. It would've saved me countless hours lost in confusion and dead ends. Chisom Nwokwu delivers a rare combination: comprehensive coverage of data engineering, grounded in clarity, relevance, and real-world experience.

Each chapter invites readers deeper into the world of data engineering—from broad concepts to advanced techniques, all the way to practical steps for entering the field. With a thoughtful structure, well-chosen topics, and clear, accessible examples, this book makes the journey both exciting and informative. It's remarkable how much Chisom has packed into just a bit over 300 pages.

With data volumes growing exponentially, and businesses racing to turn information into a competitive edge—especially in the age of artificial intelligence—data engineering has become indispensable . . . and so has the knowledge captured in this book.

Whether you're just stepping into the world of data engineering or looking to sharpen your understanding of the role, this book delivers clarity, depth, and practical insight in equal measure. Chisom has created something special:

a resource that's both technically solid and genuinely enjoyable to read. I'm confident it will inspire many to not only understand the field but to thrive in it. Enjoy the journey.

—Slawomir Tulski,
Data Engineering Manager, Meta (Prev)

Introduction

Data is more than just numbers and text; it's the foundation of modern decision-making, innovation, and intelligent systems. Data is everywhere, from the personalized recommendations we see online while shopping to the analytics that drive billion-dollar businesses. But data alone isn't enough. Behind the scenes are professionals who collect, clean, transform, and deliver data where it needs to go. These professionals are data engineers, and this book is your invitation to learn about data engineering.

The field of data engineering is growing at lightning speed, especially with the rise of artificial intelligence systems, which rely on quality data. Many people are eager to break into this field but find it difficult to navigate their learning journey. Others may already be working in tech- or data-adjacent roles but lack the foundational understanding of how modern data systems are designed, built, and maintained.

Data Engineering for Beginners is a comprehensive, beginner-friendly guide designed to help engineers, analysts, and industry professionals grasp the fundamentals of data engineering, learn necessary concepts with real-world scenarios, and ultimately launch a career with a well-defined roadmap.

This book is unique because it offers a clear and accessible introduction to complex and often intimidating concepts. Most resources on data engineering assume a certain level of prior knowledge or experience, making it difficult for true beginners to find a starting point.

I believe the strength of an engineer is understanding the rudiments of a topic, and that is what this book plans to achieve. It takes you on an intentional learning journey from understanding various data formats to designing databases, to learning how to secure data systems, to building architectures that scale.

With the rise of AI, data engineering has become even more popular. AI models also rely on vast amounts of high-quality data for training and operations, which would involve complex data processing and integration. Organizations are now keen on investing in data platforms and professionals who can manage those platforms, driving greater competition in the market.

What Does This Book Cover?

This book serves as a complete roadmap, starting from the basics and progressing to more advanced topics, providing a solid foundation for building your knowledge as you read.

Chapter 1: Understanding Data

This chapter explores the various forms of data: structured, semi-structured, and unstructured data, their advantages and their limitations. It also covers a brief history of data and the impact of data across several industries.

Chapter 2: Introduction to Data Engineering

This chapter introduces you to the world of data engineering, what it is, why it matters, and how it has evolved. You'll learn about the role of a data engineer, the key stages of the data engineering life cycle, and how engineers navigate stakeholder needs to deliver real business value.

Chapter 3: Database Fundamentals

This chapter covers the essentials of databases, what they are, and how they store data. You'll learn the difference between relational and NoSQL databases, and explore when to use each. We'll also introduce the major types of NoSQL databases and their use cases and explain the ACID principles that ensure data integrity. This chapter gives you the tools to choose and work with the right database for your project needs.

Chapter 4: SQL Fundamentals

After discussing relational databases, we need to learn how to interact with them. This chapter is all about mastering SQL, starting with the basics, then build up to more powerful tools and advanced techniques like subqueries and window functions. You'll also learn how to set up a SQL environment to practice writing and running your queries.

Chapter 5: Database Design

This chapter covers the principles of good schema design. We begin by exploring how to model data based on real-world requirements and best practices. You'll learn how to understand and apply cardinality, design entity relationship diagrams (ERDs), and make smart decisions about normalization and denormalization to balance performance with data integrity.

Chapter 6: Data Warehouses, Data Lakes, and Data Lakehouses

This chapter introduces you to the world of data storage at scale, focusing on data warehouses, data lakes, and the hybrid data lakehouse architecture. You'll learn how to design analytical models like star and snowflake schemas and explore data marts.

Chapter 7: Data Pipelines

In this chapter, you'll learn the core methods of ingesting data, from traditional batch loads to real-time streaming. You will learn concepts like windowing for managing time in streaming, and architectural patterns like Lambda that combine batch and stream processing. This chapter also unpacks data orchestration, scheduling, and automation.

Chapter 8: Data Quality

This chapter focuses on data quality. You'll learn about common causes of bad data and the real impact poor quality can have on business decisions and the key data quality dimensions.

Chapter 9: Data Security

In this chapter, you'll learn core security principles and how to safeguard data both at rest and in transit. The chapter covers key concepts like authentication and authorization, as well as the basics of encryption and data masking to keep sensitive information safe.

Chapter 10: Data Governance

This chapter unpacks the essential concept of data governance through a simple, relatable analogy. You'll learn about policies and processes that ensure data is managed responsibly and compliantly, along with common regulations.

Chapter 11: Big Data and Distributed Systems

This chapter introduces you to the exciting world of big data, starting with its fundamentals and the famous 5 V's—volume, velocity, variety, veracity, and value—that define big data challenges. You'll also explore popular big data frameworks like Apache Spark and Hadoop.

Chapter 12: Data Engineering on the Cloud

In this chapter, you'll start by understanding what the cloud is and how it compares to traditional on-premises setups for data storage and processing. The chapter breaks down cloud service models: IaaS, PaaS, and SaaS. You'll explore different storage types, object, block, and file storage, and learn how to leverage cloud compute services for data transformation.

Chapter 13: Building a Career in Data Engineering

This chapter gives you career tips. You'll have a clear understanding of the various data engineering roles available and how to identify which fits your skills and interests best. You'll learn strategies to ace interviews, including both technical challenges and behavioral questions.

Appendix: Sample Interview Questions

Get ready to test your knowledge! This appendix includes a curated set of common data engineering interview questions, complete with explanations. Topics span SQL, data modeling, pipeline design, and Apache Spark, giving you a well-rounded prep experience.

Data Engineering Glossary

To cap things off, you'll explore a glossary of key terms, tools, and acronyms.

Who Should Read This Book?

In 2021, I started a new role as a software engineer, which required me to build and manage data platforms. Before this role, I had little or no background in data. For the first few months, I struggled to understand a lot of concepts. While I was successful in my deliverables, my foundation was faulty. Driven by curiosity, I started asking questions, engaging with industry experts, and deepening my expertise in the field. This journey sparked a passion in me that inspired the creation of this book, to share the knowledge I had acquired.

This book is for curious beginners, anyone starting their career or pivoting into data engineering. This book was written specifically for you; it's a roadmap that gives you a solid starting point. It breaks down data engineering concepts with clear explanations and practical examples, giving you a strong foundation. I remember how intimidating it was when I first started, and I wanted to create something that feels like a friendly guide, not a textbook.

This book is also for software engineers, data analysts and scientists, and AI engineers in the room who keep hearing about data engineering at work but aren't quite sure what it entails. Maybe you're already writing SQL or deploying models but you don't understand how the data gets cleaned, transformed, and served to you. This book shows you what's happening behind the scenes, so you can speak the language, contribute more effectively to cross-functional teams, and create more impact in your role.

Then there are the career switchers, people who are trying to find their footing in tech. Data engineering is one of the most practical, foundational paths in the data world, and this book is your first step into the world of data, with no prior knowledge required.

Data Engineering for Beginners is both a learning tool and a reference that I hope you'll come back to again and again. It contains real-world examples, interview tips, and scenarios that reflect the day-to-day life of a data engineer, preparing you to thrive in your first role and throughout your data engineering career. It's written as a roadmap, so you can read each chapter sequentially or skip ahead if you're already conversant with those concepts. The labs are available to help you put your knowledge into practice.

Congratulations on taking your first step into data engineering, but it doesn't end here. Keep learning, growing, and building!

Understanding Data

Data is often referred to as the new oil. In today's world, data powers almost every decision we make and shapes the innovations that define industries. The word "data" is derived from the Latin word "datum" (singular), meaning "something given" or "a thing given." This reflects the idea that data consists of pieces of information that are provided or recorded as they are observed, without interpretation or analysis. In its original sense, a "datum" is a single fact or piece of evidence.

Data refers to raw, unorganized facts or information that can be processed or analyzed to derive meaning. These facts can be in the form of numbers, text, images, audio, or any other measurable elements. Data on its own does not have meaning until it is structured and interpreted. Once organized and processed, data can provide insights, inform decision-making, and be used for a variety of purposes, such as scientific research, business analytics, or technological development. In this chapter, we're going to explore the fundamentals of data and its different forms, and discuss its importance. This will build a solid foundation for subsequent chapters in this book.

WHAT YOU WILL LEARN IN THIS CHAPTER:

➤   The growing importance of data throughout history

➤   The advantages and limitations of different types of data

➤   How data is used in different industries

➤   The role of data engineering

A Brief History of Data

The first time I encountered the term "data" was in high school, and I heard it even more frequently in college. Instructors would often refer to data as "raw facts," which is accurate. However, the concept of data has evolved and holds different meanings for various individuals, particularly for older generations. The history of data stretches back much further than we often realize. Data has existed for centuries, in forms different from what we know today. Throughout history, people have continuously sought innovative ways to harness and benefit from data. Exploring the evolution of data over time, we can appreciate the impact data has had on science, technology, and social good.

Data in 19,000 BCE: The Great Baboon and Abacus

According to Wikipedia,[1] the first use of data dates back to 20,000 BCE, with the discovery of the Ishango bone in the Congo region. This tool was a baboon bone marked with notches, speculated by some scholars to have been used for counting or tracking, possibly representing one of the earliest forms of recorded data.

At that time, calculators, pens, and paper—things we take for granted today—did not yet exist. This prehistoric tool is considered the earliest known evidence of tallying, or recording, information. Another tool that was also common at this time was the abacus, which is quite familiar in our learning curricula today. The abacus is a simple device used for arithmetic calculations. It was believed to be invented by the Babylonians as early as 2400 BCE. The abacus was widely used in Asia and Europe for centuries and is still used today in some parts of the world.

Data in the 1600s: Public Health Statistics

In 1640, data began to gain some form of interpretation. John Grant, a hatmaker, started collecting information about deaths in London, information such as the number of deaths, mortality rates among age groups, and the cause of death. He conducted the first recorded experiment in statistical data analysis, and he was able to predict life expectancies, analyze death rates between genders, and eventually devise an early warning system for the bubonic plague, which was ravaging Europe at the time. London started issuing a weekly report called "Bills of Mortality." Grant became known as the Father of Statistics, laying a foundation for modern demographic research.

Data in the 1800s: The U.S. Census

In the 1800s, the emergence of data processing was prompted by the U.S. Census. The population was growing rapidly; the census process was becoming increasingly complex, and traditional methods of data collection and processing were no longer effective. Due to the volume of data, it was almost impossible to process information manually on time. To solve this problem, Herman Hollerith, a German American statistician and an employee of the U.S. Census Bureau, devised the Hollerith Tabulating Machine. This machine used punch cards to input data. A punch card is normally a type of stiff paper, onto which a machine would create holes in specific locations, and this could process data much more quickly than traditional methods. According to *Wired*,[2] the U.S. Census Bureau used a tabulating machine for the first time during the 1890 census, cutting processing time down from eight years to just two. This innovation not only saved the government millions in logistics costs but also improved accuracy by reducing human errors.

Data in the 1900s: The Concept of Storage

As data was now being processed in the 1800s, the concept of storage came up as there was an increasing need to store greater amounts of data to be collected and processed. To address this need, new storage technologies emerged such as magnetic tape and cloud storage, which played a significant role.

German engineer Fritz Pfleumer[3] invented the first magnetic tape in 1928. This technology allowed for data to be stored magnetically on tape, and it was used extensively for audio and video recordings. This idea inspired the invention of floppy disks and hard disk drives later on.

Dr. Joseph Carl Robnett Licklider, a visionary computer scientist, was considered one of the pioneers of cloud computing. According to the Internet Hall of Fame,[4] in the 1960s he introduced the idea of a network of interconnected computers capable of communicating and sharing resources. His groundbreaking concept eventually paved the way for cloud storage, which is now a vital technology for data storage and management.

In the 1970s, British computer scientist Edgar F. Codd developed the popular relational data management framework. This framework allowed for the storage and retrieval of data in a more efficient and structured manner, making it easier for organizations to manage large amounts of data.

Data in the 1990s: Data and the Internet

The advent of the Internet in the 1990s marked a major transformation in how data was collected, interpreted, and stored. It enabled the collection of a much broader array of data from diverse sources, which could then be shared and analyzed by individuals worldwide, regardless of geographic location. At this time, Tim Berners-Lee introduced the World Wide Web. Before the web was introduced, sharing information on the Internet was limited to computer experts, but Berners-Lee created a system whereby documents and resources could be linked together through hypertext, making it easy to navigate from one page to another. Now, people can access information, communicate, and collaborate on a global scale like never before. The World Wide Web became the backbone of the modern Internet.

Types of Data

Data is often categorized based on structure, format, or the context in which they are used. This is important to note because we interact with different types of data in different ways. Based on how data is structured (not the type of values it holds), here are some common categories.

Structured Data

Structured data refers to data that is highly organized and easily searchable in databases or spreadsheets. It follows a predefined model, typically with rows and columns. Each column has a specific data type (e.g., integers, dates, strings), and each row represents a unique record. This rigid structure ensures easy access and retrieval.

Examples of structured data include:

- Financial systems (e.g., banking transactions)
- Customer databases (e.g., CRM systems)
- Inventory management systems
- Log files from servers
- Excel spreadsheets

Structured data comes with a lot of advantages. It is neatly organized in rows and columns, making it easy to retrieve, query, and analyze with SQL and other traditional tools. The rigid schema ensures that data is consistent and accurate, and that it follows predefined formats, which helps maintain data integrity. Due to predefined schemas, structured data supports strong validation and data types, which helps maintain its integrity. In terms of scalability, databases that are structured are well established and can be highly scalable for specific applications like transaction processing.

> *Schema: A schema is a blueprint or structure that defines how data is organized in a database.*

> *Integrity: The accuracy, consistency, and reliability of data*

Structured data also has its limitations. Because structured data follows a strict schema, it lacks flexibility. Any changes to the structure, such as adding new columns, may require significant effort. It is also not well suited for handling rich, complex data like images, audio, or free-form text. Structured data also requires a defined schema upfront, which can limit how the data evolves in the future.

Unstructured Data

Unstructured data refers to data that doesn't have a predefined format or structure. This type of data is often text-heavy or multimedia content, and it requires more complex tools like natural language processing (NLP) or machine learning for analysis.

Examples of unstructured data include:

- Emails and chat messages
- Social media posts
- Multimedia content (images, videos, audio)
- Documents (PDFs, Microsoft Word files)

Unstructured data can include anything from text, images, and audio, to videos, making it extremely versatile. The majority of data generated today is unstructured, and this type of data can provide deeper insights when analyzed correctly (e.g., social media content, logs, or multimedia). Unlike structured data, unstructured data does not require a fixed schema, which allows for easy storage and flexibility in how the data is collected and stored. Unstructured data often contains valuable insights that go beyond the confines of structured data's rigid format, such as sentiment in text, behavior in logs, or patterns in images and video. Techniques like natural language processing (NLP), computer vision, and deep learning rely on unstructured data to derive insights.

Most times, unstructured data is difficult to analyze and extracting meaningful insights is complex and requires advanced techniques like machine learning, which can lead to significant computational resources and time compared to structured data. Unstructured data (e.g., large video files, logs) can also be massive in size, leading to storage issues and higher costs for storage systems. Without a schema to enforce validation and rules, unstructured data can lack integrity or consistency, making it harder to manage. Querying unstructured data often involves indexing and searching through large, complex datasets, which can be slow and require specialized algorithms.

Semi-structured Data

Semi-structured data is data that does not conform to a formal structure but that has some organizational properties that make it easier to parse. It doesn't adhere to a fixed schema, but it has tags, metadata, or markers that provide a loose structure. You can think of semi-structured data as a mixture of both structured and unstructured data.

Examples of semi-structured data include:

- JSON and XML files
- Email metadata
- HTML and web pages
- YAML files
- IoT/sensor data

Common formats like JavaScript Object Notation (JSON) and Extensible Markup Language (XML) are widely used for exchanging data across systems, especially in APIs. Like unstructured data, semi-structured data does not require a predefined schema, which allows for flexibility in storing and handling data of various types. Data formats like XML and JSON provide structure with tags, allowing for easier parsing and transformation compared to unstructured data. Let's look at an example of how data is represented in JSON and XML.

JSON is a format that represents data as key-value pairs. An object is a group of key-value pairs, enclosed in curly braces, {}. JSON is more structured than plain text but less rigid than a relational table:

```
{
  "name": "Ada",
  "age": 30,
  "isStudent": false
}
```

XML uses a tree-like structure made up of elements (tags), which can contain values, attributes, or other elements:

```
<person>
  <name>Ada</name>
  <age>30</age>
</person>
```

Semi-structured data can handle complex and nested data formats, making it suitable for modern applications. To address scalability issues, NoSQL databases and cloud storage systems are designed to efficiently store semi-structured data, often at scale.

While more organized than unstructured data, semi-structured data still requires parsing and processing techniques that are more complex than structured data querying. Querying and indexing semi-structured data can be less efficient than querying structured data in relational databases. Since semi-structured data can vary from record to record, it can lead to inconsistencies, making analysis and data integrity more difficult to maintain. While tools exist for processing semi-structured data, they are not as standardized or mature as those for structured data, meaning that handling this data can involve custom or specialized solutions. Table 1-1 compares structured, unstructured, and semi-structured data.

Table 1-1: Comparing Structured, Unstructured, and Semi-structured Data

FEATURE	STRUCTURED	UNSTRUCTURED	SEMI-STRUCTURED
Format	Tabular, fixed rows and columns like Excel sheets	Free-form, like plain text, images, or audio	Hierarchical or tagged format like JSON files
Schema	Rigid and predefined schema	No formal schema or metadata	Schema exists but is flexible and self-describing
Storage systems	Relational databases	Filesystems or object storage	NoSQL databases
Ease of analysis	Easy to analyze with SQL and business intelligence tools	Requires advanced methods like natural language processing (NLP)	Needs parsing, flattening, or schema-on-read tools

Why Is Data Important?

Data is no longer just a byproduct of operations—it's playing a critical role in key sectors worldwide, making it one of the most valuable assets. From healthcare to supply chain, and from transportation to artificial intelligence (AI), data is reshaping how decisions are made and creating a lot of value. Let's explore how data is impacting these sectors.

Healthcare

One of the most promising developments in modern healthcare is *predictive healthcare*, where algorithms use vast amounts of data to predict potential health risks before they happen. With this, a doctor treating a diabetic patient can analyze patterns in their blood sugar levels, lifestyle, and even family medical history. Data systems now flag early signs of complications, which allows doctors to intervene early and potentially prevent a severe health crisis.

Another area where data is making a significant impact is in clinical decision-making. The volume of medical research, treatment options, and patient outcomes is overwhelming for any individual doctor to keep up with. But by analyzing health data at scale, we can uncover trends and insights that would have been impossible to see. AI and machine learning models can now analyze thousands of medical records to identify which treatments work best for specific conditions or even uncover rare side effects of a drug that may not have been apparent in initial clinical trials, all with the help of data.

While these innovations are great, one of the biggest challenges in the healthcare industry has always been the difficulty of accessing up-to-date patient information. The problem isn't the lack of data but how fragmented it is across different systems. But now, with health data being integrated from multiple sources, healthcare providers have a comprehensive view of a patient's health, allowing them to provide more coordinated treatment.

Supply Chain

A supply chain is a network of people, activities, and resources involved in the creation and delivery of a product or service from the raw materials to the end customer. In supply chain management, a common challenge has been visibility. Companies have lacked real-time insights into where their products were, how they are moving, and when they were going to arrive. This lack of transparency creates a lot of inefficiencies and delays in the long run.

But with data, organizations have been able to set up real-time tracking using data from sensors, and Internet of Things (IoT) devices embedded in products and shipments, which has fundamentally changed how companies approach inventory management, helping them have more visibility on their processes. They can also predict exactly how much stock they need, where it should be stored, and when to replenish, thus reducing waste. During the global supply chain disruptions caused by the COVID-19 pandemic, data-driven insights became important. Companies that leveraged data to predict shipping delays were able to stay ahead of the curve and save costs.

Transportation and Logistics

Years ago, getting from point A to B was a complete hassle. But today, you can use your mobile device to book a ride and have a driver locate you seamlessly. Companies like Uber started building data systems that collect and analyze real-time data like location, traffic patterns, rider behavior, surge demand, and even weather conditions, making transportation smarter and more personalized.

The impact of data on transportation didn't end there. We're also seeing the rise of self-driving cars. These vehicles rely on huge amounts of sensor data, like cameras and GPS systems, to make split-second decisions. But it's not just about collecting that data—it's about learning from it. Every mile a self-driving car travels generates terabytes of data that feed back into machine learning models, helping the system get better at identifying obstacles. Before this, autonomous driving was just science fiction. Now, thanks to the constant flow of real-world driving data, we're getting closer to safe, driverless transportation at scale.

Artificial Intelligence

Data is the lifeblood that fuels the development of AI systems, and it's currently driving the rapid advancements we're seeing across AI today. When you think about AI and its evolution, especially when we talk about large language models (LLMs) or AI products, it's clear how far we've come in such a short time.

Earlier, AI was quite limited. For example, language models in their early days had difficulty understanding context and generating coherent text that made sense because the data they were trained on was very sparse and these models generated outputs that were far from perfect. As data volumes increased, we started to see massive datasets emerging—text, images, videos, and real-time information from a variety of sources, allowing AI models to train on much larger and more complex datasets.

For example, in LLMs, models like GPT have been able to learn billions of words across countless contexts, picking up on language, tone, and even cultural context. The real breakthrough came with the ability to use data to fine-tune models. Now, instead of general-purpose, one-size-fits-all AI systems, data allows us to tailor AI models to specific industries or problems. Data didn't just improve AI; it has evolved AI from basic automation tools to powerful systems that drive decision-making.

Data and Information

Initially, we defined data as raw, unprocessed facts and figures, but we also need to understand what information means. Information is data that has been processed, organized, and structured, giving a meaningful interpretation. In the digital world, information can be regarded as business financial reports, monthly bank statements, sales visualizations, and so much more. But before we can extract information, data must be processed and organized.

This is where data engineering comes in. It plays a critical role in transforming raw data into information and helps to ensure that raw data—often unstructured and scattered across various sources—is organized, cleaned, and transformed into a format that can be easily turned into actionable insights. When we discussed the importance of data in healthcare earlier, we mentioned that the greatest challenge health facilities faced was fragmented data. In hospitals, patient records are one of the most valuable, sensitive types of data, and you would typically have them scattered across electronic health records (EHRs), lab results, prescriptions, doctors' notes, and even data from wearables. If a patient relocates from one city to another, their medical records are scattered across different hospitals, specialists, and labs; because a centralized system doesn't exist for this, they would have to have multiple tests run all over again, which isn't efficient.

Another good example is the National Health Service (NHS) in the UK, which handles millions of patient records. Here, data engineers build the systems that collect all that messy data from different hospitals, GP clinics, and labs and make sure it flows into one place in a clean, organized, and secure way. Cleaning could involve removing duplicates (so one patient doesn't show up as two people); standardizing formats such as dates, names, and measurements so they're the same across records; handling missing data; and carrying out necessary transformations with the goal of getting high-quality data. Once the data is all in one place, doctors and nurses can access up-to-date and accurate records faster, which means better decisions for patients. Security is a huge part, too; data engineers help make sure only the right people can see the right information, which is extremely important for privacy.

Without data engineering, the journey from data to useful information would be inefficient, unreliable, and incomplete. Now that you have a good foundation, we'll dive deeper into this topic in our next chapter.

Summary

- Data refers to raw, unorganized facts or information that can be processed or analyzed to derive meaning.
- Data can be grouped into structured, unstructured, and semi-structured data.
- Structured data is organized in fixed formats like tables with predefined schemas. Examples are Excel spreadsheets.
- Unstructured data is raw, unorganized data in free-form formats. Examples are plain text, images, and audio.
- Semi-structured data has some organizational structure but flexible schemas, requiring parsing. Examples include JSON files.
- A schema is a blueprint or structure that defines how data is organized in a database.

- Data was first processed in the 1800s for the U.S. Census.

- Data is raw, unprocessed facts and figures, whereas information is data that has been processed and organized to provide meaning and context.

- Data is improving healthcare by providing more personalized care for patients and predictive analytics for medicine.

- Data is helping companies transform inventory management by enabling real-time tracking through sensors and IoT devices.

- In transportation, data enables real-time ride booking, smarter routes, and self-driving car technology.

- In AI, data is helping models evolve from basic automation tools to powerful systems that drive decision-making.

Notes

1. `https://en.wikipedia.org/wiki/Ishango_bone`

2. `https://www.wired.com/2007/06/dayintech-0601`

3. `https://www.historyofrecording.com/fritz-pfleumer.html`

4. `https://www.internethalloffame.org/inductee/jcr-licklider`

Introduction to Data Engineering

As organizations started working with more and more data, they ran into some big challenges—like how to scale their data systems, keep the data clean and reliable, and turn their raw data into something useful for either analytics, business insights, or machine learning initiatives. But there was one common question: How can we actually collect, store, process, and manage all this data efficiently?

In the last chapter, we looked at how data engineering is helping the healthcare industry become more efficient. In this chapter, we're going to dig deeper into how data engineering really works, what the main building blocks are, and how the systems behind the scenes are put together.

WHAT YOU WOULD LEARN IN THIS CHAPTER:

➤ The definition of data engineering and its evolution

➤ Data engineering explained using an oil refinery model

➤ The role of a data engineer in an organization

➤ An overview of the data engineering life cycle

➤ Navigating project requirements and stakeholders, and deliver business value as a data engineer

➤ The current state and importance of data engineering

Data engineering can be defined in many ways, and these definitions reflect the diverse experiences and viewpoints of various professionals in the industry. This variety in definitions makes sense because data engineering is a complex field with many different aspects.

By weaving these definitions together, we can see some similarities. Data engineering can be defined as the process of designing and maintaining systems that enable the collection, storage, and transformation of raw data into usable information for analysis and decision-making. In the field of data science and analytics, data engineering is one of the specializations. With data engineering, you can ensure that data is readily available, reliable, and structured in a way that makes it accessible to data scientists, analysts, and other stakeholders.

At its core, data engineering focuses on creating data pipelines that move data from one system to another. These pipelines are built to extract data from various sources, transform it into the required format, and load it into storage systems. Data engineering also involves optimizing these pipelines to ensure that they can handle high volumes of data efficiently and scale as needed.

Beyond just moving and transforming data, data engineering also emphasizes the importance of data quality and integrity. This means ensuring that data is clean, free of errors, and consistent across systems. Data engineers employ techniques such as validation, deduplication, and error handling to maintain the integrity of the data being processed. Security is another vital aspect, with data engineers often responsible for ensuring that sensitive or regulated data is handled in compliance with industry standards and regulations.

In addition to managing the flow and quality of data, data engineering involves making decisions about how to store data effectively. Depending on the type and volume of data, this could mean choosing between various storage technologies, such as relational databases, NoSQL databases, or distributed filesystems.

Data Engineering Explained Using an Oil Refinery Analogy

Let's imagine you work at an oil refinery as a refiner. An oil refinery is an industrial plant that refines crude oil into petroleum products such as diesel, gasoline, and heating oils. A refiner is an expert who owns, operates, or otherwise controls a refinery. An oil refinery takes in crude oil, which is raw material, and turns it into useful products like gasoline, diesel, and chemicals.

To make this happen smoothly, so many things are involved. The crude oil that comes into the refinery is messy and unrefined and cannot be used in this form until it undergoes some processes in the refinery. The refinery's expert takes the crude oil through several machines and cleans it up to remove impurities and dirt from the raw oil. They also separate the oil into different components to get different products.

Now, this refined oil is sent through a complex system of pipes and tanks to be processed. The refinery's expert also needs to make sure the oil meets certain quality standards. Lastly, the finished product is sent out to multiple stations and vendors, where they would be sold or processed further.

There are multiple ways we can relate this analogy to data engineering. Think of the crude oil like raw data, which is messy, unstructured, and not immediately useful. Just like a refiner turns crude oil into valuable products, a data engineer transforms raw data into clean, organized, and structured information that businesses can work with. The heavy machines in a refinery are like the processing tools that data engineers use to clean up errors, remove noise, and make sure the data is in shape. Just like refined oil gets delivered in different forms, maybe as jet fuel, diesel, or gas, clean data that has just been processed is delivered in ways that suit the end user, maybe as a dashboard for an analyst, an API for an app, or a file for deeper analysis.

In summary, the fundamental role of a data engineer is to pull data from multiple sources and design and build data pipelines and data stores that would aid in the processing and storing of this data.

This data is made available to downstream users like data analysts, researchers, stakeholders, and even other data engineers within the organization. The data engineer also ensures that data in an organization is accurate, consistent, reliable, and most importantly, available.

An Overview of the Data Engineering Life Cycle

The *data engineering life cycle* refers to the structured flow of how data is handled from its raw state to becoming usable and ready for consumption. It can also be defined as the end-to-end process of the movement and transformation of data within an organization. There are typically five main stages of the data engineering life cycle, which are shown in Figure 2-1. They are:

- Source systems
- Storage
- Ingestion
- Transformation
- Serving data

The data engineering life cycle usually begins with getting the data from various source systems and storing that data in a data store. This data is then transformed according to business use cases before being served to various end users. Depending on the organization and project requirements, these stages could differ, and various stages could repeat themselves during the life cycle.

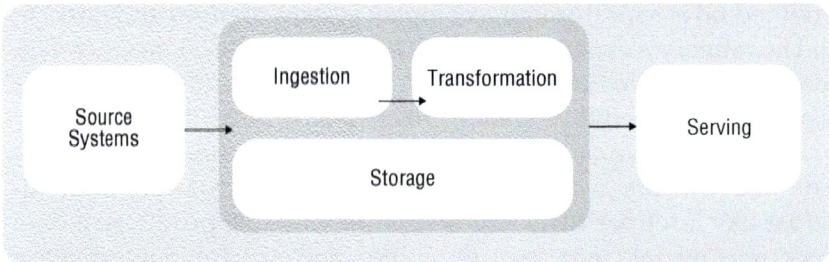

Figure 2-1: Data engineering life cycle

Source systems refer to the various origins of data that a data engineer interacts with, and these source systems can come in many forms. They could be databases, APIs, IoT devices, cloud file storage, or streaming data platforms.

Data sources are the lifeblood of any data pipeline. As a data engineer, you need to identify and understand the functionality of the source systems you're dealing with, monitor the data sources for updates or changes, and most importantly, validate data accuracy from various sources, especially when merging or aggregating data from different sources. Data from source systems could come in various formats, which could be structured, unstructured, or semi-structured. Let's discuss a few examples of what these source systems may look like:

- On a social media platform like X or Instagram, users post photos, upload videos, make comments, like, and share. Data from these actions are constantly generated by millions of users interacting with the platform. This data is usually unstructured like comments or tweets in text form, uploaded images or videos, or audio from voice notes, and this type of data doesn't follow a predefined format.

- Smart home devices such as thermostats, security cameras, or smart lighting systems continuously generate data. For example, a smart thermostat records temperature data every minute to optimize heating/cooling. This data is usually semi-structured data typically in JSON format, which is logged in real time (e.g., sensor readings, logs, status updates).

- An online shopping platform like Amazon or Shopify generates data every time a customer makes a purchase. This includes details such as items bought, payment method, shipping address, and timestamps. This could be a mix of both structured data (e.g., order details, payment records) that would come in a table-like format or semi-structured data (customer reviews that might have text, images, or videos).

Data Storage

Before ingesting data from these source systems, you need to figure out where this data would be stored. *Storage* is one major factor in a data engineering life cycle because the need for where to store data arises in multiple stages of a data pipeline. Depending on the structure and requirements, data can be stored in either a database, a data lake, or a data warehouse. A database is best suited for transactional, structured data where quick access and updates are needed; a data lake is ideal for raw, unstructured, or semi-structured data that may not have a fixed schema; and a data warehouse is designed for structured data, typically aggregated from various sources and formatted mainly for analysis and reporting. We'll be looking at these terms in detail in the coming chapters.

Choosing a Storage System

In a retail store, before restocking products, you need to make some space in the warehouse, and there are certain things you think about, like how many products are going to be bought, how much space is needed to store those products, and how these products would be accessed after storage. This is like how we think about storage systems in data engineering.

Proper data storage ensures that data is well-organized, easily accessible to users, and secure. When data is stored well, it's easy to query, which is important for smooth operations. On the other hand, when we make poor storage choices, data can get very difficult to access and slow down processing, which affects the overall performance of the system. You must consider several things when choosing a storage system:

Scalability   When you're picking a storage system, one of the first things to think about is *scalability*. Basically, you want to pick a storage system that can grow with your data, because your data *will* grow, both in size and how often it comes in with time. A scalable system means you won't have to keep pausing to reconfigure things or deal with slowdowns. It just keeps things running smoothly, even as the data piles up.

Performance   In every storage system, you can either read data or write data into the system. *Performance* in storage systems refers to the system's ability to handle data access (read) and data input (write) speeds efficiently. You need to make sure your system has good performance to ensure that the storage system can process transactions, handle queries, or respond to data retrieval requests on time.

According to the project requirements (in terms of read and write operations), fast access speeds are essential for real-time applications or high-frequency data access, whereas slower speeds may suffice for batch processing or archival storage. Achieving optimal performance is important for applications that rely on real-time or near-real-time data access, such as analytics dashboards or high-frequency trading platforms, so it's important to select storage solutions suited to the data's speed requirements.

Storage Suitability   This involves selecting and configuring the storage solution in a way that aligns with its intended purpose. It includes ensuring that the storage technology fits the system's data access and query requirements. For example, if the goal is to store large volumes of raw, unstructured data for data science or machine learning applications, an object storage would be a suitable choice, as it is scalable and cost-effective for raw data storage. Alternatively, if the focus is on running complex analytical queries on highly structured data, a cloud data warehouse would be optimal, as it's designed to handle structured data efficiently, with support for advanced querying and fast retrieval.

Access Tiers   Access tiers help you classify data storage solutions based on the frequency of data access and the speed required for retrieving that data. As you can see in Figure 2-2, each storage tier has assigned days that act as a guideline to help you decide which tier to use based on how recently the data was accessed or how often it's needed. Understanding the differences between these storage types helps you choose the right data storage solutions based on their specific needs and results in cost savings for your organization.

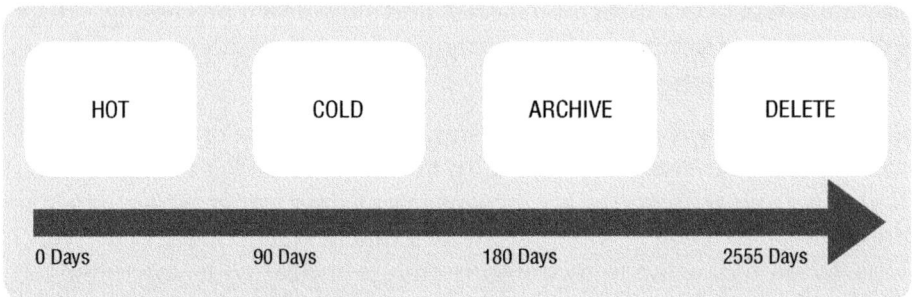

Figure 2-2: Blob storage management

Hot Storage   Used for data that needs to be accessed frequently and immediately. This includes files that are actively in use, such as application data, real-time logs, or website content. Although hot storage is the most expensive in terms of storage cost, it offers the fastest read and write speeds, making it ideal for performance-critical tasks where speed is essential.

Cold Storage   Meant for data that is accessed infrequently but still needs to be available without delay. This tier is commonly used for older reports, backups, or data that is no longer active but that may still be referenced occasionally. Cold storage is cheaper than hot storage but comes with higher costs when reading or writing data.

Archive Storage   Designed for data that is rarely accessed and that can tolerate retrieval delays of several hours. It is the most cost-effective option for long-term retention, such as storing audit logs, compliance records, or historical datasets. While storage costs are very low, retrieving data from archive storage takes time and incurs additional charges. It's best suited for information you need to keep but don't expect to use often.

In storage management, *delete* refers to the process of permanently removing data from storage. This action frees up space and eliminates ongoing storage costs. Deletion is typically used when data is no longer needed, has expired according to data retention policies, or must be removed for privacy or regulatory reasons. Once deleted, the data cannot be recovered, so it should be done with careful consideration.

Data Governance and Compliance   When you're dealing with large amounts of data, compliance is a big deal. Your storage system should not only store data, it should also help keep it safe and well managed. That means making sure the data is high-quality, you can trace where it came from, and you know how it's being used, all of which ties into good data governance. On top of that, you've got to think about legal rules, like where the data is stored geographically, so you don't run into any compliance issues. We'll dive deeper into data governance in the next few chapters.

Metadata Management   *Metadata* refers to the information that describes and provides context for data throughout its life cycle within data systems. Without metadata, you're just looking at raw numbers and text with no context. The choice of storage system needs to be designed to capture metadata about schema changes, data flows, and lineage, which enhances the organization's ability to locate, understand, and leverage data for future projects. As organizations expand and accumulate more data, having a clear, organized repository of metadata reduces the time spent on data discovery. Figure 2-3 shows two tables: The first contains records about employees, whereas the second is a metadata table that provides details about each column, such as data type, description, and other contextual information.

employee_id	first_name	last_name	nin	department_id
44	Simon	Martinez	HH 45 09 73 D	1
45	Thomas	Goldstein	SA 75 35 42 B	2
46	Eugene	Cornelsen	NE 22 63 82	2
47	Andrew	Petculescu	XY 29 87 61 A	1
48	Ruth	Stadick	MA 12 89 36 A	15
49	Barry	Scardelis	AT 20 73 18	2
50	Sidney	Hunter	HW 12 94 21 C	6
51	Jeffrey	Evans	LX 13 26 39 B	6
52	Doris	Berndt	YA 49 88 11 A	3
53	Diane	Eaton	BE 08 74 68 A	1
54	Bonnie	Hall	WW 53 77 68 A	15
55	Taylor	Li	ZE 55 22 80 B	1

Metadata

Column	Data Type	Description
employee_id	int	Primary key of a table
first_name	nvarchar(50)	Employee first name
last_name	nvarchar(50)	Employee last name
nin	nvarchar(15)	National Identification Number
position	nvarchar(50)	Current postion title, e.g., Secretary
department_id	int	Employee deparmtnet. Ref: Departments
gender	char(1)	M = Male, F = Female, Null = unknown
employment_start_date	date	Start date of employment in organization.
employment_end_date	date	Employment end date. Null if employee sti

Data

Figure 2-3: A metadata table

Data Ingestion

At this phase, you've identified both your source systems and the destination where the data will live. The next step is to figure out how to *ingest* the data, which means designing the process that connects your sources to your destination. *Ingestion* refers to gathering data from different sources, which could be databases, APIs, third-party services, or real-time streaming systems, as discussed earlier. Data from these systems can come in different formats such as JSON, CSV, XML, etc. This is the foundation of the data engineering life cycle as it brings raw data into the system, where it can later be transformed and analyzed.

There are two popular approaches used to move and process data from various sources into a data processing system or storage: batch and streaming. *Batch* ingestion involves collecting and processing data in large chunks or batches at scheduled intervals. *Streaming* ingestion involves processing data in real time or near real time as it arrives, and this is usually for real-time analytics. Both methods have their different use cases depending on the requirements of the project and can also be used together in data architectures to meet different needs for data processing and analysis. We will be looking at these concepts in detail as we move forward in the book.

Before ingesting data, there are some popular factors to consider:

- The destination of the data after ingestion
- How often the data arrives
- The format and volume of the data
- Whether you need to transform the data before it arrives at its destination

Having these key factors in mind will enable you to design your ingestion process more efficiently.

Data Ingestion Scenarios

As a data engineer, regardless of the industry, you'll find that data ingestion processes are similar. To gain a clear understanding of data ingestion, you should consider some of the typical tasks you might encounter.

Ingesting Data from a Database

In a fintech company, you can be asked to retrieve data from a relational database like MySQL, PostgreSQL, or SQL Server that has either transactional data, financial records, or customer information to make it available to other departments in the organization.

Retrieving Data from APIs

Here, you can be tasked with making social media data available for the marketing team to monitor social media trends and analyze customer engagement. Using APIs from X, Facebook, and Instagram, you establish secure connections to pull data streams directly into your data pipeline. You can also design a process that filters and structures social media metrics, such as likes, comments, and mentions, to make it accessible for analysts to measure the impact of recent campaigns.

Retrieving Data from Cloud Storage or Local Filesystems   Your company has recently migrated data storage to the cloud to support the scaling data needs of its analytics team. They've accumulated years' worth of JSON logs, CSVs of sales data, and Parquet files containing rich user behavior information. You can be asked to access these data files, clean them, and prepare them for analysis. Starting with data in JSON logs, you can develop a script that connects to the data store, iterates through directories, and extracts the necessary data.

Web Scraping for Publicly Available Data   Your company's e-commerce team is exploring a new product line and needs to analyze competitor pricing and customer sentiment for similar products. Unfortunately, the competitor's website doesn't offer an API for product data, so they enlist you to help with web scraping. As a data engineer on this project, you can design a scraping script that navigates the site to pull relevant information on product prices, descriptions, and customer reviews and use special tools to automate the collection of thousands of product reviews.

Retrieving Real-Time Data from IoT Sensors   You're working as a data engineer at Siemens, an industrial automation company, and you've been asked to retrieve real-time data from IoT sensors and industrial equipment to monitor temperature and machinery performance in real time. To streamline this data collection, you create a pipeline that ingests data directly from these sensors. With this, once the data flows into your system, you apply real-time anomaly detection algorithms to detect unusual temperature spikes or make this data available for other users.

Data Transformation

At this stage, data has been ingested and stored in a storage system. The next stage involves *transformation*, which involves cleaning and preprocessing raw data to remove inconsistencies, duplicates, and errors. The goal is to prepare the data so that it can be analyzed efficiently. Without clean, well-processed data, any insights derived from it could be misleading or inaccurate.

Data transformation ensures the data is usable and reliable for downstream tasks. It could involve aggregating data, deriving new features, or summarizing large datasets into more usable formats. Transformation can also be done at multiple stages throughout the data engineering life cycle.

Before transformation is done, the most important information to note is the business use case. Business logic and use cases help clarify the objectives of the data transformation process. They specify what the business aims to achieve with the data, guiding the transformation efforts toward those goals.

A few questions to ask at this stage:

- What transformations will make the data more valuable or usable for stakeholders?

- Are there missing values or inconsistencies in the data?

- Do I need to enrich this data with information from other sources?

- What business logic or calculations need to be applied to the data?

- Does the data need to be standardized, and how can I optimize the data for analysis or reporting?

Data Serving

This is the last stage of the data engineering life cycle, and this phase allows the organization to leverage its data effectively for major use cases like data analytics, machine learning, and other processes. Here you think about who your users are and how best to serve your data. Let's look at a few use cases in detail:

Data Analytics

Data analytics is a common use case you'll encounter as a data engineer when serving data. It involves analyzing data to identify patterns, trends, and insights. A data analyst can perform multiple types of analytics like *business* or *operational analytics*. The first step is to identify the goal of the project.

Business analytics is a combination of both historical and current data, using statistics and trend analysis to make actionable decisions for the company. An analyst will need to build dashboards and design reports, or perform ad hoc analysis of the data available depending on the requirements of stakeholders.

Dashboards: In building dashboards, analysts can present core metrics on how each area of the business is doing according to business objectives. Dashboards provide a high-level, interactive view of key performance indicators (KPIs) and metrics, allowing users to monitor trends and track progress toward specific goals—for example, a sales dashboard that shows live updates on daily revenue, conversion rates, and sales by region, with clickable filters for different time frames.

Reports: Analysts can also use this data to build reports that investigate a particular finding or problem in the organization or to answer specific questions. Reports provide detailed, static information, often presenting a comprehensive view of historical data over a specific period. They are typically used for in-depth analysis. For example, a monthly sales report that breaks down revenue, expenses, and profit margins by region and product line.

Ad hoc requests: Another common use case is ad hoc requests, one-time data inquiries that are typically initiated by business users or stakeholders to answer immediate questions.They are usually unplanned, allowing teams to act quickly on insights.

On the other hand, operational analytics is the process of analyzing real-time or near-real-time data to improve day-to-day business operations. Unlike traditional analytics, which focuses on historical data for strategic decision-making, operational analytics emphasizes immediate insights to support ongoing processes and optimize efficiency. An example of operational analytics is building dashboards to monitor the health of your application for metrics like database I/O, CPU utilization or even real-time monitoring of stock levels or sales trends.

Machine Learning

Machine learning (ML) is a branch of artificial intelligence (AI) that enables computers to learn from data and make decisions without being explicitly programmed for specific tasks. In machine learning, algorithms are trained on data to recognize patterns, classify information, and make predictions. Machine learning engineers rely on clean, processed data from data engineers that is free from errors, redundancies, and irrelevant information, allowing the model to focus on meaningful patterns. This improves the accuracy of predictions and the overall performance of the model.

Once the data is accessible, featurization comes into play. *Featurization* is the process of transforming raw data into a structured set of attributes (features) that are meaningful and useful for model training. Featurization typically requires close collaboration with ML engineers to understand the features needed for specific models and applications.

Data engineers may work with ML engineers to select relevant columns that are statistically important for the machine learning task. This would involve eliminating unnecessary columns, cleaning the data to remove missing values or outliers, and aggregating features like finding the average purchase frequency per customer, finding the total spend in the last 90 days, or finding the average session duration. After this, the features are stored in a feature store to allow easy access for ML training and real-time inference, and data engineers are also tasked with maintaining data pipelines that produce this data.

Navigating Project Requirements, Engaging Stakeholders, and Delivering Business Value

In the previous sections, we explored the various stages of the data engineering life cycle. However, before building pipelines or identifying source systems, understanding the intersection between business needs and technical work is important. This section lays the groundwork for successful data engineering projects, emphasizing the importance of requirement gathering, stakeholder engagement, and delivering business value. When you align data solutions with organizational goals, your work not only meets technical specifications but also drives strategic outcomes. We'll discuss the requirements-gathering process, identifying stakeholders, translating stakeholder requirements to system requirements, and delivering business value.

Requirements Gathering

The first step in any data engineering project is requirements gathering, where project goals and scope are defined with clarity. This phase involves collaboration with stakeholders, including business leaders, product managers, and end users, to pinpoint their needs and expectations. When clear objectives are established, data engineers create a roadmap that guides the project from inception to completion. This process not only clarifies the intended outcomes but also helps to manage stakeholder expectations and ensures that the final product aligns with the organization's vision. Defining the project scope also minimizes the risk of scope creep, which can derail timelines and budgets.

Understanding Stakeholders

Stakeholders are individuals or groups who have an interest in the project's outcome and can influence its success. Communicating effectively with stakeholders is important for ensuring that the project meets its objectives and aligns with business needs. There are two types of stakeholders you would interact with during a project: upstream and downstream stakeholders.

A Data Engineer Collaborating with a Machine Learning Engineer—A Downstream Stakeholder

Downstream stakeholders are involved later in the data engineering life cycle. They use the processed data for analysis, reporting, or operational purposes. These stakeholders could be data scientists, business intelligence professionals, executives, or machine learning engineers.

Let's say you're a data engineer working alongside a machine learning engineer (MLE) who is developing a predictive model to forecast customer churn (the rate at which customers stop doing business with a company) for your organization. The machine learning engineer requires access to process and clean datasets that will be used to train and validate the ML models. To serve the MLE effectively, you must consider several factors to ensure the data meets their needs:

- You need to clarify what specific data points the MLE requires for their model. For example, do they need customer demographics, transaction history, engagement metrics, or support interactions?

- You need to discuss the importance of historical data; the MLE may need several months or even years of data to identify patterns and trends.

- Talk about potential features that can be derived from the raw data. For instance, should you create a feature that tracks the number of support tickets raised by a customer over the last three months?

- Establish how often the MLE will need the data refreshed. For instance, do they need daily updates for model training, or is weekly sufficient?

- Discuss the acceptable latency for the model's predictions. For example, if the MLE is deploying the model for real-time predictions, you may need to ensure that the data pipeline can handle near-real-time updates.

A Data Engineer Collaborating with a Software Engineer—An Upstream Stakeholder

Upstream stakeholders are involved in the initial stages of the data engineering process. They are typically responsible for providing the data that will be processed and analyzed. These stakeholders could be software engineers who build the source systems or third-party sources you would be working with.

Imagine you are a data engineer working on a project that involves ingesting data from an application developed by a software engineer. This application collects user activity data, which your team will analyze to gain insights into user behavior. In this scenario, you need to engage effectively with the software engineer to ensure a smooth data ingestion process. Here are a few steps you can take:

- Initiate discussions with the software engineer to understand how data is generated within the application. You'll want to know what types of data are collected (e.g., user interactions, timestamps, device information) and how this data is structured.

- Discuss the expected volume of data generated by the application. Understanding the volume will help you design an efficient data pipeline that can handle incoming data without overwhelming the system.

- Clarify how frequently the data is generated and whether it's batch or streaming. This will inform decisions about how often you need to ingest data and update your datasets.

- Confirm the format in which data will be available (e.g., JSON, CSV, Avro). Understanding the format is critical for designing the ingestion process and for any necessary transformations.

- Work with the software engineer to establish a consistent schema. Agree on the names and types of fields, as well as any required metadata that should accompany the data.

- Suggest to the software engineer that they collect missing data based on the requirements of the stakeholders.

- Discuss any security measures in place for the data, including encryption and access controls. Understand how sensitive data is handled, especially if it involves personally identifiable information (PII).

- Lastly, build a relationship with the software engineer to establish open lines of communication. Discuss how you can be notified in advance of any changes that might affect data ingestion, such as application updates, schema changes, or planned outages.

Understanding System Requirements

Once you've gathered the project requirements, the next step is to translate them into specific technical details, identifying what your system needs to fulfill these requirements. System requirements fall into two main categories: functional and nonfunctional requirements.

Functional Requirements

Functional requirements refer to what the system should do. They define the specific behaviors, features, and functionalities that the system must support.

These requirements would be generated from conversations with stakeholders. Examples of functional requirements include the following:

- The system will ingest data from CSV files and JSON APIs.
- The system will perform data validation checks during ingestion to ensure data quality.
- The system will store processed data in a relational database with pre-defined schemas.
- The system will provide a user interface for users to query and visualize data.
- The system will trigger the ingestion pipeline at 2 a.m. daily.

Nonfunctional Requirements

Nonfunctional requirements are all about the quality and behavior of the system rather than specific tasks. They define the operational standards the system must meet, like performance, reliability, scalability, and more. While functional requirements tell you what the system does, nonfunctional requirements explain how well it should do those things. Examples include the following:

- The system should achieve 99.9 percent uptime to ensure continuous availability.
- The system should process data ingestion tasks within a maximum latency of five minutes.
- The system should encrypt data in transit and at rest.
- The system should be designed to scale to support a 200 percent increase in data volume over the next two years.

At the early stages of the project, especially during planning and requirements gathering, it's common for the project scope or goals to change over time. Stakeholders might realize they need additional data points, adjust business goals based on new insights, or shift priorities due to external or market changes.

Because of this, you'll often go through multiple iterations of your pipeline design, data models, or reporting structure before reaching a final, stable solution. And that's perfectly normal. To manage this change, constant and clear communication with your stakeholders is essential. It avoids reworks, because if you check in regularly, you're less likely to build something they don't need. Getting feedback early means you can make small changes instead of re-architecting later.

Best practices to stay on track include holding regular check-ins such as weekly syncs or demos, documenting requirements, and updating those requirements as they evolve.

Delivering Business Value

The goal of any data engineering project is delivering business value. The key part of your work as a data engineer is how you can find and give value to the business through the data you provide. It's easy to get caught up in the technical aspects of your work, writing scripts and picking up shiny new tools. However, it's important to step back and consider the broader perspective of your organization. By identifying its goals and objectives, you can discover ways to contribute meaningfully and drive initiatives that accelerate your organization's success.

To deliver business value, start by determining the why behind your tasks. Before jumping into coding, ask the right questions, such as: What is this data going to be used for? What decision will it influence? If you don't have a clear answer, it's worth taking a step back to clarify the purpose. Doing so ensures you're not just building for the sake of building but solving a problem that matters.

Engaging with stakeholders early is also key. Whether it's product managers, analysts, marketers, or operations teams, these are the people who depend on data to do their jobs well. Ask them what pain points they're facing, what data they wish they had, or which manual processes take up too much of their time. These conversations lead to opportunities to create tools, pipelines, or datasets that save hours of work.

Another way to drive value is to think critically about what projects you prioritize. Technical tasks will always be on your plate, but not all of them will have equal impact. Focus on work that either supports business growth or improves efficiency. Projects that save time or reduce errors are high-leverage efforts that make a visible difference.

Don't forget to communicate your impact. If you automate a pipeline that saves someone three hours a day, or if your new data model helped marketing target customers more accurately, make sure people know. Share outcomes in terms the business understands, like time saved, cost reduced, revenue gained. It helps others appreciate your work.

Finally, remember that it's not enough to just provide data—it must be usable. Invest in making your datasets clean, well documented, and easy to access. Build dashboards that tell a clear story and collaborate with analysts or business users to help them make sense of the numbers. When you make data not just available but useful, you've delivered real value.

The Current State of Data Engineering

A lot of the things we talked about sound pretty cool, but in the early days, data engineering was just primarily focused on setting up databases and handling data storage, which involved creating simple systems to collect and keep data in one place. The work was often ad hoc and manual, with engineers writing scripts to move data around without much thought to automation or scalability.

Over time, as companies collected more data and demanded quicker, more accurate insights, data engineering evolved into a field focused on building scalable data pipelines, automating data flows, and making data accessible for various business needs. By 2024, data engineering had shifted to being highly automated, with systems that pull, clean, and transform data from different sources into organized formats.

Now, data engineers design robust architectures that can handle real-time data streaming and support machine learning and AI workloads, supporting model pipelines, feature stores, and data versioning to help maintain and monitor ML models in production.

We've also seen a shift in data storage. The combination of data lakes and data warehouses into a single "lakehouse" architecture has gained popularity. Technologies like Delta Lake and Apache Iceberg are allowing organizations to store structured and unstructured data in the same environment while supporting both batch and real-time processing.

For data management, the data mesh approach is now being used to encourage decentralized data ownership across domains, allowing each team or department to treat data as a product. This shift moves data management away from centralized warehouses, letting each domain independently manage its data. New trends in data engineering also include the adoption of cloud-native platforms, which allow companies to manage data more flexibly.

There's also a growing focus on data observability and quality, with tools and practices to monitor data health and ensure accuracy across systems. In 2024, data engineering is no longer just about moving data from Point A to Point B. It's about building intelligent, automated, and scalable systems that allow companies to unlock the full potential of their data.

The Importance of Data Engineering

Data engineering is the backbone of any organization that wants to make smart, data-driven decisions. One way it's helping organizations is through integration. Without the right systems in place, data would be sitting in silos, scattered across tools and platforms, but with data engineering, we have infrastructure that lets data flow smoothly from all these different sources into one place, in a clean, reliable, and timely way

Data engineering also improves efficiency in organizations. Usually, data analysts and scientists would spend hours cleaning and wrangling data before they could start getting insights or building models. However, when a good data engineering team is set up, they can rely on data engineers for clean data and focus on high-value tasks.

Data quality is a key factor for any data-driven organization. Bad data leads to bad decisions, and those decisions can be costly. To address this, a huge part of data engineering focuses on ensuring quality at every point in its life cycle. Data engineers build in checks and validations to make sure the data is accurate and trustworthy.

Along with quality, security is also important. It's not enough to store data, it's also important to make sure the data is secure. A lot of organizations deal with sensitive information like customer details, financial records, etc. Data engineers ensure access controls, masking, and compliance with regional laws are put in place.

We've officially come to the end of this chapter; the goal was to help you understand the key building blocks of data engineering and provide a broad overview of the topic. In the upcoming chapters, we'll dive deeper into some of the topics we've touched here and explore them in more detail.

Summary

In this chapter, you learned about the following:

- Data engineering can be defined as the process of designing and maintaining systems that enable the collection, storage, and transformation of raw data into usable information for analysis and decision-making.

- Data engineering lays a good foundation for data-driven decision-making in an organization, helping organizations unify data and improve quality.

- The data engineering life cycle consists of five main stages: Source Systems, Storage, Ingestion, Transformation, and Serving.

- Source systems generate raw data followed by an ingestion process that collects moving data from source systems to storage.

- A data store is where ingested data is kept for further processing (e.g., data lakes or warehouses).

- Ingestion refers to gathering data from different sources. These sources can be databases, APIs, or third-party services. Ingestion methods can be either batch or streaming.

- The transformation stage cleans and enriches the raw data and structures it for analysis.

- The last stage of the data engineering life cycle is serving, where the processed data is made available to end users or systems through dashboards, APIs, or reports.

- Building a successful data engineering project involves understanding project requirements, communicating with stakeholders, and delivering business value.

- There are two types of stakeholders you interact with during a data engineering life cycle: upstream and downstream stakeholders.

- Upstream stakeholders are typically responsible for providing the data that will be processed and analyzed (e.g., software engineers).

- Downstream stakeholders are the people or systems that rely on the processed data after it has been ingested, transformed, and stored (e.g., data analysts).

- To understand your system requirements, you need to outline your functional requirements, which is what your system should do, and your nonfunctional requirements, which is how your system should behave.

- A good way to deliver business value is to understand the why behind your tasks, engage with your stakeholders to know their pain points, and most importantly, communicate your impact within the organization.

- The current trends in data engineering involve the use of data mesh and data lake house approaches, with more focus on data observability and quality.

Database Fundamentals

In the previous chapter, we touched on storage as a part of the data engineering life cycle. Now, let's zoom in on one of the most important tools in that stage: databases. As a data engineer, you're going to spend a lot of time working with databases, designing them and understanding how they work.

In this chapter, we'll introduce you to the foundational concepts you need to start working with databases confidently. You'll learn what they are, the different types that exist, and how to interact with them in a real-world context.

HERE'S WHAT WE'LL COVER:

- ➤ What databases are and why they matter
- ➤ The difference between relational and NoSQL databases
- ➤ Various types of NoSQL databases and their use cases
- ➤ Primary and foreign key concepts
- ➤ Interacting with databases using SQL
- ➤ Applying ACID principles
- ➤ Choosing the best type of database for your project

Databases are organized collections of data that allow for efficient storage, retrieval, and management of information. In any digital application or system, databases are the foundation for storing data, making them essential in nearly every industry. One of the key strengths of a database is that it allows data to be structured in a way that supports queries. A query is a request for information from a database. This ability to query data is what makes databases powerful for reporting, analysis, and decision-making.

The primary purpose of databases is to efficiently manage large volumes of data while ensuring that information remains consistent, accessible, and reliable. Since they provide a structured way to store and retrieve data, it makes maintaining data integrity easier, especially when multiple users access or update the data simultaneously, which makes it essential for every business.

Key Concepts of Databases

There are a few foundational concepts that are common across databases. No matter the kind of database you're working with, these concepts show up often, and understanding them would help you navigate the rest of this chapter better. They are:

- Rows
- Columns
- Schema
- Keys

Rows

A row represents a single record or entry in a database. Think of it as one complete set of information about a particular item, person, or event. For example, in a database that stores customer information, one row might contain the name, email address, phone number, and location of a single customer, and each row holds a unique set of values.

Columns

A column defines a specific type of information that will be stored across all rows. You can think of columns as the categories or fields that describe each record. In the customer example, there might be columns for Name, Email, Phone Number, and Location, and each column holds the same type of data for every row in the table.

Schema

A schema is the blueprint or structure of a database. A schema defines how data is organized, like what fields exist, what type of data is allowed, and how different parts of the database relate to each other (see Table 3-1). The schema acts like a set of rules that ensure data is stored in a consistent and meaningful way.

Table 3-1: A Database Schema

SCHEMA	DATA TYPE
CustomerID	INT
Name	VARCHAR(100)
Email	VARCHAR(255)
Phone Number	VARCHAR(15)

Keys

A key is a special piece of data used to uniquely identify or connect data records. For example, a customer ID can be used as a key to make sure each customer can be uniquely identified, even if some of their other information (like name) is the same. Keys also help link data across different parts of a database.

Types of Databases

Databases have come a long way since the early days of computing. At first, they were simple flat files like basic structures where data was stored in plain lists or tables, with no way to define relationships between pieces of information. These systems worked for small, straightforward tasks, but as the volume and complexity of data grew, they quickly became limiting.

To solve this, relational databases were introduced. Instead of one giant list, data could now be organized into multiple tables, with relationships defined between them. This made it easier to manage, query, and scale structured data. But that innovation didn't stop there. When the Internet went mainstream, data started taking on new forms, such as images, videos, and documents. NoSQL databases were built for that type of flexibility and scale, capable of handling semi-structured and unstructured data.

In this section, we'll focus on the two main types of databases: relational and NoSQL databases. You'll learn how they differ and about their use cases.

Relational Databases

Relational databases organize data into structured tables with rows and columns. If you've ever seen a Microsoft Excel sheet, that's a perfect example of what a table in a relational database looks like. In a relational database, we have what we call an *entity*, and this represents a real-world object or concept that you want to store information about. Think of a Student, Customer, or Product—these are all examples of entities. Each entity is typically modeled as a table in the database and within that table:

Each row in a relational database represents a single instance or record of the entity—for example, one specific Customer.

Each column represents an attribute, or a piece of information that all entities in the table share. For example, Customer Name, Email, or Phone Number).

Every row is one Customer, and the columns store details like Name, Address, and Phone Number:

CUSTOMER ID	NAME	EMAIL	PHONE NUMBER
1	Daniella Peters	daniellap@gmail.com	555-0125
2	Ashley Smith	ashley@hotspot.com	801-9902
3	Gabriella Hudson	gabriella@yahoo.com	567-1001

It's typical to have more than one table to represent different entities. A retail store can have separate tables for other entities like Orders, Products, Shipping, etc. In order to organize, manage, and access these tables efficiently, you can use a system. A relational database management system (RDBMS) provides the necessary tools and interface needed to manage structured data within a relational database. It allows users to store and retrieve data efficiently. Common examples of RDBMSs include MySQL, PostgreSQL, Oracle Database, and Microsoft SQL Server.

Characteristics of Relational Databases

Relational databases are built on a set of features that enable them to handle data consistency, ensure data integrity, and support complex queries. These features are:

- Primary and foreign keys
- Defined relationships between tables
- Use of Structured Query Language (SQL)
- ACID (Atomicity, Consistency, Isolation, Durability) compliance

Primary Key (PK)

A *primary key* is a specific column in a relational database table that has a unique entry for each record. These keys have no duplicates or null values, and they don't change over time. A primary key can also be referred to as a unique identifier for each record in a table, making each row in the table unique. For instance, a CustomerID in a Customer table might serve as a primary key, uniquely identifying each customer:

CUSTOMER ID (PK)	NAME	EMAIL	PHONE NUMBER
1	Daniella Peters	daniellap@gmail.com	555-0125
2	Ashley Smith	ashley@hotspot.com	801-9902
3	Gabriella Hudson	gabriella@yahoo.com	567-1001

Composite Primary Key

A *composite primary key* is a primary key that consists of two or more columns in a database table, rather than just a single column. This combination of columns is used to uniquely identify each record in the table. Each column in the composite key can contain duplicate values, but together, the values in the composite key must be unique for every row in the table. Let's look at an example of where composite keys are useful.

Suppose we have a StudentCourses table that tracks which students are enrolled in which courses. In this case, neither the StudentID nor the CourseID alone can uniquely identify a record because a student may enroll in multiple courses, and a course may have multiple students. We can use a combination of StudentID and CourseID as a composite primary key. Together, these two columns uniquely identify each record:

STUDENT ID (COMPOSITE PRIMARY KEY)	COURSE ID (COMPOSITE PRIMARY KEY)	ENROLLMENT DATE
1	CS 101	2025-01-01
1	CS 102	2025-01-05
2	CS 101	2025-01-02
2	CS 103	2025-01-07

Foreign Key (FK)

A *foreign key* is a field in one table that establishes relationships between tables. For example, an Orders table might include a CustomerID as a foreign key that references the CustomerID in the Customer table, linking orders to the specific customers who placed them:

Customer Table

CUSTOMER ID (PK)	NAME	EMAIL	PHONE NUMBER
1	Daniella Peters	daniellap@gmail.com	123-456-7890
2	Audrey Smith	audrey@gmail.com	987-654-3210

Orders Table

ORDER ID (PK)	CUSTOMER ID (FK)	ORDER DATE	AMOUNT
101	1	2024-01-01	$200
102	1	2024-01-05	$250
103	2	2024-01-03	$150

In this example, the OrderID uniquely identifies each order and CustomerID in the Orders table refers to CustomerID in the Customer table, linking the order to the customer who placed it. This linking is necessary for building relationships between tables.

Relationships

A unique characteristic of relational databases is *relationships*. Relationships define how data in one table is linked to data in another table. Instead of dumping all your data into one giant table, we split it into separate tables and then link them together using primary keys and foreign keys.

As discussed earlier, a primary key is the unique ID for each record in a table and the foreign key is what lets another table point back to it. We will be looking at different types of relationships like one-to-one, one-to-many, and many-to-many, later in this chapter.

Structured Query Language (SQL)

SQL (Structured Query Language) is a domain-specific language used to manage and manipulate data in relational databases. It provides a way to interact with these databases, allowing users to retrieve, insert, update, and delete data. Relational databases store data in tables, which are organized into rows (records) and columns (attributes). SQL is designed to operate within this tabular structure.

SQL allows users to specify what data they want without needing to detail how the database should fetch it. The RDBMS handles the underlying processes, which is efficient for complex queries.

SQL Commands

SQL commands can be broadly categorized into different types, each serving a specific purpose, as shown in Figure 3-1. To help you understand these concepts, let's assume you're working as a data engineer in a retail store and you're in charge of everything happening in the stores database.

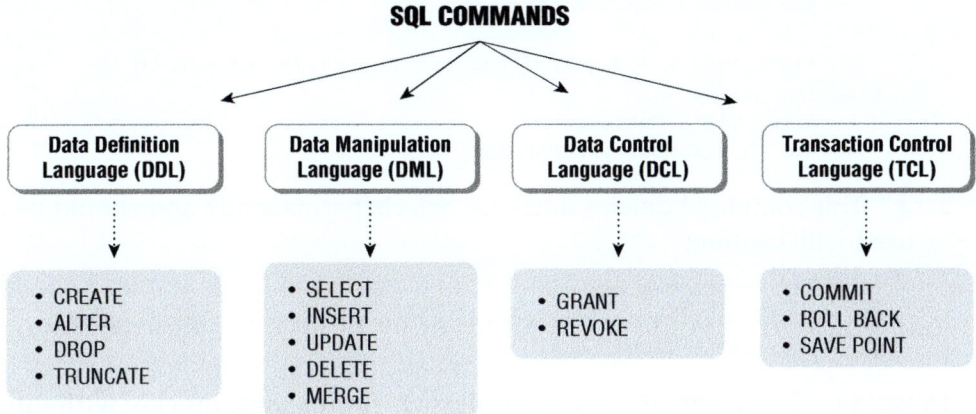

Figure 3-1: SQL commands

Data Definition Language (DDL)

Data Definition Language is used to define and manage the structure of database objects such as tables, indexes, and schemas. Before the store's operations can start, you need a structure to store your information. DDL commands are generally used for setting up or altering the framework of a database and its objects. These commands are as follows:

CREATE This command is used to create new database objects like tables, indexes, and views. In this example, you'll use this command to create tables for different entities you have:

```
CREATE TABLE TableName (
    ID INT PRIMARY KEY,
    Column1 VARCHAR(50),
    Column2 VARCHAR(50),
    Column3 VARCHAR(100)
);

#This creates a new table to store customer information.
CREATE TABLE Customer (
    CustomerID INT PRIMARY KEY,
    FirstName VARCHAR(50),
    LastName VARCHAR(50),
```

```
       Email VARCHAR(100),
       CreatedDate DATE DEFAULT CURRENT_DATE
);
```

ALTER   This command modifies an existing database object. As the data needs of your project changes, this keyword is useful for adding new columns:

```
ALTER TABLE TableName
ADD Column4 VARCHAR(15);


#This adds a new column for customer phone numbers to an
existing table.
ALTER TABLE Customer
ADD PhoneNumber VARCHAR(15);
```

DROP   This command deletes database objects permanently and should be used with caution:

```
DROP TABLE TableName;
#This deletes the OldRecords table that's no longer needed.
DROP TABLE OldRecords;
```

TRUNCATE   This command removes all rows from a table quickly without deleting the table structure, meaning the table remains available for future use and also frees up space while keeping the schema intact.

```
TRUNCATE TABLE TableName;


#This removes all data from the Logs table without deleting
the table structure.
TRUNCATE TABLE Logs;
```

Data Manipulation Language (DML)

Now the store opens, and customers start shopping. You need to add new customer information, update stock levels, and record purchases. Data Manipulation Language (DML) is used to work with the data within tables, focusing on the actual records inside the database. DML commands allow for the retrieval, insertion, updating, and deletion of data. These commands are as follows:

SELECT   This statement retrieves data from the database. It's the most commonly used SQL command, allowing you to specify columns you need to retrieve and apply conditions:

```
SELECT column1, column2, ...
FROM table_name;
#This retrieve customer names and emails.
SELECT FirstName, LastName, Email
FROM Customer;
```

INSERT This command adds new rows of data to a specific table:

```
INSERT INTO TableName (ID, Column1, Column2, Column3)
VALUES (1, 'Value1', 'Value2', 'Value3');

#This adds a new customer to the Customer table.
INSERT INTO Customer (CustomerID, FirstName, LastName, Email)
VALUES (1, 'John', 'Doe', 'john.doe@example.com');
```

UPDATE This command modifies existing data in a table, with specific conditions:

```
UPDATE TableName
SET Column3 = 'newvalue'
WHERE ID = 1;
#This updates a customer's email, where the CustomerID is 1
UPDATE Customer
SET Email = 'new.email@example.com'
WHERE CustomerID = 1;
#This updates the stock once a customer buys an item
UPDATE products
SET quantity_in_stock = quantity_in_stock - 1
WHERE product_id = 1;
```

DELETE This command removes rows from a table based on specified conditions:

```
DELETE FROM TableName
WHERE ID = 1;

#This removes a specific customer by ID.
DELETE FROM Customer
WHERE CustomerID = 1;
```

Data Control Language (DCL)

Not everyone should have full access to the database. You might want the cashier to only view products and customers, but only the store manager can update stock levels. Data Control Language (DCL) is used to control access to data within the database, managing permissions and security. These commands help ensure that users have the correct level of access to specific data and database objects. These commands are as follows:

GRANT This command gives users specific permissions to interact with database objects:

```
-- This allows the cashier to read product and customer data
GRANT SELECT ON products TO cashier;
GRANT SELECT ON customer TO cashier;
```

REVOKE   This command removes permissions from users:

```
-- This revokes stock update rights from an intern
REVOKE UPDATE ON products FROM intern;
```

Transaction Control Language (TCL)

If a customer walks into the store and wants to buy several products in one order, your system must update the inventory carefully so that you don't accidentally reduce stock for some items but not others. Transaction Control Language (TCL) manages transactions within the database. A *transaction* is a sequence of operations executed as a single unit, and TCL commands help ensure that these operations are handled consistently, especially in the event of errors or interruptions. These commands are as follows:

COMMIT   This command saves all changes made in the current transaction to the database:

```
#This query updates the stock for all products both and
commits the change, BEGIN or BEGIN TRANSACTION is used in some SQL
dialects to explicitly start a transaction.
BEGIN;
UPDATE products
SET quantity_in_stock = quantity_in_stock - 2
WHERE product_id = 1;

UPDATE products
SET quantity_in_stock = quantity_in_stock - 1
WHERE product_id = 2;
COMMIT;
```

ROLLBACK   This command undoes changes made in the current transaction if there's an error:

```
#This cancels all changes and ensures inventory stays the same
BEGIN;
UPDATE products
SET quantity_in_stock = quantity_in_stock - 2
WHERE product_id = 1;

ROLLBACK;
```

SAVEPOINT   This command sets a save point within a transaction, allowing partial rollbacks to specific stages. In this query, assuming a customer buys three products, you update stock for the first two products successfully and create a savepoint, like a safety checkpoint. If updating the third product fails due to an error, you can undo just the last step and keep the first two.

```
BEGIN;

UPDATE products
SET quantity_in_stock = quantity_in_stock - 1
```

```
WHERE product_id = 1;   -- Sold 1 Glow Serum

SAVEPOINT first_two_updated;

UPDATE products
SET quantity_in_stock = quantity_in_stock - 1
WHERE product_id = 2;

-- Error happens here with product_id 3

# Undo last update only
ROLLBACK TO first_two_updated;

# Confirm the successful updates
COMMIT;
```

We've covered some common SQL commands you'll use in your day-to-day work, but in the next chapter, you'll learn how to write SQL queries that interact with your database and help you analyze data.

Atomicity, Consistency, Isolation, and Durability (ACID) Compliance

The retail store you're working in is having a Black Friday sale and customers are flooding the site to grab discounted items, with popular items selling out fast. Two different customers add the last item to their carts and try to check out at the same time.

Without proper safeguards, both transactions might go through, resulting in overselling. Worse, one customer might be charged for the product even though the order fails to complete due to a system glitch. In some cases, your database might crash midway through a transaction, leaving your system in an inconsistent and unreliable state. These kinds of problems can create serious issues, like lost sales and refunds. From a technical standpoint, they lead to data corruption and a system that's hard to maintain.

Relational databases prevent these issues by following ACID compliance, a set of four properties that ensure data is reliable, consistent, and has integrity, especially under high pressure or simultaneous activity. ACID stands for Atomicity, Consistency, Isolation, and Durability.

What Do We Mean by Data Integrity, Reliability, and Consistency?

- Integrity means the data is accurate, complete, and protected from unauthorized changes. For instance, an order cannot exist without a valid customer.
- Reliability means the data is dependable; if a customer places an order, they can trust that it will be saved and available when they check back later.

- Consistency means the data remains logically valid throughout the system. For example, if a customer buys a product, the inventory count must decrease accordingly.

Let's take a look at the ACID properties in detail, scenarios where they are used, and how they can be implemented in a relational database. Figure 3-2 will help you to remember what each of them means.

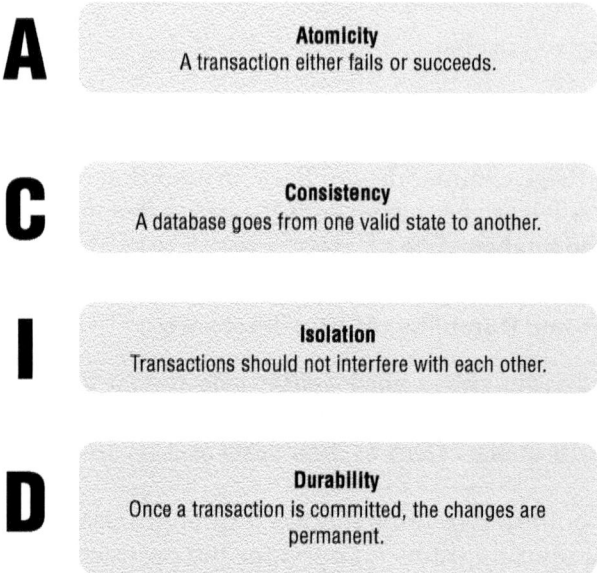

A

Atomicity
A transaction either fails or succeeds.

C

Consistency
A database goes from one valid state to another.

I

Isolation
Transactions should not interfere with each other.

D

Durability
Once a transaction is committed, the changes are permanent.

Figure 3-2: ACID properties

Atomicity

In the context of atomicity, a transaction is an indivisible unit of work. This means that either all parts of the transaction succeed, or none of them is applied. If any part of the transaction fails, the entire transaction is rolled back.

For example, suppose a customer is checking out with items worth $500 in their cart. During the checkout process, the system needs to perform two key actions: deduct the items from the inventory and charge the customer's payment method. If either of these actions fails, say the payment is declined, the inventory should not be updated. You don't want to reduce stock for an order that was never completed. Atomicity ensures that both actions must succeed together, or none at all.

Relational databases use transaction logs to record changes made during a transaction. If a failure occurs, the log ensures a rollback to undo partial changes. Additionally, as we discussed earlier, database API functions like

BEGIN TRANSACTION, COMMIT, and ROLLBACK ensure that all operations within a transaction boundary are atomic.

This query ensures that a series of operations are executed as a single, atomic unit. The transaction begins with BEGIN TRANSACTION, then deducts three units of a product (with product_id = 101) from the inventory and inserts a new order into the Orders table. The COMMIT statement ensures that both actions are permanently saved to the database only if both succeed. If any part of the transaction fails, perhaps due to a stock mismatch or payment failure, the database will roll back to its previous state, preventing partial updates and maintaining data integrity:

```
BEGIN TRANSACTION;

UPDATE inventory
SET stock = stock - 3
WHERE product_id = 101;

INSERT INTO orders (customer_id, product_id, quantity, amount)
VALUES (42, 101, 3, 500);

COMMIT; -- Ensures both inventory updates and order creation succeed
together
```

```
BEGIN TRANSACTION;
   UPDATE accounts SET balance = balance - 500 WHERE id = 1; -
Debit
   UPDATE accounts SET balance = balance + 500 WHERE id = 2; -
Credit
   COMMIT; -- Ensures both operations succeed together
```

Consistency

In *consistency*, a transaction should bring the database from one valid state to another. The database must adhere to defined rules at all times for it to be consistent. For example, an e-commerce site can enforce a constraint that the total stock count cannot be negative. If the stock count is 10 and a customer attempts to purchase 15 items, the transaction should fail because it violates the consistency rule.

Relational database schemas enforce rules like primary keys, foreign keys, and unique constraints to maintain consistency. Keywords like CHECK ensure that data adheres to business rules.

This query creates a products table in a SQL database with three columns: id, name, and stock. The stock column represents the quantity of the product in stock and is constrained by a CHECK condition that ensures the value is never negative. This CHECK constraint enforces data consistency, guaranteeing that the stock value remains logically valid and aligns with business rules, preventing invalid entries like negative stock quantities:

```
CREATE TABLE products (
    id INT PRIMARY KEY,
    name VARCHAR(100),
    stock INT CHECK (stock >= 0) -- Consistency constraint
);
```

Isolation

Isolation states that transactions that run concurrently should not interfere with each other. The outcome of a transaction should not depend on another transaction running simultaneously. For instance, if two users try to book the last available ticket for a concert, only one transaction succeeds. The database prevents the other from proceeding by isolating the transactions.

Relational databases support configurable levels using the READ UNCOMMITTED, READ COMMITTED, REPEATABLE READ, and SERIALIZABLE keywords to control the extent of isolation between transactions.

In the query, the SET TRANSACTION ISOLATION LEVEL SERIALIZABLE sets the transaction isolation level to SERIALIZABLE. SERIALIZABLE is the highest isolation level, which ensures that no other transactions can access the data being worked on until the current transaction is completed. At this level, the transaction is fully isolated from others, making it behave as if it were the only one executing in the system.

The transaction begins with BEGIN TRANSACTION, marking the start of the process. It first reads the balance of an account using SELECT, and then deducts 500 from the balance using the UPDATE statement. The isolation level is set to SERIALIZABLE, which ensures that no other transaction can read or modify the account's balance while the transaction is in progress. Finally, the transaction is committed with COMMIT, making the changes permanent. This approach guarantees the highest level of data consistency and integrity, ensuring that the account balance is updated accurately without interference from other transactions:

```
SET TRANSACTION ISOLATION LEVEL SERIALIZABLE;
BEGIN TRANSACTION;
SELECT balance FROM accounts WHERE id = 1;
UPDATE accounts SET balance = balance - 500 WHERE id = 1;
COMMIT;
```

Durability

Once a transaction is committed, the changes are permanent, even in the event of a system crash. For instance, if a customer pays for an online order, and the transaction is committed and the system crashes immediately after the commit, the payment data remains saved when the system is restored.

Relational databases achieve this using Write-Ahead Logging (WAL), where changes are first written to a log file on disk before being applied to the database. This ensures durability even if the system crashes. Databases also have *checkpoints*, periodic snapshots of the database state to ensure quick recovery after a crash.

The following query updates the status of an order to `'paid'` within a transaction. This means the change is applied atomically and changes persist after a commit, ensuring reliable database behavior.

```
BEGIN TRANSACTION;
UPDATE orders
SET status = 'paid'
WHERE id = 101;
#This keyword ensures the change persists even if the server crashes
COMMIT;
```

NoSQL Databases

Early in my career, I used to think that all databases were structured like relational databases, with rows and columns. But as I later discovered, databases can take on many different forms beyond just tables. *NoSQL databases*, which means "Not only SQL," became popular when the Internet was introduced in the mid-1990s. Data from applications came in several forms—structured, unstructured, and semi-structured—and schema definition became nearly impossible. In response to the weakness of traditional SQL databases, NoSQL databases allowed developers to store data in an unstructured and more flexible way than standard relational databases.

The acronym NoSQL was first used in 1998 by Carlo Strozzi when naming his open source relational database that didn't use standard SQL. In 2006, Google introduced a paper on BigTable, a wide-column database that stores data in columns rather than rows, designed to support massive, distributed storage systems. Google's paper highlighted the potential of NoSQL databases to manage vast amounts of data across distributed servers as a solution to traditional relational databases, which struggled with scale and flexibility in certain applications.

Around 2009, people started gaining more interest in NoSQL databases, and document-oriented databases like MongoDB and CouchDB came about. They provided a schema-less structure ideal for storing unstructured and semi-structured data, enabling developers to efficiently manage data that didn't consistently fit neatly into rows and columns.

The Agile methodology also gained popularity, and developers started thinking of ways they could iterate quickly and make changes on the go. NoSQL databases align well with these demands. Developers could now update their database schemas on the fly, keeping pace with changing application needs instead of being locked into a rigid structure.

The rise of cloud computing also fueled NoSQL's popularity. As developers used cloud platforms like AWS, Google Cloud, and Microsoft Azure, they sought database solutions that supported distributed, scalable storage across multiple servers and regions. NoSQL databases are optimized for these cloud environments, which help to maintain application resilience and scale by distributing data across servers.

Key Characteristics of NoSQL Databases

NoSQL databases offer a set of unique features that make them well suited for handling large-scale data workloads. Unlike relational databases, they emphasize flexibility, scalability, and high performance over strict consistency and relationships. In this section, we'll explore the key characteristics of NoSQL databases:

Multimodel Support   NoSQL databases are *multimodel* because they can support different types of data structures, like documents, key-value pairs, graphs, or columns, all in one database. In a company, data can come in many forms, and with a NoSQL database, data engineers can store and retrieve these different data types in one place. This reduces complexity and makes data management more efficient since there's no need to manage multiple databases. Think of a multimodel database like a Swiss Army knife; rather than using separate tools for different tasks, a multimodel database lets you handle various types of data in a single system.

Distributed Architecture   A NoSQL database is considered distributed in nature not simply because it spreads data, but because its design philosophy and goals prioritize scalability, availability, and flexibility. It's important to note that data distribution itself is not unique to NoSQL; relational databases (RDBMSs) can also distribute data. However, what sets NoSQL apart is that distribution is a foundational aspect of its architecture.

Let's use as an example a social media application used by millions of people worldwide. If all its data were stored on a single server, that server could quickly become overloaded, leading to downtime. By distributing data across multiple servers, the application can better handle high traffic and maintain uptime.

For data engineers, this distributed setup offers the advantage of horizontal scalability; they can add more servers as needed instead of upgrading to more powerful (and often more expensive) hardware. This approach also helps with balancing workloads and maintaining fast response times, even under heavy data loads and user demand.

Flexible Schema   In traditional databases, like a relational database, a *schema* has to be defined ahead of time and is usually fixed. However, in NoSQL databases, data can be stored without a schema, making it easier to change the format as needed. A common scenario in data engineering is working with data from multiple sources and having their formats change over time. With a flexible schema, data engineers can quickly adapt to these changes without reworking the database structure, allowing them to handle evolving data sources.

High Availability   NoSQL databases are designed to stay up and running as much as possible, even if parts of the system fail. They achieve this by automatically replicating data across several servers. In a company setting, some applications must be available at all times, especially customer-facing ones. For data engineers, a high-availability setup means they don't have to worry about the database going down if one server fails. This kind of setup maintains data access without any interruptions.

Partition Tolerance   Partition tolerance ensures that the NoSQL databases can still operate and work smoothly even if communication is temporarily lost between some parts (or partitions) or a minor network issue occurs. Partition tolerance is essential when handling large, distributed systems; in situations where one part of the system loses connection, the rest can still function without causing a disruption.

Fast Development   Fast development refers to the ability to quickly build, modify, and deploy applications. This is important in Agile environments where businesses need to roll out features rapidly, respond to market changes, or experiment with new ideas. In traditional databases, you often need to set up a strict structure (schema) for data before development. This means planning each table, field, and relationship, which can slow down the process if requirements change.

NoSQL databases, however, offer flexible schema designs that allow developers to store data without predefining the structure. This flexibility speeds up the process of prototyping, testing, and deploying new features. For data engineers, fast development with NoSQL databases means they can quickly adapt to new data sources or formats, integrate data from various systems, and add new features without making time-consuming changes to the database schema. This agility allows them to support fast-paced development teams, making it easier to keep up with business demands.

Types of NoSQL Databases

There are a variety of databases you can use for NoSQL workloads, depending on the requirements of the project. The type of NoSQL database you choose largely depends on your project's unique needs. In this section, we'll examine the primary types of NoSQL databases and explore their unique features and real-world use cases. The primary types of NoSQL databases are as follows:

Document Databases   Document databases store data in documents, usually in formats like JSON, XML, or BSON (Binary JSON). In relational databases, each row in a table must follow the predefined table schema and columns with specified data types. However, document databases do not enforce a strict schema. This means that documents within the same collection can have different fields, data types, and structures without needing to modify or redefine a schema. For example, one document in a collection could have fields like `name` and `age`, while another document could have `name`, `age`, and `address`.

Take an e-commerce platform with a variety of products. There are electronics with a lot of technical specifications, books with authors and publishers, and even apparel with size options and colors. Instead of creating multiple tables, each product could be represented as a document in a collection, with each document containing fields relevant to that specific product. Documents are grouped into collections, which roughly resemble tables in relational databases but are more flexible. In collections, you can have two similar documents with a relationship, but these documents can have additional fields.

The JSON file represents two products in an e-commerce inventory system, stored as documents in a document database. Each document contains key-value pairs, where the key represents the attribute of the product (e.g., `name`, `price`, `stock`) and the value holds the corresponding data.

The first document describes a `Wireless Mouse` with attributes like `price`, `stock`, and `features`. The second document describes a `Smartphone`, including additional attributes such as `color` and `brand`, which are specific to this product. The flexible schema allows each document to have unique attributes, showcasing the adaptability of document databases to store and manage diverse product data without a rigid structure. The unique identifier (`"_id"`) in each document ensures that each product is easily identifiable and accessible.

```
"_id": "product1",
"name": "Wireless Mouse",
"category": "Electronics",
```

```
    "price": 29.99,
    "stock": 150,
    "features": ["Wireless", "Ergonomic", "Rechargeable"]
}


{
    "_id": "product2",
    "name": "Smartphone",
    "category": "Electronics",
    "price": 599.99,
    "stock": 50,
    "features": ["5G", "OLED Display", "128GB Storage"],
    "color": "Black",
    "brand": "BrandX"
}
```

Document databases are mostly used when:

▪ You're working with semi-structured data, like customer profiles, product catalogs, or IoT sensor data.

▪ You need flexible schemas where each record doesn't have to follow a rigid structure.

▪ You want to store complex data with nested arrays or objects, as in the case of e-commerce, where each product might have unique specifications.

Document databases can also get cumbersome to manage and query when the documents become very large, and they are not suited for transactional operations.

Graph Databases   Graph databases store data in nodes and edges, representing entities and the relationships between them. This structure is ideal for analyzing connections, because it allows for efficient queries based on relationships, often better than relational databases where complex joins are needed for similar queries.

Figure 3-3 shows a graph representation of user relationships in a social media context, showing follow and unfollow actions between users. Each circle represents a user node, and the arrows (edges) represent the relationships between them.

Graph databases are useful when:

▪ You're working with data that's highly interconnected, like social networks, recommendation systems, or fraud detection. For a social networking site, every user is connected to other users via `"friend"` relationships. If you want to find `"friends of friends"` or see how two people are indirectly connected, a graph database efficiently allows these queries by following the edges (relationships) between nodes (users).

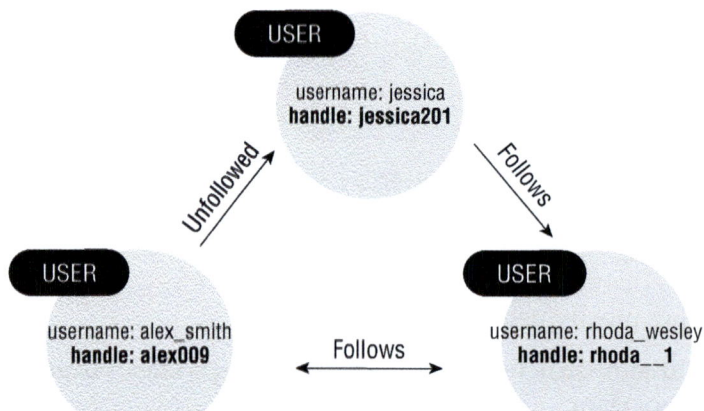

Figure 3-3: Representation of relationships in a graph database for a social media application

- You need to run complex queries on relationships, such as finding the shortest path between two entities or identifying clusters within a network.

Graph databases are not optimized for handling large volumes of unconnected data, so they are less efficient for data without many relationships. They also have limited vendor support and a smaller community compared to other NoSQL databases and are somewhat complex to manage and optimize if you're unfamiliar with graph theory.

Key-Value Databases   Key-value databases store data as pairs of keys and values. This is one of the simplest database types, where each key is unique and used to retrieve its corresponding value. Values can be anything from simple data types to complex objects, depending on the database.

In our example, the data represents three distinct entries where each key is associated with a JSON object as its value. The key `"user:56789"` maps to Bob's user profile, containing his name, age, and email. The key `"product:9876"` stores information about a product, a TechCorp Smartphone priced at $699.99. The key `"session:abc123"` holds session-related data, linking it to Bob's user ID, along with the session's expiration timestamp and current status as `"active"`. Each entry is a simple and independent object, which is typical in key-value stores that prioritize fast lookups and scalability.

User Profile

```
Key: "user:56789"
Value: {"name": "Bob", "age": 28, "email": "bob@example.com"}
```

Product Information

```
Key: "product:9876"
Value: {"name": "Smartphone", "brand": "TechCorp", "price":
699.99}
```

Session Data

```
Key: "session:abc123"
Value: {"user_id": "user:56789", "expires_at": "2024-12-
05T12:00:00Z", "status": "active"}
```

Key-value (KV) databases are useful when:

- You need a caching solution, such as temporarily storing frequently accessed data in memory to reduce load on the primary database and improve application performance. For example, systems like Redis are widely used as in-memory KV stores to cache session data, user preferences, or API responses, enabling applications to serve repeated requests much more quickly.

- You need quick access to data and don't require complex querying capabilities.

- You're storing session information, user profiles, shopping carts, or any other data that can be retrieved by a unique key. For instance, in an online shopping website where each customer has a shopping cart, you can assign a unique key (like the customer ID) to each cart, and the cart's contents are the value. When the customer adds or removes items, you only need to update this value, making the process fast and efficient.

- You're handling data that is transient or frequently changing, as key-value databases are optimized for speed and low latency.

Key-value databases are optimized for speed and simplicity, but they come with some limitations. Because data is accessed directly by its key, they have limited support for advanced querying (reading data from the database) or combining data, like calculating totals or averages across many records. Additionally, key-value stores are not well suited for scenarios that require complex filtering or managing relationships between different pieces of data. Since each entry is independent, linking related data across keys can be difficult and may result in data duplication. These trade-offs make key-value databases less ideal for applications that require rich querying or relational data modeling.

Columnar (Column-Family) Databases   Columnar databases store data in columns rather than rows. This allows for highly efficient reads on specific columns, as data is physically stored in columns, making it ideal for analytical queries that need to scan large datasets. Since columnar databases store similar data types together, they achieve high compression rates and excel at queries that involve aggregates and large scans over specific columns.

Here's what a typical column-based storage would look like compared to a row-based design. In row-based storage, all the values for a single record are stored together in one row and each row represents a complete record:

Row-Based Storage

```
[1, Alice, 30, 70000], [2, Bob, 45, 90000], [3, Carol, 29,
80000]
```

In contrast, column-based storage groups the same attribute from multiple records together into columns. Now, all the IDs are stored together, all the names together, and so on. This design is beneficial for analytical queries where operations are performed on a single column, like finding the average salary. Since only the relevant columns need to be accessed and loaded into memory, it makes processing faster and more efficient.

Column-Based Storage

```
[1, 2, 3], [Alice, Bob, Carol], [30, 45, 29], [70000, 90000,
80000]
```

Columnar databases are useful when:

- You're handling time-series data, logs, or data from IoT devices where writes are frequent, and reads are for specific columns.
- You need high availability and scalability for distributed applications.
- You want fast retrieval of aggregated data for analytics purposes, since reading columns instead of rows is efficient for large datasets.

For an application monitoring system, you're collecting metrics (CPU usage, memory, response times) from thousands of servers every second. By storing each metric in its column, it's easy to pull aggregated data quickly (like average CPU usage over the past hour) without reading all the rows.

Columnar databases have some disadvantages, as they are not intuitive to query for those familiar with traditional relational databases. They are less suitable for transactions and scenarios requiring high data consistency, and the schema design for columnar databases can be complex, since it often requires careful planning to achieve performance benefits.

Choosing Between Relational and NoSQL Databases

When starting a project, picking the right database is important. This section will help you decide when to use a relational database versus a NoSQL database based on your data and application needs. Let's break down the key factors to consider.

Start with Your Data's Structure

The first thing to consider is your data structure. Ask yourself whether the data you're working with is highly structured and consistent. If it is, a relational database is probably your best bet. These databases use tables with strict schemas, which is perfect when you know your data types ahead of time. On the flip side, if your data is more flexible or doesn't have a fixed format—say you're storing JSON documents, user profiles that vary in fields, or log data—then NoSQL databases give you that freedom. NoSQL doesn't enforce rigid schemas, so you can evolve your data model as your app grows.

Think About the Relationships in Your Data

Relational databases shine when your data has lots of connections, like users tied to orders, products tied to categories, and so on. That's because they're designed to handle joins efficiently. You can run complex queries across multiple tables and get exactly the results you want. But if your data is more self-contained, like storing blog posts, sensor readings, or user settings, NoSQL might be a better fit. You won't need to join across tables because each record often holds everything it needs.

How Fast Do You Need to Move?

Speed matters. So think about whether you're building a quick minimum valuable product (MVP) or designing for a long-term system. If you're moving fast, especially during prototyping, NoSQL can be less of a headache. You don't need to spend time defining tables and enforcing constraints. You just toss in your documents and go. It's super helpful when you're still figuring out your data model. But if you're designing a system meant to scale predictably and last long-term, especially with business-critical data, relational databases give you integrity, consistency, and years of battle-tested reliability.

How Do You Need to Query Your Data?

If your team, or future you, needs to write complex, ad hoc queries or do deep analysis, relational databases win hands down. SQL is super powerful and standard across platforms, so your queries are readable and portable. NoSQL, in contrast, often lacks that flexibility. You can still query, but it's usually simpler and more limited. Some NoSQL systems require you to know exactly how you'll access the data in advance, so you design around your read/write patterns from day one.

Scaling and Performance

With NoSQL databases, you can scale horizontally. That means you can add more servers as your app grows, especially when dealing with massive volumes of traffic and data. Relational databases can grow to handle more data and users, but usually by making one server more powerful, like adding more CPU, RAM, or faster disks. This is called *vertical scaling*. When many users read data, it's easier to handle by adding things like read replicas (copies of the data that handle read requests), so reading scales better. But when many users need to write or update data, it's harder to scale because all those writes have to be carefully managed on the main server to keep data correct. So relational databases can slow down or reach limits if write traffic gets too heavy. In summary, if you're expecting explosive growth and need to serve millions of users, NoSQL can be a better choice for scaling.

Transaction and Strong Consistency Needs

If your app needs ACID transactions, like banking apps or anything that deals with money, relational databases are your best choice. They make sure that data changes are always valid, even in the face of errors or crashes. Most NoSQL databases sacrifice some level of consistency for performance and scalability. You get eventual consistency in many of them, which means data might take a bit to sync across nodes. That's fine for something like a user profile update—but not ideal for transferring $100.

In choosing the right database, it's not either/or. Many modern systems use both. You might store transactional data in a relational database and logs in a NoSQL store. You don't need to pick one forever. Just make sure you understand your data, your use case, and how your app will grow, and most importantly, ask lots of questions!

Summary

- Databases are organized collections of data that allow for efficient storage, retrieval, and management of information. One of the key strengths of a database is that it allows data to be structured in a way that supports queries.

- There are four concepts common to all databases: rows, columns, keys, and schemas.

- A row represents a single record or entry in a database, a column defines a specific type of information that will be stored across all rows, a schema is the blueprint or structure of a database, and a key is a special piece of data used to uniquely identify or connect data records.

- There are two main types of databases: relational and NoSQL databases. Relational databases organize data into structured tables with rows and columns. NoSQL databases allow engineers to store data in an unstructured and more flexible way than standard relational databases.

- The characteristics of relational databases include primary and foreign keys, relationships, the use of SQL, and ACID compliance.

- A primary key is a specific column in a relational database table that has a unique entry for each record. A foreign key is a field in one table that establishes relationships between tables.

- Relationships in relational databases define how data in one table is linked to data in another table.

- SQL is a domain-specific language used to manage and manipulate data in relational databases. Its statements are typically categorized into four types: DDL (Data Definition Language), DML (Data Manipulation Language), TCL (Transaction Control Language), and DCL (Data Control Language).

- In ACID compliance, *atomicity* means a transaction is an indivisible unit of work, *consistency* ensures a transaction brings the database from one valid state to another, *isolation* states that transactions that run concurrently should not interfere with each other, and *durability* ensures that once a transaction is committed, the changes are permanent, even in the event of a system crash.

- Key characteristics of NoSQL databases include multimodel support, distributed architecture, high availability, flexible schema, and fast deployment.

- Various types of NoSQL databases include document databases, graph databases, key-value databases, and columnar (Column-Family) databases.

SQL Fundamentals

In the previous chapter, you learned about the foundations of databases, what they are and how they're structured. Now it's time to explore SQL, the language used to communicate with relational databases. As a data engineer, you'll find that SQL will become one of your most-used tools. Whether you're extracting insights, transforming data, or building pipelines, you'll need to write queries. In this chapter, we're going to walk you through SQL fundamentals and look at simple code examples. By the end of this chapter, you'll be able to analyze data and apply what you've learned using a database management system.

HERE'S WHAT WE'LL COVER:

➤ What SQL is and why it's important

➤ Basic SELECT queries

➤ Filtering using the WHERE statement and logical operators

➤ Using JOINs to combine data

➤ Aggregating data with GROUP BY and functions

➤ Writing subqueries and using window functions

➤ Setting up SQL Server and running queries

➤ Best practices for writing clean and efficient SQL

Introduction to SQL

SQL is a programming language used to communicate with and manage data stored in relational databases. Think of it as a tool used to ask questions and give instructions to a database. To maintain clarity and consistency throughout this chapter, we'll rely on two tables for most of our examples: a Customer table that stores customer information and an Orders table that stores all orders and the total amount for the store.

Customer Table

CUSTOMER_ID	CUSTOMER_NAME	STATUS
1	Ada Herbert	Gold
2	Grace Turing	Gold
3	Alan Hopper	Bronze
4	Margaret Bill	Silver

Orders Table

ORDER_ID	CUSTOMER_ ID	TOTAL_ AMOUNT	SHIPPING_ COUNTRY	PAYMENT_ METHOD	ORDER_ DATE
101	1	200.0	USA	Credit	2025-01-02
102	1	100.0	UK	Credit	2025-02-15
103	2	400.0	USA	Coupon	2025-01-30
104	5	150.0	Canada	Credit	NULL

Basic SQL Clauses

Let's begin with the most common and essential SQL commands, the SELECT statement, the AS statement, and the WHERE statement. The SQL queries in this chapter are written using standard SQL syntax. If you're using another database system like PostgreSQL, you may need to make slight adjustments based on dialect differences.

SELECT *Statement*

The SELECT statement is used to retrieve data from a table. You can either list specific columns you want to see or use * to select all columns. The syntax for SELECT is as follows:

```
SELECT column1, column2, ...
FROM table_name;
```

This query gets all orders from the Orders table:

```
SELECT * FROM orders;
```

ORDER_ID	CUSTOMER_ID	TOTAL_AMOUNT	SHIPPING_COUNTRY	PAYMENT_METHOD	SHIPPED_DATE
101	1	200.0	USA	Credit	2025-01-02
102	1	100.0	UK	Credit	2025-02-15
103	2	400.0	USA	Coupon	2025-01-30
104	5	150.0	Canada	Credit	NULL

This query gets only `order_id` and `total_amount`:

```
SELECT order_id, total_amount
FROM orders;
```

ORDER_ID	TOTAL_AMOUNT
101	200.0
102	100.0
103	400.0
104	150.0

AS *Statement*

The AS statement is used to give a temporary name (alias) to a column or table, making the output easier to read or shortening long names.

```
SELECT column_name AS alias_name
FROM table_name;
```

This query displays the `total_amount` as `amount_paid`:

```
SELECT order_id, total_amount AS amount_paid
FROM orders;
```

ORDER_ID	AMOUNT_PAID
101	200.0
102	100.0
103	400.0
104	150.0

WHERE Statement

The WHERE statement filters rows that meet a certain condition. It helps you retrieve only the data you need.

```
SELECT column1, column2
FROM table_name
WHERE condition;
```

This query gets all orders with a total amount greater than 100:

```
SELECT order_id, total_amount
FROM orders
WHERE total_amount > 100;
```

ORDER_ID	TOTAL_AMOUNT
101	200.0
103	400.0
104	150.0

This query gets all orders shipped to the United States:

```
SELECT order_id, shipping_country
FROM orders
WHERE shipping_country = 'USA';
```

ORDER_ID	SHIPPING_COUNTRY
101	USA
103	USA

Comparison Operators

Comparison operators are used in the WHERE clause to build conditions that filter rows. They allow comparisons, check for values in a set, or match patterns.

DESCRIPTION	OPERATOR
Equal to	=
Not equal to	<> or !=
Greater than	>

DESCRIPTION	OPERATOR
Less than	<
Greater than or equal to	>=
Less than or equal to	<=

This query finds orders where the total amount is not equal to 200:

```
SELECT order_id, total_amount
FROM orders
WHERE total_amount != 200;
```

ORDER_ID	TOTAL_AMOUNT
102	100.0
103	400.0
104	150.0

LIKE Statement

The LIKE operator in SQL is used to search for a specified pattern in a column, often with text data. It's commonly used in WHERE clauses to filter rows based on partial matches.

The LIKE operator works with two special wildcard characters: the percent sign (%) and the underscore (_). The % matches zero or more characters, and the _ matches exactly one character.

This query finds all orders paid with a method that starts with credit:

```
SELECT order_id, customer_id, shipping_country, payment_method
FROM orders
WHERE payment_method LIKE 'Credit%';
```

ORDER_ID	CUSTOMER_ID	SHIPPING_COUNTRY	PAYMENT_METHOD
101	1	USA	Credit
102	1	UK	Credit
104	5	Canada	Credit

This query finds payment methods with Pay in the middle:

```
SELECT DISTINCT payment_method
FROM orders
WHERE payment_method LIKE '%Pay%';
```

This query matches names with exactly three letters where the second and third letters are da:

```
SELECT * FROM customers
WHERE name LIKE '_da';
```

CUSTOMER_ID	CUSTOMER_NAME
1	Ada Herbert

IN Statement

The IN statement is used when you want to match a value against a list of values. It's cleaner than writing a bunch of OR conditions.

This query finds customers that are either Gold or Bronze:

```
SELECT customer_id, customer_name, status
FROM customer
WHERE status IN (Gold, Bronze);
```

CUSTOMER_ID	CUSTOMER_NAME	STATUS
1	Ada Herbert	Gold
2	Grace Turing	Gold
3	Alan Hopper	Bronze

This is the same as writing this:

```
SELECT order_id, status
FROM orders
WHERE status = 'Shipped' OR status = 'Pending' OR status = 'Delivered'
```

BETWEEN Statement

BETWEEN is used to filter values within a range, and it's inclusive of both ends. This statement is helpful when you want to get a specific range of values, especially dates.

This query finds orders with a total amount between $100 and $300:

```
SELECT order_id, customer_id, total_amount
FROM orders
WHERE total_amount BETWEEN 100 AND 300;
```

ORDER_ID	CUSTOMER_ID	TOTAL_AMOUNT
101	1	200.0
102	1	100.0
104	5	150.0

This query gets all orders placed between January 1 and January 31, 2025:

```
SELECT order_id, total_amount, order_date
FROM orders
WHERE shipped_date BETWEEN '2025-01-01' AND '2025-01-31';
```

ORDER_ID	TOTAL_AMOUNT	SHIPPED_DATE
101	200.0	2025-01-02
103	400.0	2025-01-30

Logical Operators

Logical operators in SQL are used to combine multiple conditions in a WHERE clause and return rows based on whether those conditions evaluate to TRUE, FALSE, or UNKNOWN.

AND Statement

The AND statement combines two conditions and returns TRUE only if *both* conditions are true.

This query returns credit orders that were made in the United States:

```
SELECT * FROM orders
WHERE payment_method = 'Credit' AND shipping_country = 'USA';
```

ORDER_ID	CUSTOMER_ ID	TOTAL_ AMOUNT	SHIPPING_ COUNTRY	PAYMENT_ METHOD	SHIPPED_ DATE
101	1	200.0	USA	Credit	2025-01-02

OR Statement

The OR statement combines two conditions and returns TRUE if *at least one* condition is true.

This query returns orders from either the United States or Canada:

```
SELECT * FROM orders
WHERE shipping_country = 'USA' OR shipping_country = 'Canada';
```

ORDER_ID	CUSTOMER_ID	TOTAL_AMOUNT	SHIPPING_COUNTRY	PAYMENT_METHOD	SHIPPED_DATE
101	1	200.0	USA	Credit	2025-01-02
103	2	400.0	USA	Coupon	2025-01-30
104	5	150.0	Canada	Credit	NULL

NOT Statement

The NOT statement is used to negate a condition. It returns the opposite of the condition it's applied to.

This query returns a list of all employees who are not in the HR department:

```
SELECT * FROM orders
WHERE NOT payment_method = 'Credit';
```

ORDER_ID	CUSTOMER_ID	TOTAL_AMOUNT	SHIPPING_COUNTRY	PAYMENT_METHOD	SHIPPED_DATE
103	2	400.0	USA	Coupon	2025-01-30

IS NULL and IS NOT NULL Statements

In SQL, NULL means a value is missing or not recorded. IS NULL and IS NOT NULL help us filter for missing values accordingly.

This query helps us find all orders that haven't been shipped yet, and we can do this by checking records that have a shipped_date of NULL:

```
SELECT order_id, shipped_date
FROM orders
WHERE shipped_date IS NULL;
```

ORDER_ID	CUSTOMER_ID	TOTAL_AMOUNT	SHIPPING_COUNTRY	PAYMENT_METHOD	SHIPPED_DATE
104	5	150.0	Canada	Credit	NULL

This query finds all orders that have been shipped, using IS NOT NULL:

```
SELECT order_id, shipped_date
FROM orders
WHERE shipped_date IS NOT NULL;
```

ORDER_ID	CUSTOMER_ID	TOTAL_AMOUNT	SHIPPING_COUNTRY	PAYMENT_METHOD	SHIPPED_DATE
101	1	200.0	USA	Credit	2025-01-02
102	1	100.0	UK	Credit	2025-02-15
103	2	400.0	USA	Coupon	2025-01-30

Sorting and Limiting

These clauses help organize and reduce the data returned by your queries, especially when dealing with large datasets. To achieve this, we can use the ORDER BY, LIMIT, or TOP statement.

ORDER BY

This is used to sort query results by one or more columns. You can sort in ascending (ASC, which is the default) or descending (DESC) order.

```
SELECT column1, column2
FROM table_name
ORDER BY column1 [ASC|DESC];
```

This query sorts orders by total_amount in ascending order, and this puts the lowest amount on the first row:

```
SELECT order_id, total_amount
FROM orders
ORDER BY total_amount ASC;
```

ORDER_ID	TOTAL_AMOUNT
102	100.0
104	150.0
101	200.0
103	400.0

This query sorts by `shipped_date` in descending order to get the most recent order that was shipped:

```
SELECT order_id, shipped_date
FROM orders
ORDER BY shipped_date DESC;
```

ORDER_ID	SHIPPED_DATE
102	2025-02-15
103	2025-01-30
101	2025-01-02
104	NULL

LIMIT or TOP

These clauses restrict the number of rows returned in a result set. The syntax differs slightly depending on the database.

This query returns the first two highest orders:

```
SELECT order_id, total_amount
FROM orders
ORDER BY total_amount DESC
TOP 2;
```

ORDER_ID	TOTAL_AMOUNT
103	400.0
101	200.0

Aggregate Functions

Aggregate functions perform calculations on a set (group) of rows and return a single value. They're commonly used in reports, summaries, and dashboards.

- `COUNT`
- `AVG`
- `SUM`
- `MIN & MAX`

COUNT()

This returns the number of rows that match a particular condition or returns the count of all the rows using (*).

This query counts the total number of orders:

```
SELECT COUNT(*) AS number_of_orders
FROM orders;
```

NUMBER_OF_ORDERS
4

SUM()

The SUM statement returns the total (sum) of a numeric column.

This query gets the total revenue from the Orders table:

```
SELECT SUM(total_amount) AS total_revenue
FROM orders;
```

TOTAL_REVENUE
850.0

AVG()

The AVG() statement returns the average value of a numeric column.

This query calculates the average order value from the Orders table:

```
SELECT AVG(total_amount) AS average_order_value
FROM orders;
```

AVG_ORDER_VALUE
212.5

MAX() and MIN()

MAX() returns the highest value and MIN() returns the lowest value in a column.

This code returns the highest order value:

```
SELECT MAX(total_amount) AS highest_order
FROM orders;
```

HIGHEST_ORDER
850.0

This code returns the earliest order date:

```
SELECT MIN(order_date) AS first_order_date
FROM orders;
```

EARLIEST_ORDER
850.0

GROUP BY

Use the Group By statement when you want to group rows that have the same values in specified columns so that you can apply an aggregate function like SUM, COUNT, or AVG. It's like saying, "Group this data by customer, or country, or status, and give me totals or averages for each group."

This code counts the number of orders per shipping country:

```
SELECT shipping_country, COUNT(*) AS order_count
FROM orders
GROUP BY shipping_country;
```

SHIPPING_COUNTRY	ORDER_COUNT
USA	2
UK	1
Canada	1

This query calculates the total revenue per customer:

```
SELECT customer_id, SUM(total_amount) AS total_spent
FROM orders
GROUP BY customer_id;
```

CUSTOMER_ID	TOTAL_SPENT
1	300
2	400
5	150

To avoid errors, always note that every column in the SELECT clause that isn't part of an aggregate function *must* be included in the GROUP BY clause.

HAVING

The HAVING clause works like the WHERE clause, but it's used after data has been grouped. While WHERE filters individual rows before grouping, HAVING filters entire groups based on aggregate functions like SUM(), COUNT(), or AVG(). Since aggregate functions aren't allowed in WHERE, we use HAVING instead.

This code shows only countries with more than five orders:

```
SELECT shipping_country, COUNT(*) AS order_count
FROM orders
GROUP BY shipping_country
HAVING COUNT(*) > 5;
```

SHIPPING_COUNTRY	ORDER_COUNT
USA	6

This code shows customers who spent over $200 total:

```
SELECT customer_id, SUM(total_amount) AS total_spent
FROM orders
GROUP BY customer_id
HAVING SUM(total_amount) > 200;
```

CUSTOMER_ID	TOTAL_SPENT
1	300
2	400

In summary, use *GROUP BY* to group rows by a category and use *HAVING* to filter those grouped results based on aggregated values.

Understanding Joins

Imagine your company has two tables, one called Orders, which shows information about each order, and another called Customers, which stores customer details, and you need to find the name of the customer who placed order #1005. You would need to combine data from both tables to get this data, and that's where joins come in.

Customers Table

CUSTOMER_ID	CUSTOMER_NAME	STATUS
1	Ada Herbert	Gold
2	Grace Turing	Gold
3	Alan Hopper	Bronze
4	Margaret Bill	Silver

Orders Table

ORDER_ ID	CUSTOMER_ ID	TOTAL_ AMOUNT	SHIPPING_ COUNTRY	PAYMENT_ METHOD	ORDER_ DATE
101	1	200.0	USA	Credit	2025-01-02
102	1	100.0	UK	Credit	2025-02-15
103	2	400.0	USA	Coupon	2025-01-30
104	5	150.0	Canada	Credit	NULL

A *join* in SQL lets you pull information from two or more tables based on a related column between them. Using a join, you can match rows from one table to rows in another table where a shared column (usually an ID) lines up. Let's walk through the four main types of joins using a simple example.

INNER JOIN

An INNER JOIN is the most common type of join. It returns only the rows where there's a *match* in both tables. In Figure 4-1, the shaded area in the middle represents the matching rows, which are records that exist in both tables based on a common column. To get all orders that have a valid customer, using the Customers and Orders table, you'd write this query:

```
SELECT
    orders.order_id,
    customers.customer_name,
    orders.total_amount
```

```
FROM orders
INNER JOIN customers
    ON orders.customer_id = customers.customer_id;
```

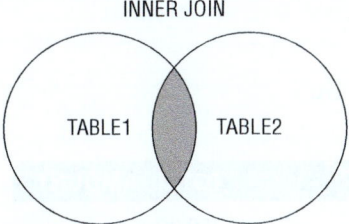

Figure 4-1: Inner join

Now, only customers who have matching orders would appear in the output. Alan and Margaret don't appear, and Order #104 is also excluded because customer 5 doesn't exist.

CUSTOMER_NAME	ORDER_ID	TOTAL_AMOUNT
Ada Herbert	101	250.00
Ada Herbert	102	100.00
Grace Turing	103	400.00

LEFT JOIN

In Figure 4-2, a LEFT JOIN returns *all rows* from the first (left) table and the *matched* **rows** from the second (right) table. If there's no match, the result will show NULL for the missing pieces.

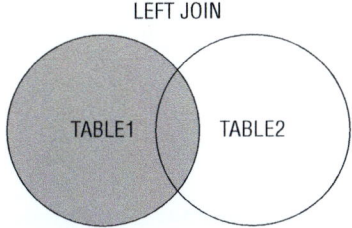

Figure 4-2: LEFT JOIN

A LEFT JOIN is useful when data might be missing in the second table but you still want to keep everything from the first. We use a LEFT JOIN when we want to retrieve a complete list of all customers, including those who haven't placed any orders yet.

```
SELECT
    customers.customer_id,
    customers.customer_name,
    orders.order_id,
    orders.total_amount
FROM customers
LEFT JOIN orders
    ON customers.customer_id = orders.customer_id;
```

CUSTOMER_ID	CUSTOMER_NAME	ORDER_ID	TOTAL_AMOUNT
1	Ada Herbert	101	250.00
1	Ada Herbert	102	100.00
2	Grace Turing	103	400.00
3	Alan Hopper	NULL	NULL
4	Margaret Bill	NULL	NULL

Customers like Alan and Margaret haven't made any purchases yet, so their order_id and total_amount appear as NULL. Now we can identify inactive customers who've signed up but never placed an order and even target marketing campaigns to them.

RIGHT JOIN

A RIGHT JOIN is the opposite of a LEFT JOIN. As shown in Figure 4-3, a RIGHT JOIN gives you all the rows from the second (right) table, and the matching rows from the first (left) table.

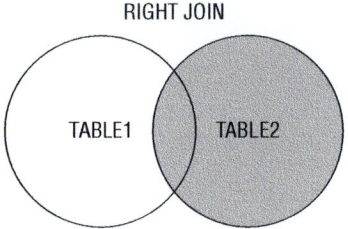

Figure 4-3: RIGHT JOIN

Imagine you're working on cleaning up historical sales data. Due to a migration from an old system, some orders exist without a matching customer profile; maybe the customer data was lost or never recorded properly. Now, you will want to list all orders, including those where the customer details are missing, so the data team can investigate or clean it up. This is where a RIGHT JOIN comes in handy; it ensures all records from the Orders table are included, even if there's no match in the customers table.

```
SELECT
    customers.customer_name,
    orders.order_id,
    orders.total_amount
FROM customers
RIGHT JOIN orders
    ON customers.customer_id = orders.customer_id;
```

CUSTOMER_ID	CUSTOMER_NAME	ORDER_ID	TOTAL_AMOUNT
1	Ada Herbert	101	250.00
1	Ada Herbert	102	100.00
2	Grace Turing	103	400.00
NULL	NULL	104	150.00

Order 104 was placed without matching order records, possibly due to the migration. RIGHT JOINs are not used as often, but they're a good choice if your focus is on the second table.

FULL OUTER JOIN

A FULL OUTER JOIN returns all rows from both tables, as seen in Figure 4-4. If there's no match, you'll see NULL for the missing pieces on either side.

FULL OUTER JOIN

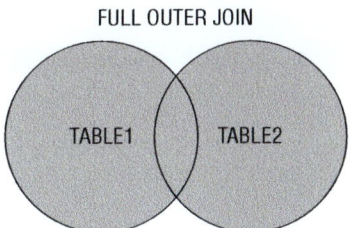

Figure 4-4: FULL OUTER JOIN

Using our tables, you might be tasked with generating a comprehensive report that shows all customers and all orders, even if they don't line up, so the team can identify data mismatches and clean things up.

```
SELECT
    customers.customer_name,
    orders.order_id,
    orders.total_amount
```

```
FROM customers
FULL OUTER JOIN orders
    ON customers.customer_id = orders.customer_id;
```

CUSTOMER_NAME	ORDER_ID	TOTAL_AMOUNT
Ada Herbert	101	250.00
Ada Herbert	102	100.00
Grace Turing	103	400.00
Alan Hopper	NULL	NULL
Margaret Bill	NULL	NULL
NULL	104	150.00

Subqueries

Let's say you want to find the customer with the highest order total. You can't answer this directly with just one simple query, because first, you need to find the highest order total, then use that value to find the customer who made it.

This is when we use a subquery. A *subquery* is a query inside another query. It's useful when you need to retrieve an intermediate result, like the maximum value, a filtered list, or a calculated metric, then use that result in your main query to drive further analysis. Let's use a subquery to figure out our problem.

This query finds customers with the highest order total:

```
SELECT
    customers.customer_name,
    orders.order_id,
    orders.total_amount
FROM orders
JOIN customers
    ON orders.customer_id = customers.customer_id
WHERE orders.total_amount = (
    SELECT MAX(total_amount)
    FROM orders
);
```

CUSTOMER_NAME	ORDER_ID	TOTAL_AMOUNT
Grace Turing	103	400

The subquery (inner query) finds the highest `total_amount` across all orders. The `WHERE` clause filters the results to show only the order(s) that match the highest total found in the subquery.

Common Table Expressions (CTEs)

A subquery is a query nested inside another query. It's great for quick, one-off filters or calculations but can get hard to read if complex or repeated. To solve this, we use a common table expression (CTE), which is a named temporary result set defined at the start of your query using WITH. It makes your SQL easier to read, debug, and maintain, especially when you reuse the same logic multiple times or build multistep queries.

The syntax for the subquery looks like this:

```
WITH cte_name AS (
    -- Your inner query here
)
SELECT * FROM cte_name;
```

Let's calculate the average order amount, using a subquery versus a CTE. Using a subquery, we calculated the average order amount twice on both queries:

```
SELECT *
FROM orders
WHERE total_amount > (
    SELECT AVG(total_amount) FROM orders
);

SELECT COUNT(*)
FROM orders
WHERE total_amount > (
    SELECT AVG(total_amount) FROM orders
);
```

Using a CTE means you write that logic once and refer to it by name, rather than nesting subqueries repeatedly.

```
WITH avg_order AS (
    SELECT AVG(total_amount) AS average_amount
    FROM orders
)
```

AVERAGE_AMOUNT
212.5

This query gets the order that is greater than or equal to the average amount of all orders:

```
SELECT *
FROM orders, avg_order
WHERE orders.total_amount >= avg_order.average_amount;
```

ORDER_ID	CUSTOMER_ ID	TOTAL_ AMOUNT	SHIPPING_ COUNTRY	PAYMENT_ METHOD	ORDER_ DATE
103	2	400.0	USA	Coupon	2025-01-30

This query gets the number of records that have total amounts greater than or equal to the average amount of all orders:

```
SELECT COUNT(*)
FROM orders, avg_order
WHERE orders.total_amount > avg_order.average_amount;
```

COUNT
1

Set Operations

Set operators are SQL commands that let you combine results from two or more queries into a single result set by treating those results like mathematical sets. They are UNION, INTERSECT, and EXCEPT.

Set operations are helpful when you want to merge data from different queries or tables, to find commonalities or differences between datasets, or to simplify complex queries that involve multiple result sets.

An important thing to note before using set operations is that the combined queries must have the same number of columns and the columns must be of compatible data types. The order of columns also matters because the set operator compares rows positionally. Let's explore each of them with examples.

UNION

UNION combines the results of two queries into a single result set, removes duplicate rows by default, and returns all distinct rows that appear in either query. This query gets a list of all customers who have either placed an order or are listed in the Customers table, excluding duplicates:

```
SELECT customer_id FROM customers
UNION
SELECT customer_id FROM orders;
```

CUSTOMER_ID
1
2

CUSTOMER_ID
3
4
5

UNION ALL

UNION ALL in SQL is used to combine the results of two or more SELECT statements into a single result set. Unlike UNION (which removes duplicates), UNION ALL returns every row, even if some are exact duplicates, which makes it faster than UNION because it doesn't sort or check for duplicates. This query gets a list of all customers who have either placed an order or are listed in the Customers table, including duplicates:

```
SELECT customer_id FROM customers
UNION ALL
SELECT customer_id FROM orders;
```

CUSTOMER_ID
1
2
3
4
1
1
2
5

INTERSECT

INTERSECT returns only the rows that appear in both queries and also removes duplicates. Let's find customers who have placed orders:

```
SELECT customer_id FROM customers
INTERSECT
SELECT customer_id FROM orders;
```

CUSTOMER_ID
1
2

EXCEPT

EXCEPT returns rows from the first query that do *not* appear in the second query. This query finds customers who exist in the Customers table but who have never placed an order:

```
SELECT customer_id FROM customers
EXCEPT
SELECT customer_id FROM orders;
```

CUSTOMER_ID
3
4

Window Functions

Window functions in SQL perform calculations across a set of rows related to the current row. It does this without collapsing rows like GROUP BY does. There are several types of window functions:

- Ranking functions
- Aggregate functions
- Value functions

Ranking Functions

These functions assign a position or order to each row within a group. You can use rank functions to answer questions like these:

- Who are the top three performers in each department?
- What is the rank of each product based on sales within a region?

In SQL, there are three types of ranking functions:

- ROW_NUMBER()
- RANK()
- DENSE_RANK()

ROW_NUMBER()

Let's use an employee table with employees, their region, and respective sales.

EMPLOYEE	REGION	SALES
David	West	900
Eve	West	800
Frank	West	800
Grace	West	700
Bob	East	600
Alice	East	500
Charlie	East	500
Hannah	East	400

Using this query, the ROW_NUMBER statement assigns a unique row number to each row within a specific group, based on a defined order:

```
SELECT
  employee, region, sales,
  ROW_NUMBER() OVER (PARTITION BY region ORDER BY sales DESC) AS row_num
FROM sales;
```

Let's explain the various parts of this statement:

```
ROW_NUMBER() OVER (PARTITION BY region ORDER BY sales DESC) AS row_num
```

OVER()   Defines the window of rows the function operates on.

PARTITION BY   Resets the row numbering for each region. So, employees in different regions will have separate sequences starting with 1.

ORDER BY   Sorts the rows in each partition by sales in descending order. The highest sales get row_num = 1.

EMPLOYEE	REGION	SALES	ROW_NUM
David	West	900	1
Eve	West	800	2
Frank	West	800	3
Grace	West	700	4
Bob	East	600	1
Alice	East	500	2
Charlie	East	500	3
Hannah	East	400	4

RANK()

RANK() assigns the same rank to tied rows and skips ranks after a tie; that is, if two people tie for rank 2, the next rank will be 4. This is important when you want to reflect actual competition rankings where ties affect positions.

A good example is a sports competition or tournament, where if two players tie for second place, no one is ranked third; the next competitor is fourth. This approach helps maintain fairness and accurately represents the standings when multiple participants achieve the same score or result.

```
SELECT
   employee, region, sales,
   RANK() OVER (PARTITION BY region ORDER BY sales DESC) AS rank
FROM sales;
```

EMPLOYEE	REGION	SALES	RANK
David	West	900	1
Eve	West	800	2
Frank	West	800	2
Grace	West	700	4
Bob	East	600	1
Alice	East	500	2
Charlie	East	500	2
Hannah	East	400	4

This preserves the idea that those tied share the second-place position, and the next place is effectively the fourth position.

DENSE_RANK()

DENSE_RANK assigns a ranking number to rows within a partition, based on the specified order, without skipping ranks when there are ties. It's useful when you want to avoid gaps in your ranking sequence, and it also keeps the ranking continuous, even with ties.

EMPLOYEE	REGION	SALES	DENSE_RANK
David	West	900	1
Eve	West	800	2
Frank	West	800	2
Grace	West	700	3

EMPLOYEE	REGION	SALES	DENSE_RANK
Bob	East	600	1
Alice	East	500	2
Charlie	East	500	2
Hannah	East	400	3

Aggregate Functions

We discussed aggregate functions like SUM(), AVG(), MIN(), MAX(), and COUNT() earlier, but when used in a window function, they operate across a set of rows (a window). Instead of returning one row per group, they return a value for every row, while still considering the group. This function is useful when you want to compare each row to a group total or average while still keeping the full row detail.

EMPLOYEE	REGION	SALES
David	West	900
Eve	West	800
Frank	West	800
Grace	West	700
Bob	East	600
Alice	East	500
Charlie	East	500
Hannah	East	400

```
SELECT
    employee, region, sales,
    DENSE_RANK() OVER (PARTITION BY region ORDER BY sales DESC) AS rank
FROM sales;
```

EMPLOYEE	REGION	SALES	TOTAL_SALES_REGION	AVG_SALES_REGION
David	West	900	3,200	800
Eve	West	800	3,200	800

EMPLOYEE	REGION	SALES	TOTAL_SALES_REGION	AVG_SALES_REGION
Frank	West	800	3,200	800
Grace	West	700	3,200	800
Bob	East	600	2,000	500
Alice	East	500	2,000	500
Charlie	East	500	2,000	500
Hannah	East	400	2,000	500

Here, `total_sales_region` is the sum of sales within each region, and `avg_sales_region` is the average sales within each region. We can use this approach to easily compare each employee's sales with the average sales amount in the region.

Value Functions

Value functions return values from other rows in the result set without collapsing rows. These functions allow you to compare current rows with previous/next rows or to compute running totals, differences, and trends, all while preserving every row. Common value functions include `LAG()` and `LEAD()`, which are useful for analyzing sequential data or tracking changes over time.

LAG()

The `LAG()` function is used to access data from a previous row in the same result set without using a self-join. This function is particularly useful when comparing a current row with its previous one, like checking how sales changed compared to the previous month. You can specify how many rows behind to look (the default is 1), and even a default value if the previous row doesn't exist.

Let's introduce a month column into the table.

ID	MONTH	SALES
1	Jan	1,000
2	Feb	1,200
3	Mar	1,100

```
SELECT
  month,
  sales,
  LAG(sales) OVER (ORDER BY month) AS prev_month_sales
FROM sales;
```

Here, `LAG()` has gotten the previous month's sales value for easy comparison.

ID	MONTH	SALES	PREV_MONTH_SALES
1	Jan	1,000	NULL
2	Feb	1,200	1,000
3	Mar	1,100	1,200

LEAD()

The `LEAD()` function retrieves data from a future row in the result set. This function is useful when you want to compare current values with upcoming ones, such as when you're forecasting or analyzing trends between current and next entries.

```
SELECT
  month,
  sales,
  LEAD(sales) OVER (ORDER BY month) AS next_month_sales
FROM sales;
```

ID	MONTH	SALES	NEXT_MONTH_SALES
1	Jan	1,000	1,200
2	Feb	1,200	1,100
3	Mar	1,100	NULL

Lab: Setting Up SQL Server and Running SQL Queries

In this lab, you'll be creating the tables we used in this chapter from scratch in MySQL Server Studio and running your queries directly on the server. This hands-on approach will give you a clear understanding of what it's like to build tables and perform analysis on them. Let's begin.

Step 1: Download and Install SQL Server

1. Go to the official Microsoft SQL Server download page at `www.microsoft.com/en-us/sql-server/sql-server-downloads`

2. Under Express Edition (Free), click Download Now (or choose Developer Edition for full features; free for nonproduction use).

3. Run the installer and follow these steps:
   a. Choose Basic installation for simplicity.
   b. Accept the license terms.
   c. Wait for the installation to complete.

Step 2: Download and Install SQL Server Management Studio (SSMS)

1. Go to `https://learn.microsoft.com/en-us/sql/ssms/download-sql-server-management-studio-ssms`.

2. Download the latest SSMS installer.

3. Run the installer and follow the instructions to install.

Step 3: Connect to Your SQL Server Instance

1. Open SQL Server Management Studio (SSMS).

2. In the Connect To Server window, specify the following:
   a. Server type: Database Engine
   b. Server name: localhost or .\SQLEXPRESS (for Express edition)
   c. Authentication: Windows Authentication (or SQL Server Authentication if you created a login)

3. Click Connect.

Step 4: Create Database

1. Right-click Database, and create a new database called **RetailStoreDB**.

2. Double-click RetailStoreDB and create a new table.

Step 5: Create Tables

1. On the blank document, enter this code to create the Customer table and then click Run:

```
CREATE TABLE Customer (
  customer_id INT PRIMARY KEY,
  customer_name VARCHAR(100),
  status VARCHAR(20)
);
```

2. In the left panel, you should see dbo.Customer, confirming that your table now exists.

3. Clear the editor, enter the following command for the Orders table, and click Run.

```
CREATE TABLE Orders (
    order_id INT PRIMARY KEY,
    customer_id INT,
    total_amount DECIMAL(10, 2),
        shipping_country VARCHAR(50),
```

```
        payment_method VARCHAR(20),
        order_date DATE,
        FOREIGN KEY (customer_id) REFERENCES Customer
(customer_id)
        );
```

Step 6: Insert Data into Tables

1. Clear your editor and enter this code to insert data into your Customer table:

```
    INSERT INTO Customer (customer_id, customer_name, status)
VALUES
    (1, 'Ada Herbert', 'Gold'),
    (2, 'Grace Turing', 'Gold'),
    (3, 'Alan Hopper', 'Bronze'),
    (4, 'Margaret Bill', 'Silver');
```

2. Click Run.

3. Run this code to confirm your data has been inserted:

```
    SELECT *
    FROM Customers
```

4. Clear the editor and enter the following code to populate your Orders table:

```
    INSERT INTO Orders (order_id, customer_id, total_amount,
shipping_country, payment_method, order_date) VALUES
    (101, 1, 200.00, 'USA', 'Credit', '2025-01-02'),
    (102, 1, 100.00, 'UK', 'Credit', '2025-02-15'),
    (103, 2, 400.00, 'USA', 'Coupon', '2025-01-30'),
    (104, 5, 150.00, 'Canada', 'Credit', NULL);
```

5. Run this code to verify that your tables were created correctly and your data was inserted as expected:

```
    SELECT *
    FROM Orders
```

Step 7: Practice SQL Queries

Now that you've created your tables and inserted the data, go ahead and run the queries from this lesson to deepen your understanding. All the code from this chapter is available in this GitHub repository: https://github.com/ Sommie09/sql-chapter-examples. Try out SELECT, WHERE, JOIN, and GROUP BY clauses to explore different patterns and gain familiarity with result sets.

Best Practices for Writing Efficient SQL Queries

You're going to be writing a lot of SQL queries during your day-to-day, and the way you write those queries can make or break the performance. Writing efficient SQL isn't just about getting correct results; it's about getting them fast, with minimal strain on your database. Your goal is to make queries readable, maintainable, and optimized for scale. In this section, we'll explore best practices that help you write SQL that's both clean and high-performing so that your pipelines run smoothly.

Write Clear Queries   Clarity is key in SQL, especially when working in teams or returning to your code later. Stick to consistent formatting, capitalize SQL keywords, and indent. Always use descriptive names for tables and columns, and avoid ambiguous or overly abbreviated aliases. Doing so makes your queries easier to read and maintain, especially as complexity grows.

Avoid SELECT *   Using SELECT * pulls in unnecessary data, which can hurt the performance of your queries and make them less explicit. Always select only the columns you need. This not only improves performance by reducing I/O and memory usage, but it also makes the intent of your query clearer to others.

Filter and Limit Early   When possible, reduce the dataset as early as you can in the query. Applying filters before joins or aggregations reduces the number of rows being processed, which improves performance. Similarly, if you're only interested in a small number of results, use limits to avoid processing unnecessary rows.

Use CTEs and Subqueries for Modularity   Common table expressions (CTEs) and subqueries help break down complex logic into modular, understandable blocks. This makes debugging and future changes easier, though you should be mindful of performance implications, especially if CTEs are used repeatedly.

Test and Optimize   Don't assume a query is efficient; test it on real or large datasets and analyze how the database engine executes your query.

Summary

- SQL is a programming language used to communicate with and manage data stored in relational databases.

- The SELECT statement retrieves data from a table. You can specify the columns you want or use * to select all columns.

- Operators are used in the WHERE clause to build conditions that filter rows. They are =, <, >, <=, >=, and !=.

- Logical operators in SQL are used to combine multiple conditions in a WHERE clause; these operators are AND, OR, and NOT.

- Sorting and limiting clauses help organize and reduce the data returned by your queries, especially when dealing with large datasets. These clauses are ORDER BY, LIMIT, and TOP.

- Aggregate functions calculate on a set (group) of rows and return a single value. These functions are COUNT(), AVG(), SUM(), MIN(), and MAX().

- A join in SQL lets you pull information from two or more tables based on a related column between them. We have INNER JOIN, LEFT JOIN, RIGHT JOIN, and FULL JOIN.

- A subquery is a query inside another query. It's useful when you need to retrieve an intermediate result.

- A common table expression (CTE) is a named temporary result set defined at the start of your query using WITH.

- Set operators are SQL commands that let you combine results from two or more queries into a single result set. They are UNION, INTERSECT, and EXCEPT.

- Window functions in SQL perform calculations across a set of rows related to the current row. They are divided into ranking, aggregate, and value functions.

- When writing SQL queries, always use descriptive names for tables and columns, and avoid ambiguous aliases. When possible, reduce the dataset as early as you can in the query using filters.

Database Design

A well-designed database is the backbone of any reliable system. It determines how efficiently data is stored, how easily it's retrieved, and how well the system scales as users and data grow. Without thoughtful design, even the best applications can suffer from data redundancy and performance issues.

Database design acts as the foundation for how data flows through a system. Just like architects need blueprints before construction begins, engineers need a clear plan for how data will be structured and maintained. This plan guides everything from table creation and relationships to how queries and updates are handled, ensuring the system remains maintainable and scalable over time.

As business needs change and new features are introduced, data volume grows. A well-designed database should accommodate those changes with minimal disruption. So as you go through this chapter, whether you're designing from scratch or maintaining existing databases, always remember that design is not just about creating tables and building models. It's about creating a solid, efficient, and flexible foundation for everything else that comes after.

In this section, we'll walk you through the principles and practices that make up strong database design, from gathering requirements to defining data models, setting up relationships, and optimizing for performance. You'll learn how to structure data in a way that supports both the business and the technology behind it. These topics include:

- How to model data
- Various stages of data modeling

- Data modeling best practices
- Understanding cardinality
- Designing an entity relationship diagram (ERD)
- Normalization and denormalization
- Rules of normalization
- Database optimization strategies

Data Modeling

Data modeling is the process of designing a blueprint that represents how data is organized, structured, and related within a system. It defines the relationships between different pieces of data, ensuring they are stored efficiently and can be accessed in meaningful ways. This process helps guide the creation of databases, data warehouses, and other data storage systems.

As discussed in the previous chapter, a schema refers to the structure that defines the organization of data within a database. It includes tables, columns, data types, and the relationships between them. While data modeling is the conceptual process of designing how data should be represented, the schema is the actual implementation of that design in a database. In other words, the schema is a tangible version of the data model, a way of translating the design into a physical structure that a database can use to store and manage data.

Why Do We Need to Model Data?

Let's look at a simple instance where building a data model would come in handy. Imagine you own a bakery and you take orders from customers. A customer named, Emily Johnson comes to the store to pick up her order. The store staff tries to search for her name in the system, but they see three different Emilys: Emily J, Johnson, Emily, and emily_j01. This confusion could lead to giving out the wrong order or not finding the order at all.

The bakery shop can solve this by linking every order to a CustomerID and generating a unique OrderID. Doing so makes it easy to find orders without relying solely on names. The staff can quickly retrieve Emily's order using her OrderID or CustomerID, eliminating any confusion.

Beyond just convenience, this structure supports the concept of ACID principles, which we discussed in previous chapters. These principles also guide good database design:

- In ACID principles, *atomicity* ensures that an order is either fully processed or not at all. A good data model enforces foreign key relationships.

So when creating an order, if there's no valid CustomerID, the whole transaction fails and does not partially save, which prevents broken or half-finished data.

- *Consistency* enforces rules, like requiring every order to be linked to a valid CustomerID. If someone tries to insert an Order with a fake CustomerID, the model rejects it, thus maintaining consistent, valid data.

- *Isolation* makes sure that two staff members adding orders for different Emilys at the same time don't overwrite or corrupt each other's data. Because each order is tied to a unique OrderID and CustomerID, the database won't mix them up. The structure helps different users' transactions run safely in parallel.

- *Durability* guarantees that once an order is saved, it won't disappear even if the system crashes. The model itself doesn't ensure durability, but it works with the database engine to make sure valid, complete data is written.

In this way, good data modeling not only helps organize information but also ensures that critical rules for data integrity and reliability are enforced.

Data models are built around business needs, so the first step before building a data model is to gather requirements from stakeholders. These business needs are integrated into planning in order to design a blueprint of what the database would look like.

A successful data model should:

- Map real-world business concepts like customers, orders, and products to data structures in a database.

- Create relationships between the data and maintain data integrity.

- Be flexible enough to adapt to changing requirements over time.

Types of Data Modeling

Data modeling can be categorized into different types based on the scope and level of detail they represent. These types help ensure that data is structured appropriately for the system's needs, whether it's for a simple database, a data warehouse, or a more complex enterprise system. The three primary types of data modeling are conceptual, logical, and physical.

Conceptual Data Model

A *conceptual data model* provides a high-level structure of business concepts and their relationships, focusing on how data is represented in the real world. It is defined by business stakeholders and data architects to capture initial project requirements, business rules, and entity relationships.

These models, also known as *domain models*, are abstract and independent of hardware, software, or database technologies. The goal is to organize and define the scope of business concepts, as well as establish data relationships, without detailing physical implementation or data processing flows.

Imagine a large retail company that is planning to launch a new online store. The leadership team needs a high-level overview of the key data entities involved, like customers, products, orders, and payments. They gather stakeholders from various departments, including marketing, sales, and IT, to define the relationships between these entities without focusing on technical details. The goal is to ensure everyone understands the data structure and how different parts of the business interact. A conceptual data model looks at the bigger picture without necessarily going into the details of how the database system would function.

Let's look at a conceptual data model for an e-commerce business.

Entities:

- Customer: Represents individuals who shop on the platform
- Product: Represents items available for sale
- Order: Represents customer purchases
- Payment: Represents transactions for orders

Relationships:

- A *customer* can place multiple orders.
- An *order* can have multiple *products*, and a *product* can be part of multiple *orders*.
- Each *order* is linked to a single *payment* transaction.

Business rules:

- Each *customer* must have at least one registered *payment* method.
- *Products* have a set inventory quantity that must be updated with each order.
- *Orders* cannot be processed without a valid payment.

Logical Data Model

A logical data model goes a step further by providing more detail about the concepts and relationships stated in the conceptual data model. In this stage, the attributes for each entity are defined. It serves as a bridge between the conceptual model and the physical model.

Using the retail company we spoke about earlier, after agreeing on the conceptual model, a logical model would be the details of these entities. We need to specify attributes such as customer names, email addresses, product categories, and payment methods.

The logical model also defines relationships like one customer placing many orders or one order containing multiple products. This model becomes the blueprint for database development, helping the team decide how data will be structured without considering specific database technologies.

For our example, here are the entities with their attributes:

- Customer (CustomerID, Name, Email)
- Order (OrderID, Date, TotalAmount)
- Product (ProductID, Name, Price)

Entity Relationship Diagrams (ERDs)

We've explored the logical data model, which defines entities and attributes. Our next step is to visualize these elements. Entity relationship diagrams (ERDs) are a key tool for representing logical data models in a clear, visual format. They help us map out how different entities relate to one another and ensure that the structure aligns with business requirements before any database is built.

An ERD visually represents the data structure of a system. It illustrates entities, attributes, and relationships between entities, making it a foundational tool in relational database design. Entity diagrams simplify complex data structures for stakeholders, serve as a blueprint for database creation, and most importantly, enable technical and nontechnical teams to understand data requirements.

The process of designing an ERD typically involves defining entities, their attributes, the relationships between them, and the cardinality of those relationships. Let's discuss each in detail.

Entities

Entities represent real-world objects or concepts that are significant to the business and need to be tracked in a database. Each entity is typically a noun and corresponds to a table in a database. Entities can be formed by identifying the core objects your business needs to manage, naming them using singular, descriptive terms (e.g., Customer instead of Customers), and ensuring entities are distinct and not overlapping (e.g., Employee and Manager can be separate if they have different attributes).

Here are some examples:

- In a retail system: Customer, Product, Order
- In a school system: Student, Teacher, Course

Attributes

Attributes describe properties or characteristics of an entity. Each attribute corresponds to a column in a database table. To form an attribute, you identify the key pieces of information you need to capture about each entity; use clear, meaningful names; and ensure attributes are atomic, meaning they cannot be broken down further—for instance, FullName might be split into FirstName and LastName.

Relationships

Relationships define how entities are connected. As discussed in the previous chapters, they show how data in one table relates to data in another. They are often represented using primary and foreign keys. It is intuitive to form relationships when you think about how entities can relate to each other in a real-world setting. To form these relationships, you must think about the appropriate cardinality and, additionally, implement foreign keys in your database to establish these relationships in a physical database model.

Cardinality

As seen in Figure 5-1, cardinality refers to the number of relationships between two entities in a database. It defines how many instances of one entity can be associated with instances of another entity.

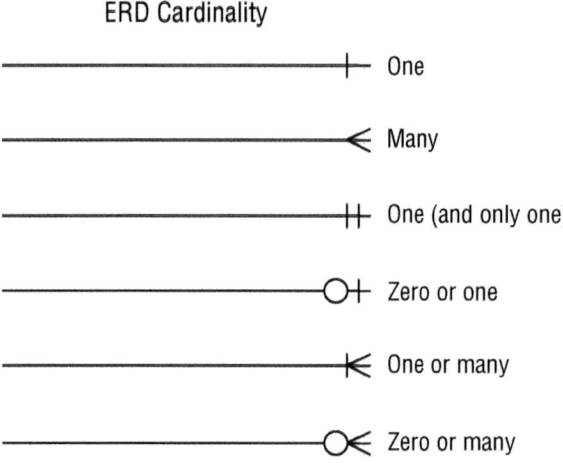

ERD Cardinality

One

Many

One (and only one)

Zero or one

One or many

Zero or many

Figure 5-1: Types of cardinality

Here are the types of cardinality:

- One-to-One (1:1): Each entity instance in Entity A is related to one entity instance in Entity B. This is used when entities have a unique and direct relationship, such as a company's employee ID linked to a security badge or a person having one passport.

- One-to-Many (1:N): One entity instance in Entity A can relate to many instances in Entity B. This is common in transactional systems, like e-commerce platforms where one customer can make several purchases.

- Many-to-many (M:N): Multiple instances in Entity A can relate to multiple instances in Entity B. Many-to-many relationships are typically used in scenarios involving multiple associations, such as students enrolling in multiple courses and each course having many students.

Designing an Entity Relationship Diagram

Figure 5-2 shows an ERD for an online shopping system. Each box contains an entity name, its attributes, and a primary and foreign key where necessary. Notice that some symbols represent cardinality, as we discussed earlier. Let's look at each entity in more detail.

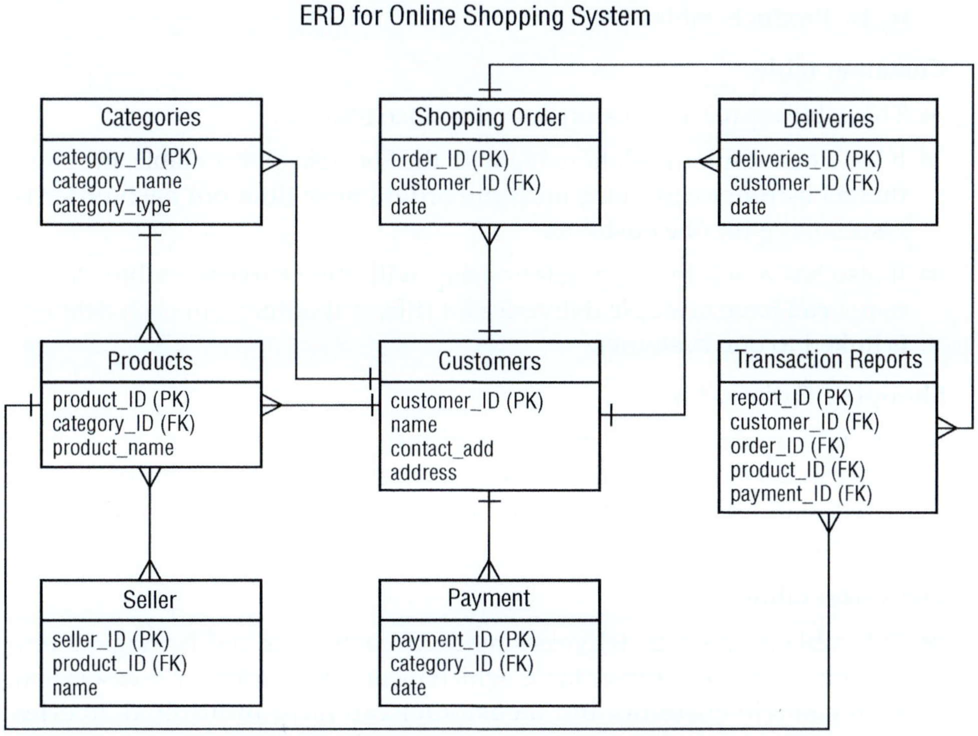

Figure 5-2: Entity relationship diagram for an online shopping system

Category table:

- This table represents different categories of products.
- It has a one-to-many relationship with the Products table, which means that a category like Electronics can have multiple products such as laptops, smartphones, and headphones.
- It has a one-to-many relationship with the Payment table, which allows payments made for products. For instance, the fashion category can be grouped together for revenue analysis.

Products table:

- This table represents Products available for sale.
- It has a one-to-many relationship with the Seller table, which means that a product like Lenovo can be sold by Seller A and Seller B, each having their own seller ID and attributes.

Seller table:

- This table represents sellers who sell products and belongs to one product in the Products table.

Customer table:

- This table represents customers who place orders.
- It has a one-to-many relationship with the Shopping Order table, meaning that a customer can place multiple orders over time but each order is associated with one customer.
- It also has a one-to-many relationship with the Deliveries table. A customer can have multiple deliveries for different orders, but each delivery is linked to one customer.

Shopping Order table:

- This table represents orders placed by customers and belongs to one customer in the Customer table, which means each shopping order is associated with a single customer but a customer can have multiple orders over time.

Deliveries table:

- This table represents deliveries made to customers and belongs to one customer in the Customer table, which means each delivery is associated with a single customer but a customer can have multiple deliveries over time.

Payment table:

- This table represents payments made for products and belongs to one category in the Categories table.

Transaction Reports table:

- This table provides a summary of transactions involving customers, orders, products, and payments along with a foreign key to reference these tables. This table would be useful for aggregating data from the Customers, Shopping Order, Products, and Payment tables.

- For instance, a transaction report could indicate that Customer A purchased Product X via Order Y and paid through Payment Z.

Physical Data Model

A physical data model is the most detailed stage of data modeling. It translates the logical data model into an implementable database design. It specifies how data will be stored, managed, and accessed in a specific database management system (DBMS). Unlike conceptual and logical models, the physical model considers the technical aspects, including storage structures, indexing, and constraints.

The retail company now needs to implement their physical model using a specific database technology, let's say PostgreSQL. The data engineers create a physical data model that defines tables, columns, data types, indexes, and partitions. They also specify primary and foreign keys for each table. According to the table, the physical model is the final, detailed plan for the database, ensuring it meets performance, scalability, and security requirements when deployed in production.

COLUMN NAME	DATA TYPE	CONSTRAINT
CustomerID	INT	PRIMARY KEY
Name	VARCHAR(100)	NOT NULL
Email	VARCHAR(100)	UNIQUE
Age	INT	CHECK (Age > 18)
OrderID	INT	FOREIGN KEY

In physical data modeling, one of the most important decisions you'll make is choosing the appropriate data type for each column. A data type defines what kind of data a column can store, like numbers, text, or dates. These choices might seem small, but they have real consequences on how much storage your database uses, how fast queries run, and how accurate your data remains over time. Let's break them down into categories:

Numeric Data Types   These are used when you need to store numbers. SQL gives you several options, depending on the size and precision you need. They include:

INT/INTEGER   Integers can store whole numbers. It usually takes up 4 bytes and works well for things like IDs, as long as the values stay within the limit of about 2 billion.

SMALLINT/TINYINT/BIGINT   These are variants of integers that use less or more space. For example, BIGINT can store much larger values (up to 9 quintillion), but takes 8 bytes.

FLOAT/REAL/DOUBLE   These can store approximate decimal values. They are fast but not always exact.

DECIMAL/NUMERIC   Stores exact decimal values. Perfect for financial data because they avoid rounding errors.

String (Character) Data Types   These types store text, like names, addresses, or notes:

CHAR(n)   This data type is used for fixed-length strings. If you define CHAR(10) and only store yes, SQL still stores 10 characters, padding the rest with spaces.

VARCHAR(n)   This data type stores variable-length strings up to a max length n. If you define VARCHAR(100) and store yes, it only uses three characters. This is more efficient for unpredictable text.

TEXT/CLOB   These data types are used for very long text (like articles or descriptions). They are less efficient for indexing and querying, so avoid them unless absolutely necessary.

Date and Time Data Types   These data types are used to track when something happens:

DATE   This data type stores only the calendar date (e.g., 2025-05-18).

TIME   This data type stores only the time of day (e.g., 14:30:00).

DATETIME/TIMESTAMP   This data type stores both date and time. DATETIME is often time zone–agnostic, while TIMESTAMP usually stores values relative to UTC.

Boolean Data Types   BOOLEAN/BOOL data types store TRUE or FALSE values but are not supported in all databases natively; some use TINYINT(1) under the hood.

Normalization

Let's assume that we have a table named Orders in an online store's database that is used to store customer information. In its initial, non-normalized form, the Orders table might look like this:

ORDER ID	CUSTOMER ID	CUSTOMER NAME	CUSTOMER ADDRESS	PRODUCT NAME	QUANTITY	ORDER DATE
1001	1	Jessica	405 Whitehouse St, NY, USA	Laptop	1	2024-11-20
1002	2	Lily	456 Elm St, LA, USA	Smartphone	2	2024-11-21
1003	1	Jessica	405 Whitehouse St, NY, USA	Headphones	1	2024-11-22
1004	3	Ben	789 Oak St, Chicago, USA	Laptop	1	2024-11-22

We have a few problems with this table:

- Jessica's address is repeated for every order she makes. If Jessica places multiple orders, her address information is stored multiple times and this wastes storage space.

- If Jessica changes her address—maybe she moves to a new home—we need to ensure that the address is updated in every order record for her. If we miss updating even one record, the system will have inconsistent data, leading to errors in customer communication or shipping.

How does normalization solve this?

- With the Customer table and the Orders table created, the customer's address is now stored only once in the Customer table rather than being repeated for every order. This reduces redundancy and storage usage.

- If Alice changes her address, we only need to update the Customer table. This change will automatically apply to all of Alice's orders without having to modify each order record individually, making maintenance more efficient.

- By storing the address in only one place, the risk of inconsistent data is eliminated. Every time a customer places an order, the correct address is used from the Customer table.

- There's no risk of having outdated or incorrect address information across different rows because the address is always retrieved from the Customer table.

Here is the Customer table:

CUSTOMER ID	CUSTOMER NAME	CUSTOMER ADDRESS
1	Jessica	405 Whitehouse St, NY, USA
2	Lily	456 Elm St, LA, USA
3	Ben	789 Oak St, Chicago, USA

And here is the Orders table:

ORDER ID	CUSTOMER ID	PRODUCT NAME	PRODUCT QUANTITY	ORDER DATE
1001	1	Laptop	1	2024-11-20
1002	2	Smartphone	2	2024-11-21
1003	1	Headphones	1	2024-11-22
1004	3	Laptop	1	2024-11-22

Normalization is one of those key principles in database design that keeps things clean and efficient. The idea is simple: We don't want to store the same piece of information in multiple places. Why? Because it takes up unnecessary space and can easily lead to mistakes and redundancy. It also helps to improve data integrity by organizing data into separate tables and reducing the risk of errors.

Rules of Normalization

The rules of normalization are guidelines for organizing data in a relational database. These rules are divided into *normal forms (NF)*, with each form addressing specific types of data anomalies, each ensuring redundancy and data integrity. As a data engineer, you might find that understanding the concept of normal forms can be confusing, but in this section, we'll simplify the rules of normalization and make it easy for you to recognize and apply each one.

First Normal Form: 1NF

The first normal form ensures all columns contain atomic values—that is, indivisible values. This means each cell should hold only a single piece of information, not a list or a set of values. Another attribute is that each row must be unique, and no duplicate rows are allowed. Let's take a look at an example.

The following table stores information about customers and their phone numbers. But there's an issue: If you look closely at the PhoneNumber column, Bailey has two different numbers in one column, which doesn't adhere to the 1NF rule.

CUSTOMER ID	NAME	PHONE NUMBER
1	Bailey	123-456, 987-654
2	Ashley	555-789

This new table is now 1NF compliant because the PhoneNumber column now contains atomic values.

CUSTOMER ID	NAME	PHONE NUMBER
1	Bailey	123-456
1	Bailey	987-654
2	Ashley	555-789

The 1NF rules don't just enforce structure; they also support the Atomicity and Consistency principles of ACID. By making sure each value is atomic and properly separated, databases can handle updates and queries more reliably, without risking partial updates or mismatched records. In 1NF, atomic means each field in a table contains only one value—for example, one phone number per cell. In ACID, atomicity means a transaction must either complete fully or not at all. When your data is structured with atomic values, thanks to 1NF it's easier for a transaction to meet the atomicity requirement because you don't have to worry about partially updating a list of values in a single cell, because each update touches only one clean, separate value.

1NF also helps enforce data consistency by eliminating duplicate rows and ensuring each field is clearly defined. In ACID, consistency means that a transaction brings the database from one valid state to another, maintaining integrity constraints. If your tables are not in 1NF—for example, if one column stores multiple phone numbers—it's much easier for inconsistent states to occur. One part of the application might update one number but forget the other, violating business rules. 1NF enforces a structure that helps keep your data valid and predictable, which supports transactional consistency.

While 1NF is a normalization rule, and ACID is a set of transactional guarantees, they support each other indirectly.

Second Normal Form: 2NF

The second normal form achieves the 1NF and removes partial dependencies. Partial dependencies occur when a column that is not part of any candidate key depends on part of a composite primary key rather than the whole key, and this is common only in tables with composite primary keys. As discussed in the previous chapters, a composite primary key is a primary key that is formed by combining two or more columns to uniquely identify each row in a table. This partial dependency creates a lot of inconsistencies, and 2NF helps us with this.

Assume we have a table that stores information about courses taken by students. The composite primary key is (StudentID, CourseID) because each student can take multiple courses and each course can be taken by multiple students.

The attribute CourseName depends only on CourseID, not on the entire composite key (StudentID, CourseID). Similarly, Instructor depends only on CourseID. This is a partial dependency, as CourseName and Instructor are functionally dependent on part of the primary key (CourseID) rather than the whole composite key.

Why Should Attributes Depend on the Entire Key?

In our table with a composite primary key (StudentID + CourseID), every non-key column should only depend on the whole key, not just part of it.

The primary key uniquely identifies each row in the table. If some columns (like CourseName) depend only on part of the key (like CourseID) and not the whole key (StudentID + CourseID), it means they don't belong in this table. Instead, they belong in a table where CourseID is the primary key.

The StudentCourses table looks like this:

STUDENT ID	COURSE ID	COURSE NAME	INSTRUCTOR
1	CS 101	Programming	Dr. Smith
1	CS 102	Networking	Mrs. Logan
2	CS 101	Programming	Dr. Smith

By splitting the table, we separate the Student–Course relationship from the Course details. The StudentCourses table tracks which student takes which course, and the Courses table tracks details about each course (like name and instructor). This reduces data redundancy because Programming and Dr. Smith are no longer repeated for every student taking CS 101), and it also improves data integrity; if an instructor changes for a course, you update it in one place. This is the StudentCourses table:

STUDENT ID	COURSE ID
1	CS 101
1	CS 102
1	CS 101

And this is the Courses table:

COURSE ID	COURSE NAME	INSTRUCTOR
CS 101	Programming	Dr. Smith
CS 102	Networking	Mrs. Logan

Third Normal Form: 3NF

The third normal form, 3NF, achieves 2NF and removes transitive dependencies, which is where all non-prime attributes, that is, columns that are not part of any candidate key, are only dependent on the primary key and not on any other non-prime attribute. Let's break that down with an example:

In this table, the primary key is StudentID. StateTaxCode depends on State, not directly on StudentID. This creates a transitive dependency that would look like this: StudentID → State → StateTaxCode.

This setup causes redundancy because "NY123" is repeated for every student in New York and risks inconsistency.

STUDENT ID	NAME	CITY	STATE	STATE TAX CODE
1	Jessica	New York	New York	NY123
2	Alexa	Los Angeles	California	CA456
3	Daniella	Albany	New York	NY123

Now in this new design, we have two tables: the Students table and States table. In this setup, StateTaxCode depends directly on the state in the States table. There's no more redundancy because "NY123" is stored only once for "New York".

If the tax code for a state changes, you update it in one place and most importantly, for scalability, adding a new state or modifying state information doesn't affect the Students table.

Students

STUDENT ID	NAME	CITY	STATE
1	Jessica	New York	New York
2	Alexa	Los Angeles	California
3	Daniella	Albany	New York

States

STATE	STATE TAX CODE
New York	NY123
California	CA456

Higher Normal Forms (BCNF, 4NF, 5NF)

Higher normal forms address more complex dependencies and anomalies that usually occur in large-scale and highly normalized systems. They also build upon the rules and conditions of earlier normal forms, providing stricter criteria for database design, although rarely used, it's important to also have a good understanding of them. They include Boyce-Codd Normal Form (BCNF), Fourth Normal Form (4NF), and Fifth Normal Form (5NF).

Boyce-Codd Normal Form (BCNF)

In the Boye-Codd Normal Form:

- The table must already be in 3NF.
- For every functional dependency □ → □, □ must be a superkey (i.e., □ uniquely identifies every row in the table). A functional dependency is when one set of columns (A) determines another set of columns (B).
- For example, in a table of students, if StudentID determines StudentName, that's a functional dependency. If A determines B, then A must be a superkey.
- A superkey is any column (or combination of columns) that can uniquely identify every row in the table. In simpler terms: If one thing (A) decides another thing (B), that "thing" (A) must be able to uniquely identify all rows in the table.

In this table, the Instructor is dependent on the Department, because an instructor is always associated with one department. But the Instructor is not a superkey because it cannot uniquely identify rows. After all, Dr. Andrew might teach multiple courses.

COURSE ID	INSTRUCTOR	DEPARTMENT
CS 101	Dr. Andrew	Computer Science
CS 102	Mrs. Kayla	Computer Science
ENG 103	Mr. Stephen	Engineering

To make all functional dependencies link directly to superkeys, we must split the tables: the Instructor_Department table and the Course_Instructor table. In summary, every determinant (a column or set of columns that determines another attribute) must be a candidate key. Boyce-Codd Normal Form (BNCH) can be used in transactional systems where data integrity is critical, and we can also regard BCNF as a stricter version of 3NF.

Instructor_Department table

INSTRUCTOR	DEPARTMENT
Dr. Andrew	Computer Science
Mrs. Kayla	Computer Science
Mr. Stephen	Engineering

Course_Instructor table

COURSE ID	INSTRUCTOR
CS 101	Dr. Andrew

COURSE ID	INSTRUCTOR
CS 102	Mrs. Kayla
ENG 101	Mr. Stephen

Fourth Normal Form (4NF):

For a table to be in 4NF, the table must already be in BCNF and all multivalued dependencies must be removed. A *multivalued dependency* occurs when a single attribute determines two or more independent values (attributes). These should be separated into distinct tables.

The following table tracks students, the languages they speak, and the sports they play. There are a couple of multivalue dependencies here. A student can speak multiple languages and a student can play multiple sports. The problem here is that the languages a student speaks are independent of the sports they play. This would result in redundant data where every combination of language and sport is listed for each student.

STUDENT ID	LANGUAGE	SPORT
1	English	Basketball
1	French	Basketball
1	English	Football
1	French	Football

To eliminate that redundancy, we split the above table into two tables, Languages and Sports. With this change, we can add a new language or sport for a student without duplicating unrelated data. 4NF improves database integrity by ensuring independent relationships are stored in separate tables. If such dependencies don't exist in your schema, you might not need to normalize to 4NF. Languages table

STUDENT ID	LANGUAGE
1	English
1	French

Sports table

STUDENT ID	SPORTS
1	Basketball
1	Football

Fifth Normal Form (5NF)

5NF is a level of database normalization aimed at eliminating redundancy by breaking down tables into smaller ones without losing data integrity. A table is in 5NF if and only if every nontrivial join dependency in the table is implied by the candidate keys. A join dependency occurs when a table can be broken into two or more smaller tables, which can then be joined together to re-create the original table. The goal is to ensure that data is represented in the most atomic way possible and that all relationships are captured without redundancies.

Let's look at the Employee table that follows. Here, the combination of Employee, Skill, and Project shows a multivalued dependency because skills and projects are independent facts associated with an employee. But this table has some issues:

- Skills and projects for each employee are listed repeatedly, causing redundancy.

- If Alexa gets assigned a new project, we need to repeat her skills for the new project.

- Removing a project could inadvertently delete all skill information for an employee.

Employee table

EMPLOYEE	SKILL	PROJECT
Alexa	SQL	Alpha
Alexa	Python	Alpha
Bella	SQL	Alpha
Bella	Python	Beta

By breaking this table into smaller tables, all anomalies are eliminated:

- We can add a new skill or project without duplicating other information.

- Updating a skill or project doesn't require repetitive changes.

- Deleting one project won't lose information about skills or employees.

- Most importantly, we can join the Employee_Project table with the Project_Tasks table using the Project column to identify which employees are linked to which tasks via their projects.

Employee_Task table

EMPLOYEE	TASK
Alexa	SQL
Alexa	Python
Bella	SQL
Bella	Python

Employee_Project table

EMPLOYEE	PROJECT
Alexa	Alpha
Bella	Alpha
Bella	Beta

Project_Tasks table

PROJECT	TASK
Alpha	SQL
Alpha	Python
Beta	Python

5NF ensures that tables are broken into smaller tables to eliminate redundancy caused by multivalued dependencies. While 5NF is not always necessary in a typical database design, it is important in cases of complex relationships and large enterprise systems.

Downsides of Normalization

We've discussed the benefits of normalization in detail, but normalization also has its downsides:

- Normalized databases often require multiple joins to fetch related data, which can slow down query performance for complex datasets or high-traffic applications.

- Normalization requires a thorough understanding of data relationships, making database design more time-consuming. While normalization is ideal for transactional systems, it may not be efficient in certain scenarios, and this is where denormalization comes in.

Denormalization

Denormalization is the process of combining separate tables into one to reduce the need for complex joins during queries. Additionally, calculated or aggregated data may be stored directly in tables instead of computing it on demand. It is essentially the opposite of normalization, where a database is organized to reduce redundancy and improve data integrity.

Denormalization handles reporting use cases where read performance is prioritized over write performance. With fewer joins on tables, query logic becomes simpler and easier to write. Denormalized tables also store precomputed data, and this speeds up data retrieval critical for large-scale reporting systems.

This is what a denormalized table would look like:

ORDER ID	CUSTOMER ID	CUSTOMER NAME	PRODUCT ID	PRODUCT NAME	QUANTITY	ORDER DATE	TOTAL PRICE
101	C001	Alexa	P001	Laptop	1	2025-12-04	1000
102	C002	Daniella	P002	SmartPhone	2	2025-12-03	1200
103	C001	Alexa	P003	Headphone	1	2025-12-03	200

This table is denormalized because:

- CustomerName is repeated for CustomerID C001, meaning customer info is duplicated across rows.

- ProductName is repeated for each order instead of referencing a Products table.

- TotalPrice is calculated and stored, avoiding the need to calculate it on-the-fly using (Price * Quantity). For instance, the cost of two Smartphones has been calculated as 1200.

While normalization helps maintain data integrity and reduce redundancy, some real-world systems actually benefit from denormalized data due to performance needs and faster read times:

Analytical and Reporting Systems   A *data warehouse* is a centralized repository designed to store, process, and manage large volumes of data collected from various sources. In data warehouses or OLAP (online analytical processing) systems, data is denormalized for read-heavy workloads and analytical queries. The goal in these systems is to simplify the retrieval of aggregated or summarized data for reporting and decision-making purposes. Analytical systems prioritize the speed of complex queries overwrite efficiency, making denormalization favorable choice. We will be looking at data warehouses in detail later in this book.

Real-Time Applications Real-time applications such as stock trading systems or IoT (Internet of Things) platforms require low-latency data reads. Denormalization is used here to avoid the lag in performance associated with frequent joins, because data needed for a single operation is often stored together, eliminating the need to join multiple tables during query execution.

Distributed Systems In distributed databases, data is partitioned and stored across multiple nodes. Denormalization ensures that all the data required for a query resides on a single node, reducing latency and network overhead that would come up. Distributed systems prioritize availability, and denormalization aligns with this model by simplifying data retrieval, even if consistency across nodes is delayed.

Data Modeling Best Practices

Data modeling is the foundation of an efficient data system, ensuring that data is organized, accessible, and optimized for both performance and scalability. A solid data model helps us organize data in a way that makes sense for the business and keeps things efficient. Let's look at best practices for creating effective data models for business needs.

Define the Grain

The *grain* of a table specifies the level of detail represented by each row. It answers the question, What does one row in the table represent? Is it one transaction? One customer per month? Or one product per store, per day?

Imagine you're building a sales table. You have to decide if each row should represent an individual transaction, like one order placed at a specific time or if it should represent something more aggregated, like total sales per store per day. This decision defines your grain.

One row = One transaction

ORDER_ID	STORE_ID	PRODUCT_ID	QUANTITY	PRICE	ORDER_DATE
1234	01	P001	2	20.00	2025-05-17 10:32 AM

One row = one day of sales per store

STORE_ID	SALE_DATE	TOTAL_SALES	TOTAL_TRANSACTIONS
01	2025-05-17	1500.00	5

You can't mix grains in the same table, so if the grain isn't clear, your data model becomes inconsistent and downstream reports become unreliable. Choosing the right grain is also a collaborative process. You don't decide it in a vacuum. You work with business stakeholders, product managers, and analysts to understand how the data will be used. What are the key questions the business is trying to answer? What kind of analysis needs to happen?

Sometimes, a fine-grained level (like one row per transaction) is what you need when you want flexibility and detail. Other times, an aggregated level (like one row per day per product) can make querying and performance more efficient, especially for reporting use cases.

Normalize Now, Denormalize Later

When you're starting out on a project, especially in the early stages of designing your data model, your top priority should be to normalize the data. That means structuring it cleanly into separate, related tables where each piece of information is stored only once. This keeps your data consistent and makes it easier to maintain in the long run.

As discussed earlier, instead of storing customer names and emails with every order, you keep that customer information in one Customer table and reference it from your Orders table. This structure is easier to understand and ensures that if a customer's email changes, you update it in only one place.

Now, as your application matures and your data grows, something interesting happens. You start to notice performance bottlenecks. Your application might start making a lot of JOINs across multiple tables to serve a single user request. Here's where denormalization comes in.

Denormalization is a conscious decision to optimize for performance by combining or duplicating data to reduce the number of complex JOINs needed. For example, you might add a customer's name directly into the Orders table if it's something you frequently display together, even if it breaks strict normalization.

The key here is, you don't start with denormalization. You first get your structure clean and correct. Then, based on actual performance needs, you denormalize in a targeted way. It's a trade-off; you're giving up some maintainability to gain speed where it matters.

Choose the Right Data Types

As discussed earlier, selecting the right data type is one of the most important decisions you make during physical data modeling. It might seem like a minor detail, but it directly impacts how your database performs, how much storage it uses, and how reliably it scales.

Each data type defines the boundaries and behavior of your data. If you choose well, your system runs efficiently, your queries perform better, and your storage usage stays lean. If you choose poorly, you may face a range of problems.

For example, consider a database that tracks user login timestamps. Using DATETIME might seem fine at first, but in many systems, it occupies more space than TIMESTAMP. If you don't need time zone support, switching to TIMESTAMP can save significant storage, especially at scale.

In another case, a financial system uses INT for transaction IDs. As the system grows and transaction volume increases, it eventually exceeds the limit for INT, resulting in runtime errors or even system crashes. In situations like this, BIGINT is a safer choice for fields expected to grow significantly over time.

Here are some other common considerations:

- Use INTEGER instead of FLOAT for primary keys or IDs because integers provide exact values and use less space, whereas floats are approximate and not ideal for joins or indexing.

- Prefer VARCHAR(255) over TEXT when string lengths are predictable. TEXT types are less efficient to index and can lead to wasted storage.

- Be mindful of precision; using the wrong numeric type (like FLOAT for financial data) can cause rounding errors and data inaccuracies.

- Avoid overly flexible types like VARCHAR if your data follows a strict format. It's better to define constraints that protect the quality and consistency of your data.

Proper Naming Conventions

Good naming is about clarity, consistency, and communication. When you name your tables and columns well, you're making processes easier, not just for yourself, but for everyone who will work with that system after you.

Imagine opening a database and seeing a table called tbl001, with columns like c1, c2, or field_x. You'd have no clue without digging into the data, and that slows everyone down. On the other hand, if the table is called Customers, and it has columns like First_Name, Last_Name, and Account_ID, the intent is immediately obvious. That's what good naming does—it removes friction and reduces guesswork.

Adopt a naming convention and stick with it. Whether that's snake_case for column names (like account_id) or PascalCase for table names (like TransactionHistory), consistency is key. This way, when someone moves from one part of the database to another, they're not relearning the rules each time.

Database Optimization

Sepora is a rapidly growing e-commerce platform that specializes in same-day delivery. The company has a central relational database used to store its product inventory, customer information, order details, and delivery schedules. Initially, Sepora handled a few hundred transactions per day efficiently. As the business expanded, the number of daily transactions surged to thousands, but the database structure remained unchanged.

On Christmas Eve, they had a holiday sale, and the website traffic skyrocketed. Customers had a bad experience searching for products because the pages weren't loading fast enough. The database server got overwhelmed because every query, especially for popular products, was sent to the same server, causing a lot of bottlenecks.

As a data engineer working at Sepora, what can you do?

As your database grows in size and complexity, you may start to notice slower performance and reduced responsiveness. These challenges are common, especially in large-scale systems, where the volume of data and number of queries can quickly become overwhelming. To keep your systems running efficiently, it's important to apply techniques that can address those issues. Database optimization to the rescue! It's the process of improving how well your database performs, ensuring it remains fast and scalable as it grows. In this section, we'll walk you through key optimization techniques:

- Indexing
- Partitioning
- Sharding
- Views

Indexing

Indexing is the process of creating a data structure (called an index) that improves the speed of data retrieval operations in a database table. Instead of scanning every row, the database can use the index to quickly locate the data it needs, making queries more efficient. Indexing helps us improve query performance by reducing the amount of data scanned, especially while handling large datasets where full table scans are inefficient.

In the e-commerce platform we talked about earlier, indexing helps in situations where users frequently search for products by name or category. If the database stores millions of product details without an index, a query to find a product by name would scan the entire table, leading to high latency (delay), but with an index on the product_name column, the database can quickly locate the relevant rows.

Let's see how this would work.

The first step is to create a table:

```
CREATE TABLE products (
    id SERIAL PRIMARY KEY,
    name VARCHAR(255) NOT NULL,
    category VARCHAR(100),
    price DECIMAL(10, 2),
    stock_quantity INT
);
```

After defining your table, you add indexes to optimize queries that are expected to be frequent or slow—for example, if users often search products by name.

```
CREATE INDEX idx_product_name ON products(name);
```

Now when you query, the database engine uses the index you created on name to quickly find matching rows, rather than scanning every row in the products table.

```
SELECT * FROM products WHERE name = 'Laptop';
```

Partitioning

Say you visit a large library with thousands of books and your task is to find a specific book quickly. If all the books were placed randomly on one massive shelf, searching for a particular book would take forever. But to make the search easier, the librarian organizes the books into sections based on categories like Fiction, Nonfiction, Science, and History. The librarian can also divide the books using certain criteria, like dividing books by year of publication (e.g., 1900–1950, 1951–2000), dividing books by genre (e.g., Fiction, Science, History) or randomly distributing books into sections by assigning them a unique identifier, which is referred to as *hashing*.

Partitioning involves dividing a large table in a database into smaller, more manageable pieces known as *partitions*, stored separately. The database uses partition logic to determine where data is stored and retrieved. Partitioning improves query performance by restricting scans to specific partitions.

In the e-commerce store we talked about, let's assume their launch day was in the year 2005. The sales table of the store would contain transaction data from 2005 to the present day. To efficiently manage this massive dataset and optimize query performance, you as the data engineer might decide to partition the sales table by year of the sale:

```
CREATE TABLE sales (
    sale_id INT PRIMARY KEY,
    sale_date DATE,
```

```
    amount DECIMAL(10, 2)
) PARTITION BY RANGE (YEAR(sale_date)) (
    PARTITION p0 VALUES LESS THAN (2000),
    PARTITION p1 VALUES LESS THAN (2010),
    PARTITION p2 VALUES LESS THAN (2020),
    PARTITION p3 VALUES LESS THAN (MAXVALUE)
);
```

In the SQL query, data would be automatically stored in different partitions based on the year in the sale_date column.

- Sales from before the year 2000 go into p0.
- Sales from 2000 to 2009 go into p1.
- Sales from 2010 to 2019 go into p2.
- Sales from 2020 on go into p3.

To get the total sales for the year 2021, you'd query the sales table and filter by the sale_date column; with our partitioning strategy, we won't need to search the entire table.

```
SELECT SUM(amount) AS total_sales
FROM sales
WHERE sale_date BETWEEN '2021-01-01' AND '2021-12-31';
```

Sharding

Sharding is a database optimization strategy used when your data becomes too large to handle efficiently on a single server. It works by horizontally partitioning data across multiple databases or nodes, each of which holds just a portion of the overall data, known as a *shard*. This approach helps applications scale horizontally and reduces the risk of one server becoming a performance bottleneck.

You'll often see sharding in action on platforms like social media apps, which serve billions of users. Instead of placing all user data in one central location, they shard the data, sometimes by region or user ID, so information is stored closer to users. This significantly reduces latency and improves performance for things like region-specific queries or content delivery.

Choose a Sharding Key

One of the most important decisions when sharding is selecting the right sharding key, the value that determines how data gets divided across shards. A well-chosen key ensures data is evenly distributed, which helps balance load and maintain performance. Common sharding keys include UserID, OrderID, or even Region, depending on how your application is used.

Configuring Multiple Shards

Each shard in a sharded architecture is essentially a separate database instance. These shards usually share the same schema, but each one holds a different slice of the data. For example, if you're storing user data, Shard 1 might contain users with IDs from 1 to 1,000,000, while Shard 2 could hold users from 1,000,001 to 2,000,000. This setup reduces the load on any single database and makes it easier to scale your application horizontally.

Let's see how sharding is implemented across data. To start, we define a basic schema for the users table. This structure will typically be replicated across all shards:

```
CREATE TABLE users (
    user_id INT PRIMARY KEY,
    name VARCHAR(100),
    email VARCHAR(100),
    region VARCHAR(50)
);
```

This table will exist in each shard, but each shard will store only a portion of the users based on the sharding key, in this case, user_id. For example:

■ Shard 1 holds rows where user_id is between 1 and 1,000,000.

■ Shard 2 holds rows where user_id is between 1,000,001 and 2,000,000.

By distributing the data this way, we prevent bottlenecks and enable the system to handle higher loads, especially useful in high-traffic systems like social platforms, e-commerce apps, or streaming services.

Now that we've split our user data across multiple shards, a big question comes up: How does the application know which shard to query? That's where sharding logic comes in. Suppose you're using a very simple sharding rule:

■ If user_id % 2 = 0, the user belongs to shard1.

■ If user_id % 2 = 1, the user belongs to shard2.

This is a hash-based sharding strategy. It evenly distributes users between two shards based on the parity of their user ID. Here's what the logic might look like in Python:

```python
# Determine the shard for a given user_id
def get_shard(user_id):
    if user_id % 2 == 0:
        return "shard1"
    else:
        return "shard2"

#Sample query
```

```
user_id = 12345
shard = get_shard(user_id)

#Run SQL code according to the shard
if shard == "shard1":
    execute_query("SELECT * FROM shard1.users WHERE user_id = 12345")
else:
    execute_query("SELECT * FROM shard2.users WHERE user_id = 12345")
```

This logic allows your application to route queries to the correct database, avoiding unnecessary load on other shards and improving performance. In production systems, this sharding logic is often abstracted away inside a shard manager, middleware, or ORM layer so engineers don't have to manually write conditional logic like this every time.

Difference Between Sharding and Partitioning

At first glance, sharding and partitioning might seem like the same thing because both involve breaking large datasets into smaller pieces. But the key difference lies in where the data lives.

Partitioning happens within one database server. You're dividing a large table into smaller segments (called *partitions*), but it all still lives in the same physical system. These partitions are often based on criteria like dates, regions, or product categories. This approach is used when you've got a huge orders table, and you partition it by month to make queries for recent orders faster. It improves query performance and data management within one server.

While sharding goes a step further, it spreads the data across multiple physical databases or servers. Each shard holds a subset of the data, often based on a sharding key like user_id or region. It's mostly used when user base has grown into the hundreds of millions, and your single database can't handle the load anymore. It then enables horizontal scaling, fault isolation, and better geographical performance.

Views

Views are like virtual tables created from the results of an SQL query. Instead of rewriting complex queries or joins over and over, you define a view once and reuse it wherever you need. This not only saves time but also makes your code cleaner and easier to maintain. Views can handle complicated joins, filters, and aggregations behind the scenes, so when you query a view, you're working with a simplified and consistent dataset.

Also, from a security standpoint, views are powerful because they let you control what data users can see. You can restrict access to sensitive columns or rows by exposing only certain parts of the underlying tables through the view, adding an extra layer of protection. Let's explore how to work with views.

Creating a View

This view filters out only the employees in the Engineering department:

```
CREATE VIEW EngineeringEmployees AS
SELECT id, name, salary
FROM employees
WHERE department = 'Engineering';
```

Querying the View

This query retrieves the names and salaries of engineering employees who earn more than $50,000, using the view we defined earlier:

```
SELECT name, salary
FROM EngineeringEmployees
WHERE salary > 50000;
```

Materialized Views

Materialized views are like regular views but with a key difference: They store the query results physically. While a regular view runs the query fresh every time you access it, a materialized view saves the results when it's created or refreshed. This means that for queries that are run frequently and don't need real-time updates, like summary reports or dashboards, materialized views can boost performance significantly by avoiding repeated computations. However, because the data is stored, materialized views need to be refreshed whenever the underlying data changes, either on a schedule or triggered by certain events. Let's look at how materialized views work.

Creating a Materialized View

This query creates a materialized view that stores the total value of orders greater than $1,000.

```
CREATE MATERIALIZED VIEW HighValueOrders AS
SELECT o.order_id, o.customer_id, SUM(oi.quantity * oi.unit_price) AS
total_value
FROM orders o
JOIN order_items oi ON o.order_id = oi.order_id
```

```
GROUP BY o.order_id, o.customer_id
HAVING SUM(oi.quantity * oi.unit_price) > 1000;
```

Refreshing a Materialized View

Materialized views can become outdated when the underlying data changes. To keep the data current, you can refresh the materialized view:

```
REFRESH MATERIALIZED VIEW materialized_view_name;
```

Summary

- Database design is the process of structuring how data will be stored, organized, and accessed in a database. It also involves deciding what tables to create, how they relate to each other, and how to optimize for performance.

- A successful data model should map real-world business concepts to database structures, create relationships between the data, maintain data integrity, and be flexible enough to adapt to changing requirements over time.

- There are three types of data models: conceptual, logical, and physical data models. Conceptual models cover the high-level view of entities and their relationships. Logical models add attributes, whereas physical models cover the actual implementation, like tables, indexes, and storage details for a specific database.

- An entity relationship diagram (ERD) visually represents the data structure of a system. It illustrates entities, attributes, and relationships between entities.

- Cardinality refers to the number of relationships between two entities in a database. It could be one-to-one, one-to-many, or many-to-many.

- A data type defines what kind of data a column can store, like numbers, text, or dates. They are grouped into Numeric, String, Date and Time, and Boolean.

- Numeric data types are used to store numbers, String data types are used to store text, Date and Time data types are used to store dates and times, and Boolean data types are used to store `True` or `False` values.

- Normalization is the process of organizing data in a database to reduce redundancy and improve data integrity. It involves splitting large, repetitive tables into smaller, related ones and defining clear relationships between them.

- The rules of normalization are divided into six normal forms: 1NF, 2NF, 3NF, and higher normal forms like BCNF, 4NF, and 5NF.

- Denormalization is the process of combining separate tables into one to reduce the need for complex joins during queries. Systems that benefit from denormalization are analytical and reporting systems, real-time systems, and distributed systems.

- Some best practices for modeling data include defining the grain, normalizing now and denormalizing later, choosing the right data types, and using proper naming conventions.

- Database optimization is the process of improving the performance, efficiency, and scalability of a database. Optimization techniques include indexing, partitioning, sharding, and views.

Data Warehouses, Data Lakes, and Data Lakehouses

In previous chapters, we explored the fundamentals of databases, exploring how databases are structured, managed, and optimized for business operations. Databases are the backbone of data storage and retrieval for many organizations. However, traditional database systems have some limitations. This chapter will introduce you to other database solutions designed to tackle unique challenges faced by organizations.

IN THIS CHAPTER, YOU WILL LEARN ABOUT THE FOLLOWING:

- What are data warehouses and how do they work?
- Extract, transform, and load processes
- Star and Snowflake modeling techniques
- Online Transaction Processing (OLTP) and Online Analytical Processing (OLAP) systems
- Data marts and their benefits
- Storing raw data with data lakes
- The data lakehouse architecture
- Choosing between a database, a data warehouse, and a data lake
- Exploring real-world use cases

By the end of this chapter, you will have a solid foundation for understanding these key data storage paradigms, enabling you to make informed decisions while integrating them into modern data workflows. Throughout this chapter, we'll use Dough & Delight, a fictional bakery, as our retail store example. All data models and scenarios will reference this business to provide consistency and real-world context.

Data Warehouses

Our retail store, Dough & Delight, has a relational database with separate tables for tracking customer orders, pastries, prices, and transactions.

TABLE	PURPOSE
Orders	Stores general information about customer purchases, such as the order ID, customer ID, and date of the transaction
Products	Stores information about the items the bakery sells, such as product name, category, and product ID
OrderDetails	Tracks the specific items included in each order, including product ID, quantity, and order ID
Price	Maintains pricing information for each product, including product ID and unit price

At the end of the week, Dough & Delight wants to analyze the number of cupcakes that were sold. The IT team picks up this request and starts running queries on the transactional database by following these steps:

1. Querying the Orders table to retrieve orders placed within the past week

2. Filtering the Products table to identify entries related to cupcakes and joining this with OrderDetails

3. Querying the OrderDetails table to retrieve quantities of cupcakes sold using the relevant product IDs

4. Using the Price table to fetch the unit price of cupcakes if needed for revenue calculations

5. Finally, summing up the total quantity of cupcakes sold during the week

This operation would be successful, but the process has several issues. The transaction database records thousands of transactions per second. The previous query would have to read thousands of rows, filter the data, and join multiple tables to get the result. Because these databases aren't built to handle complex queries, they slow down business operations and processing time, especially during peak hours. The IT team might even be forced to run these queries at night when the system is less busy.

Another issue with traditional databases is fetching historical records. The price table contains the current price of items. If the price of a cupcake changes, the table won't record the previous prices. To know how much a cupcake was sold for at different points in the week, we won't have this data, making our result inaccurate. This limitation also makes long-term trend analysis, like year-over-year analysis, impossible with a traditional database.

These limitations arise because Dough & Delight is using a traditional database, which is optimized for Online Transaction Processing (OLTP). OLTP systems are designed to handle high volumes of short, simple transactions like placing an order, updating a product's inventory, or processing a payment. These systems are used to run the everyday operations of a business. The focus is on speed, accuracy, and consistency. For example, when a customer places an order for a cupcake, the system needs to save that order immediately, update the inventory, and confirm the purchase, all in real time.

However, OLTP systems aren't built for deeper data analysis. This is where Online Analytical Processing (OLAP) comes in. OLAP systems are designed to answer big-picture questions, such as these:

- How many cupcakes did we sell last week?
- What were our top-selling products this month?
- Are there seasonal patterns in customer purchases?

These questions usually require scanning through large amounts of historical data, joining multiple tables, and performing calculations like totals, averages, or trends. They are complex and resource-intensive, and running them on an OLTP system can slow everything down. To avoid this, many businesses separate their systems into two parts: OLTP systems for handling real-time operations and OLAP systems for analyzing data and generating insights. This separation ensures that transactions stay fast and reliable, while analysts and decision-makers can still get the reports and dashboards they need, without interfering with day-to-day business processes.

This is where a data warehouse proves valuable. A data warehouse is a special type of database optimized for analytics. It's a centralized repository designed to store large volumes of structured data that contain current and historical data from various source systems. Unlike databases, data warehouses are denormalized, and this consolidates all the data into one table and provides a unified view of the data supporting querying, reporting, and data analysis. Popular data warehouses include Amazon Redshift, Google BigQuery, Snowflake, and Microsoft Azure Synapse Analytics.

Extract, Transform, and Load (ETL)

An integral part of a data warehouse architecture is the extract, transform, and load (ETL) process, shown in Figure 6-1. In this process, data is cleaned, standardized, and enriched before being loaded into the data warehouse.

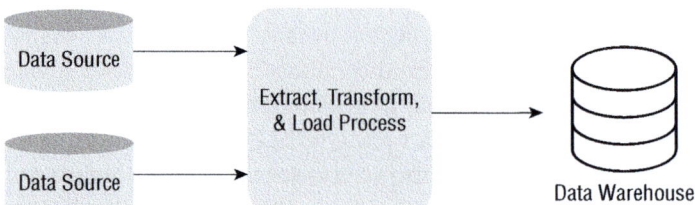

Figure 6-1: The extract, transform, and load process

Extract   In Figure 6-1, the first step in the ETL process is extraction. In this phase, data is extracted from various sources like relational databases, flat files, websites, etc. This phase also involves understanding source systems and interacting with different file formats and schemas.

Transform   The next step is to carry out transformations on the data to make it suitable for analytics. Depending on the project requirements, the transformation process might include any of the following:

Data Enrichment   Enrichment involves adding extra data with valuable information that would be helpful during analysis. For example, this enrichment makes it possible to map customer locations or analyze geographic trends better. Enriched data can also include metadata, which provides context about the data itself, such as the source, format, or time of collection, enabling a more informed analysis.

Data Reformatting   Reformatting is the process of transforming the structure of the data to better suit analytical needs. An example of this is splitting a single column into multiple fields for more granular insights or merging several columns into one.

Data Cleaning   Cleaning involves handling inconsistencies in the dataset, such as identifying missing or null values, removing duplicate entries, and correcting data points that fall outside acceptable ranges. This step ensures that the data is accurate.

Data Standardization   Data standardization is the process of making data uniform so that it follows certain rules or guidelines. This means adjusting the data to a common format or scale, so it's easier to use together—for example, converting dates and times into a standard format, such as YYYY-MM-DD or HH:mm:ss.

Data Aggregation   This is the process of combining multiple data points into a summary. It often involves applying functions like sum, average, count, or maximum/minimum to group data by certain attributes.

Load   The final step involves loading the transformed data into the data warehouse. There are two types of loading strategies:

Full Load   In this method, all the data is loaded into the data warehouse at once. It's usually done when the data warehouse is first set up or when a big update is needed. However, it can take a lot of time and resources because it moves all the data. A full load is the best choice if the data volume is small and the frequency of updates is low.

Incremental Load   This method loads only the data that has been added or changed since the last time it was loaded. It's more efficient than a full load because it transfers less data and takes less time. This method is often used for regular updates and when dealing with large datasets that grow over time.

Schema Design

A data warehouse has two common schema designs that make it optimized for querying and reporting, especially for analytical workloads. Before data is loaded into the data warehouse, this schema ensures data integrity and structure. Here's an overview of each:

Star Schema   A star schema is a common data modeling technique used in data warehousing to organize data for efficient querying. It organizes data into a central *fact* table, which stores quantitative metrics like sales or revenue, and multiple surrounding *dimension* tables, which contain descriptive attributes such as time, location, or product details.

As seen in Figure 6-2, this layout resembles a star, with the fact table at the center and dimensions radiating outward. The structure reduces the number of joins required during analysis, making it faster and more efficient for querying large datasets.

Fact Table   The fact table stores measurable data about business events (numbers). In our bakery Dough & Delight, the fact table would track sales metrics such as Quantity_Sold and Total_Sale_Amount.

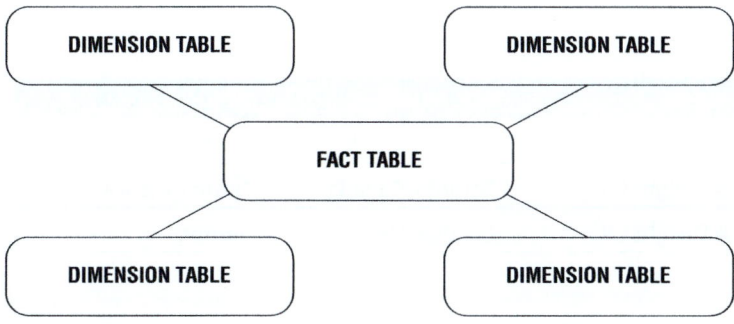

Figure 6-2: Star schema

Each record represents a unique sale, identified by SaleID. It also contains foreign keys linking to dimension tables, ProductID, CustomerID, StoreID, and DateID, which provide additional details about each sale.

Sales Fact Table

SALE ID	PRODUCT ID	CUSTOMER ID	STORE ID	DATE ID	QUANTITY_ SOLD	TOTAL_ SALE_ AMOUNT
1	101	1001	201	301	2	50.00
2	102	1002	202	302	1	30.00
3	103	1003	203	303	5	100.00

Dimension Table   The dimension tables provide descriptive information about the data in the fact table like the product, customer, store, and date.

Product Dimension Table

PRODUCT ID	PRODUCT NAME	CATEGORY	FLAVOR	PRICE
101	Cupcakes	Pastries	Vanilla	25.00
102	Donuts	Pastries	Chocolate	30.00
103	Croissants	Bread	Butter	20.00
104	Brownies	Desserts	Chocolate	25.00

Customer Dimension Table

CUSTOMER ID	CUSTOMER NAME	AGE	EMAIL	LOYALTY LEVEL
1001	Alice Smith	28	alice.smith@gmail.com	Bronze
1002	Daniella Peters	27	daniellap@gmail.com	Gold
1003	Bob Johnson	45	bj@gmail.com	Silver

Store Dimension Table

STORE ID	STORE NAME	LOCATION	REGION
201	Dough & Delight NY	New York, USA	North America
202	Dough & Delight CA	Toronto, Canada	North America
203	Dough & Delight UK	London, UK	Europe

Date Dimension Table

DATE_ID	DATE	DAY OF WEEK	MONTH	QUARTER	YEAR
301	2025-05-01	Friday	May	Q2	2025
302	2025-05-02	Saturday	May	Q2	2025
303	2025-05-03	Sunday	May	Q2	2025

By linking the sales fact table with these dimension tables, analysts can perform detailed queries. Now, using these tables, it's time to put your SQL skills to practice, so let's take a look at some queries to help you understand why data warehouses are optimized for analytics.

Example 1: Finding the Total Sales by Product

Using the existing tables, we want to get the total sales by product in a store. The following query calculates the total sales amount for each product and lists them along with the product name.

- This query joins the Sales (fact table) with the Products (dimension) table based on Product_ID.
- It sums the sales amounts for each product.
- The GROUP_BY groups the results by product name so the sales for each product are calculated separately.
- Finally, it first sorts the results (using ORDER_BY) in descending order (using DESC) by the total sales amount, showing the most sold products.

```
SELECT
    p.ProductName,
    SUM(s.Total_Sales_Amount) AS Total_Sales
FROM
    Sales s
JOIN
    Products p ON s.Product_ID = p.Product_ID
GROUP BY
    p.ProductName
ORDER BY
    Total_Sales DESC;
```

Here's the output of this query:

PRODUCT NAME	TOTAL SALES
Cupcakes	100
Donuts	75

PRODUCT NAME	TOTAL SALES
Croissants	30
Brownies	50

Let's also compare how this would have been done on a transactional database. A hypothetical transactional database table structure would have the following tables: Orders, Products, and OrderDetails (as discussed earlier). Using this table structure, this is what the query would look like:

```
SELECT
    p.ProductName,
    SUM(oi.Quantity * oi.Unit_Price) AS TotalSales
FROM
    Orders o
JOIN
    OrderDetails oi ON o.OrderID = oi.OrderID
JOIN
    Products p ON oi.ProductID = p.ProductID
GROUP BY
    p.ProductName
ORDER BY
    TotalSales DESC;
```

In a transactional database, you typically need to join three tables to get total sales by product. First, join Orders with OrderDetails to access individual product-level details within each order. Then, join OrderDetails with the Products table to retrieve the product names. This is more complex than in a data warehouse, where only a single join is often needed between a fact table and a dimension table.

Also, in contrast to a data warehouse where Total_Sales might already exist as a precomputed column, transactional systems usually store raw data. This means you must calculate the total sales at query time by multiplying Quantity * Unit_Price for each item sold.

Example 2: Finding the Sales by Region and Day of the Week

Let's calculate the total quantity of products sold per region.

- This query calculates the total quantity of products sold in each region by joining the Sales table with the Stores table using the Store_ID.

- It selects the Region from the Stores table and sums the Quantity_Sold from the Sales table, representing the total number of products sold in each region.

- The results are grouped by Region to calculate the total quantity sold for each distinct region.

- Finally, the query sorts the results in descending order based on the Total_Quantity_Sold, showing the regions with the highest total sales first.

- This helps to identify which regions are selling the most products.

```
SELECT
    st.Region,
    SUM(s.Quantity_Sold) AS Total_Quantity_Sold
FROM
    Sales s
JOIN
    Stores st ON s.StoreID = st.StoreID
GROUP BY
    st.Region
ORDER BY
    Total_Quantity_Sold DESC;
```

Here's the output of this query:

REGION	TOTAL QUANTITY SOLD
Europe	5
North America	3

North America has a total of three items sold:
- Store 201 sold 2 items.
- Store 202 sold 1 items.

Europe has a total of 5 items sold:
- Store 203 sold 5 items.

The result is grouped by the Region column from the Stores table, which displays the sum of the Quantity_Sold for each region.

In summary, the fact and dimension table structure used in data warehouses enables highly efficient summarization and aggregation. The schemas are denormalized, meaning that related data is grouped together in fewer tables. This design reduces the number of joins required for queries, making aggregations faster and easier to write and execute. Additionally, most modern data warehouses store data in a columnar format, which is specifically optimized for read-heavy operations like scanning, filtering, and aggregating across large datasets.

While traditional (OLTP) databases can support similar queries, they are not optimized for them. OLTP systems are highly normalized to minimize data redundancy and maintain data integrity, which leads to more complex joins across multiple tables during analysis. They also store data in a row-based format, which is ideal for fast lookups and frequent inserts/updates but inefficient for aggregations that touch large portions of the dataset. This means that even if a transactional database can produce the same results, it would typically do so more slowly and with greater resource consumption.

Snowflake Schema

A snowflake schema is a variation of the star schema, where the central fact table is connected to multiple-dimension tables. The only difference in the snowflake schema is that the dimension tables are further broken into sub-dimensions to eliminate redundancy. The snowflake schema in Figure 6-3 is more complex than the star schema because it involves multiple related dimension tables, which can make querying slightly more complicated.

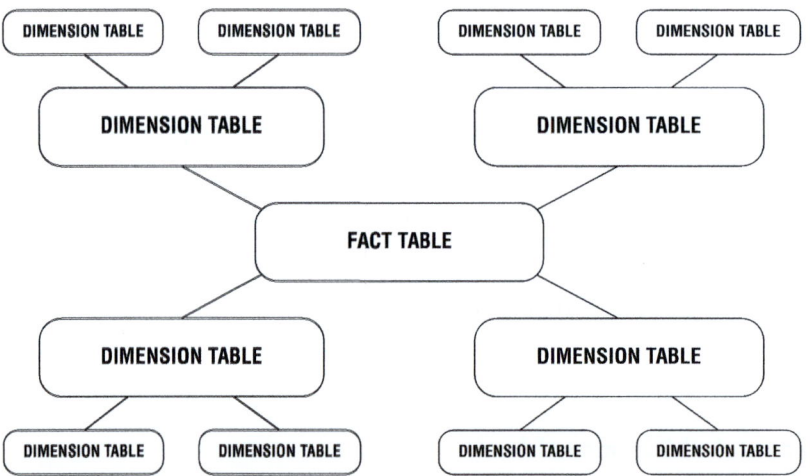

Figure 6-3: Snowflake schema

Choosing Between the Star and the Snowflake Schema

When designing a data warehouse, choosing the right schema structure is important to ensure it meets the analytical needs of the project. Both star and snowflake schema come with unique features, making them suitable for different use cases, but understanding their trade-offs is important for making decisions. We will be discussing these trade-offs under the following topics:

- Complexity
- Performance
- Normalization
- Maintenance
- Scalability

Complexity

The star schema is much simpler when comparing the complexity of star and snowflake schemas. It has a central fact table with dimensions, which are not broken down further. These dimension tables contain all the descriptive data, even if it's repetitive. This simplicity makes it intuitive to understand and quick to design.

The snowflake schema normalizes the dimension tables. Instead of storing all information in a single dimension table, the data is split into additional tables based on hierarchy qualities. For example, in a snowflake schema, a Location table might be divided into Country, State, and City tables. Designing this structure is more complex and requires a deeper understanding of relationships in the data. This is common in systems like customer relationship management (CRM), healthcare data analysis, and supply chain management, where reducing redundancy is a priority. Redundancy in a database refers to unnecessary data duplication within the database. This occurs when the same information is stored in multiple places or tables.

Performance

The star schema is an excellent choice for querying large datasets. Its denormalized structure means fewer joins are needed when combining the fact table with the dimensions, so query execution is faster. A star schema excels in analytical queries, especially where speed is critical for dashboards or reports. The snowflake schema introduces more joins because the data is spread across multiple related tables. These extra joins can slow down performance particularly with large datasets, since the database must work harder to combine the tables.

Normalization

Normalization is the major difference between these two schemas. The star schema uses minimal normalization, which means it keeps redundant data. For example, the same city name is repeated for multiple customers. While this redundancy increases storage requirements, it simplifies the schema and makes querying straightforward.

The snowflake schema is highly normalized. It removes redundancy by splitting data into smaller, related tables. This reduces duplication and saves storage space but increases complexity.

Maintenance

The star schema is easier to maintain because it has fewer tables and simpler relationships. Adding a new data field involves modifying just one or two tables, making debugging more straightforward.

Maintenance is more challenging in the snowflake schema because changes often require updating multiple related tables. Also, troubleshooting can take more time and effort if a mistake occurs, such as a missing relationship.

Scalability

The snowflake schema is more scalable because its normalized structure supports growth. Adding new attributes, dimensions, or even entirely new datasets is easier to integrate without disrupting existing tables. However, the star schema is less flexible for scaling. When adding new dimensions or attributes, it might require restructuring tables, which can be difficult as the dataset expands.

In summary, star schemas are best for simplicity, speed, and ease of use. They are ideal for scenarios where quick query performance is essential, especially with smaller to medium-sized datasets. The denormalized structure of a star schema allows for faster reads, which is useful for reporting and analysis. Snowflake schemas, due to their normalized structure, reduce redundancy and save storage space, making them better for systems that require managing hierarchical data relationships, such as an employee management system where each employee reports to a manager, forming a tree-like structure. Choosing between the two depends on your specific use case and future growth expectations.

Slowly Changing Dimensions

Our bakery, Dough & Delight, has successfully designed its data warehouse but in a few months, they discovered that historical records weren't being properly tracked. They couldn't see how records changed over time, and this created a huge gap in their dashboards. Fact tables change constantly to reflect business events, but dimension tables are not modified as frequently. When data in a dimension table changes multiple times, how do we keep track of that data?

Slowly changing dimensions (SCD) is a framework for updating and maintaining data stored in dimension tables, as dimensions change. They are important because they help us to track how a record is changing over time.

There are a lot of ways to handle slowly changing dimensions, and in this section, we will discuss the three types of slowly changing dimensions.

Slowly Changing Dimensions (Type 1)

In SCD Type 1, if a record in a dimension table changes, the existing record is overwritten. With this, the records in the dimension table always reflect the current state and no historical data is maintained.

For example, our Products Dimensions table stores information about the price of pastries sold in a Dough & Delight, and this handles changing of records using SCD Type 1. If the record of the pastry already exists in the table, it will be updated with the new information. Otherwise, the record will be inserted into the dimension table. In data engineering, updating data if it exists or inserting it otherwise is known as "upserting."

PRODUCT ID	PRODUCT NAME	PRICE
93201	cupcake	5.40
07879	croissants	8.20

If the price of cupcakes changes to 7.80, we can use SCD Type 1 to capture this change in the dimension table, producing the following result. Without SCD Type 1, the old price would remain in the dimension table, leading to outdated or incorrect pricing in reports and dashboards.

PRODUCT ID	PRODUCT NAME	PRICE
93201	cupcake	7.80
07879	croissants	8.20

SCD Type 1 ensures that the data reflects the most recent current dimension and there are no duplicate records in the table. This is also useful for real-time dashboarding, where only the current state is of interest, but since only the most recent information is stored in the table, we can't compare changes in dimensions over time. This shows that SCD Type 1 has limitations when performing historical analysis.

Slowly Changing Dimensions (Type 2)

In many businesses, it's important to keep track of how data has changed over time. For example, if the price of a cupcake changes or a supplier's address is updated, we may still want to know what the old value was and when the change happened. This is where Slowly Changing Dimensions (Type 2) comes in. In SCD Type 2, historical data is maintained by adding a new row when a dimension changes and Type 2 dimensions are the most common approach to tracking historical records. There are two ways to implement an SCD Type 2 table:

Using a Flag In this method, a column is used as a flag to show which record is active, using True if the record reflects the most current value, and False otherwise.

PRODUCT ID	PRODUCT NAME	PRICE	IS CURRENT
93201	cupcake	5.40	False
07879	croissants	8.20	True
93201	cupcake	7.80	True

In the table, when the price of a product changes, a new row is added with the value True in the IsCurrent column. To maintain historical data and accurately show the current state, the IsCurrent column for the previous record is set to False.

Using a Timestamp

When there is a need for granular data, such as revealing how customers responded to a particular price change, we can achieve this by recording transactions along with time-stamped dimension references. This allows us to analyze behavior at specific points in time. Rather than using the IsCurrent column, this uses a StartDate and an EndDate column. These dates represent the period when the dimension was the most current. The EndDate is set to null since the data in this table is the most recent.

PRODUCT ID	PRODUCT NAME	PRICE	START DATE	END DATE
93201	cupcake	5.40	2024-11-13	null
07879	croissants	8.20	2024-08-24	null

If the price of cupcakes changes to 7.80, a new record would be added. The EndDate for the first row has been updated to the last day cupcakes were 5.4. With a new record added, the EndDate of the new row would be set to null.

SCD Type 2 offers more information about data changes than SCD Type 1. In SCD Type 1, instead of checking for whether a record is active or not, you can find the most recent timestamp and fetch the active data row. You can also piece together the timestamps to get a full picture of how a row has changed over time.

PRODUCT ID	PRODUCT NAME	PRICE	START DATE	END DATE
93201	cupcake	5.40	2024-11-13	2025-01-03
07879	croissants	8.20	2024-08-24	null
93201	cupcake	7.80	2025-01-04	null

Slowly Changing Dimensions (Type 3)

In the Type 3 SCD, a column is used to indicate a change. Rather than upserting, or adding a new row to store changes, it uses current and previous columns, especially when the most recent data is important or in cases where the dimension rarely changes.

The following table contains information about warehouse details. It helps the bakery keep track of its warehouse locations for easier supply chain management. We have two columns to store the current and previous addresses for the bakery's warehouses. Since each of these warehouse addresses are still valid, the PreviousAddress column is populated with NULLs.

WAREHOUSE ID	WAREHOUSE NAME	CURRENT ADDRESS	PREVIOUS ADDRESS
562819	Cinnamon Square Depot	Parkside Avenue	NULL
930193	Butter & Flour Hub	Eastwood Plaza	NULL

If Cinnamon Square Depot changes its address, the updated table will look like the following. To account for the new address, Parkside Avenue is moved to the PreviousAddress column, and Riverside Mall takes its place in the CurrentAddress column. This means that only a single historical record for a single-dimensional attribute can be maintained.

WAREHOUSE ID	WAREHOUSE NAME	CURRENT ADDRESS	PREVIOUS ADDRESS
562819	Cinnamon Square Depot	Riverside Mall	Parkside Avenue
930193	Butter & Flour Hub	Eastwood Plaza	Null

Choosing Between Type 1, Type 2, and Type 3

How do you choose between the three types?

- Type 1, Slowly Changing Dimensions, is suitable for situations where historical tracking is unnecessary and only the latest data matters. For example, correcting a misspelled name would be an ideal use case. These changes do not impact historical reporting because the business only cares about the current state. However, it's essential to confirm with stakeholders that overwriting data aligns with business objectives, as there's no way to recover the original data after the update.

- Type 2, Slowly Changing Dimensions, preserves history by adding a new row such as metadata—start and end dates or a flag for the current version—for each change. This type is best suited for situations where maintaining a full history of changes is critical, such as tracking customer addresses or employee roles over time. It enables detailed historical analysis and allows reports to reflect the state of the data at any specific point in the past.

- Type 3, Slowly Changing Dimensions, stores limited historical information by adding new columns for previous values. This approach works well when the business needs to track only the most recent change, such as storing an employee's current and previous job titles. It is less complex than Type 2 and requires less storage since only a fixed number of changes are tracked.

Data Marts

A *data mart* is a subset of a data warehouse designed to focus on a specific business area or department within an organization. As shown in Figure 6-4, it contains a smaller set of data compared to the entire data warehouse, and this makes it easier for users to access and analyze relevant information.

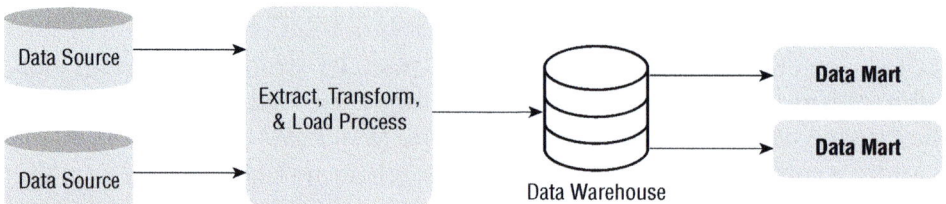

Figure 6-4: Data mart architecture

Benefits of a Data Mart

The advantages of a data mart are as follows:

- **Domain-specific focus:** Data marts allow departments in an organization to focus on the specific data they need for their operations without having to navigate the complexity of a full data warehouse.

- **Better performance:** Data marts contain a smaller subset of data, which provides a faster query performance compared to querying the entire data warehouse. This reduces the load on the main warehouse and enhances the efficiency of business operations.

- **Cost efficiency:** A data mart provides the ability to segment data and store only the relevant information needed by a department, thereby reducing the costs associated with setting up an entire data warehouse.

- **Maintenance:** Data marts are smaller and less complex than data warehouses, making them easier to maintain, especially when the volume of data isn't large.

Challenges with Data Marts

Data marts can be incredibly powerful. They give departments the flexibility to focus on their own subject areas and reporting needs. For instance, the marketing team might need a customer-focused view, whereas the finance team might want a detailed transactional data view. So, each team builds its own data mart to serve its goals. That's great, but in a large enterprise, this flexibility can become an issue because different teams would build and customize their own data marts independently, and although that solves short-term problems, it can create long-term issues.

Over time, this decentralized approach can lead to what we call *data silos*. A data silo is when different departments store and manage their data in isolation, often in separate systems or formats. These silos prevent teams from accessing each other's data, limit collaboration, and most importantly, break the consistency of your enterprise data.

When marketing's version of revenue doesn't match finance's numbers, and both differ from what operations is tracking, you lose your single source of truth. This inconsistency leads to duplicated work, skewed reports, and poor decision-making.

Your role in designing a data storage solution is to balance flexibility with structure. Yes, give teams what they need. But also ensure there's a unified data strategy, one that prevents silos and ensures reliable insights across the business.

Data Lakes

Our retail store, Dough & Delight, made a lot of sales in the past year and expanded its products to over 50 stores worldwide. Its website now has new features, such as customer reviews and product and recipe videos, and it generates more data in both structured and unstructured formats. The IT team wants to store all of this data in one bucket, and using a data lake as an additional storage solution would be the best choice for this expansion.

A *data lake* is a centralized repository that stores large volumes of structured, semi-structured, and unstructured data at any scale. Unlike a data warehouse, which organizes data into predefined schemas, a data lake allows you to store data in its raw format until needed. In terms of volume, data lakes are usually built on scalable cloud systems, meaning they can handle growing amounts of data without running out of space. With the variety of data in the data lake, the IT team can launch various initiatives like building machine learning models on customer reviews, create personalized marketing campaigns, or optimize their supply chain. Data lakes offer flexibility, scalability, and support for diverse data types, and it's also cost effective. Popular data lakes include Amazon S3, Azure Data Lake Storage, and Google Cloud Storage.

How Do Data Lakes Work?

Data lakes are designed to store large volumes of diverse data in its raw form. According to Figure 6-5, to make this data useful, it flows through several stages, from ingestion to storage, enrichment, and finally, consumption, and each stage plays a key role:

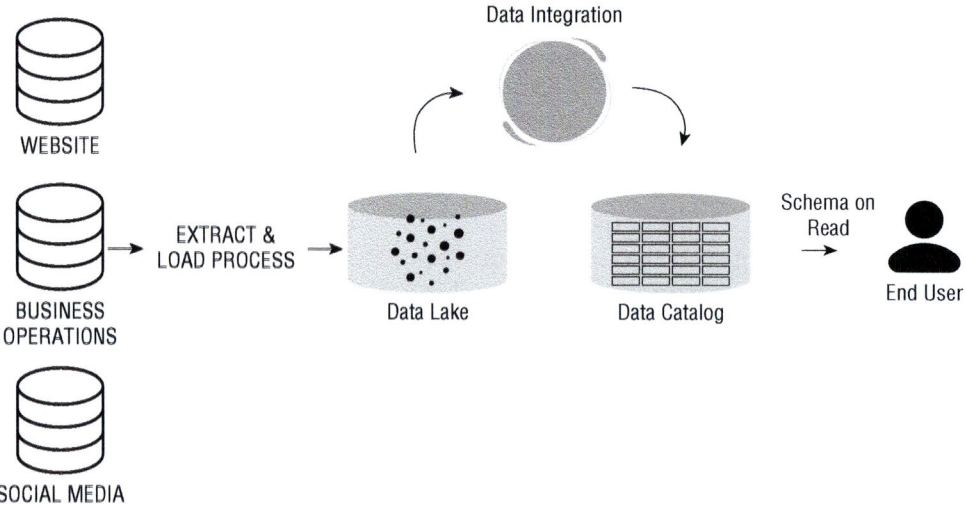

Figure 6-5: Data lake architecture

Data Sources   Data lakes gather data from multiple sources, such as transactional databases, social media platforms, websites, and more. This data can include structured information (like tables and spreadsheets), semi-structured data (like JSON or XML), and unstructured content (like images, videos, or text).

Extract, Load, and Transform (ELT) Process   Unlike data warehouses, which typically follow an extract, transform, and load (ETL) process, data lakes use an extract, load, and transform (ELT) approach. Data is extracted and directly loaded into the lake in its raw format without immediate transformation. In the data lake, the data is organized hierarchically in folders using object storage systems such as Amazon S3, Azure Blob Storage, or Hadoop Distributed File System (HDFS).

Storage Layer   The storage layer in the data lake is essential for managing data in different stages as it arrives. Once data is loaded into the data lake, it doesn't get dumped in one big pile—it passes through three different zones: the raw zone, the cleansed zone, and the curated zone.

Raw Zone   The raw zone contains unprocessed, raw data as it is ingested from various sources into the data lake. The data is stored without any modifications, cleaning, or transformation. We keep it in its original form so we can always go back to it if needed.

Cleansed Zone   Next, we move the data into the cleansed zone. Here's where we start fixing date formats, handling missing values, correcting inconsistencies, and just doing the basics that make the data usable.

We're not adding business logic yet—we're just making sure the data is accurate and structured enough for processing.

Curated Zone   The curated zone contains data that is enriched and transformed to be more business-specific and ready for consumption. This is the version of data stakeholders consume and that dashboards run on.

For instance, in Amazon S3, a widely used data lake service, users typically create separate directories (or folders) for each data zone, such as raw, cleaned, and curated. As raw data is ingested, it is stored in the appropriate user-defined folder. This deliberate organization helps maintain a structured and easily accessible data storage system.

```
s3://your-bucket-name/
    ├── raw-zone/
    │   ├── source1/
    │   │   ├── 2025-01-01/
    │   │   │   ├── data_part1.json
    │   │   │   ├── data_part2.json
    ├── cleansed-zone/
    │   ├── source1/
    │   │   ├── 2025-01-01/
    │   │   │   ├── cleaned_data_part1.json
    │   │   │   ├── cleaned_data_part2.json
    ├── curated-zone/
    │   ├── reports/
    │   │   ├── monthly_sales_2025-01.csv
    │   │   ├── monthly_sales_2025-02.csv
    │   ├── machine-learning-models/
```

Data Integration   When data first lands in a data lake, it's unorganized and raw. It hasn't been structured or labeled and, in that state, it's hard to work with. You can't expect analysts or downstream systems to make sense of it right away. That's where metadata comes in. Metadata is like a label that tells you what's inside your data, where it came from, how it's structured, and how to handle it. It doesn't change the data itself, but it adds critical context. By extracting metadata, such as schema, data types, source system, and timestamps, we turn the raw data into something we can work with. Metadata is what makes a data lake navigable.

Data Cataloging

Once we've extracted metadata from the raw data in our lake, we need to set up a catalog. A data catalog is like the library's index—it organizes all that metadata into a searchable, browsable format, typically using SQL tables or JSON documents. These catalog entries don't store the actual data; they reference it. This catalog enables end users to

- Quickly discover datasets relevant to their work
- Understand a dataset's lineage and structure without opening raw files
- Ensure they're using consistent definitions across the company

So rather than going through folders and files, they query the catalog and save time.

Schema-on-Read

With a catalog in place, a data lake uses a schema-on-read. Unlike traditional systems where the schema is fixed before data is stored (schema-on-write), in data lakes we apply a schema only when we need to access or analyze the data. This flexibility allows users to define the structure and format of the data, depending on the use case. For instance, a machine learning engineer might access data from the catalog to build predictive models, defining the schema only at the time of model training or analysis. The same dataset could be used differently by a business analyst and a data scientist, each applying their own schema at query time.

In summary, data lakes are a highly versatile solution for storing massive data volumes in structured and unstructured formats. They offer cost-effective storage for raw data, allowing organizations to retain historical data that may be valuable in the future. By leveraging a data lake, organizations establish a foundation for big data analytics, predictive modeling, machine learning, and other initiatives.

Challenges of Data Lakes

The main challenge of using a data lake is storing huge amounts of raw data without clear objectives, which can lead to a "data swamp." To prevent this, it is essential to ensure that the data stored is usable. This can be achieved through effective data cataloging, so everyone knows what data exists, where it lives, and how to access it, and strong governance frameworks to enforce data quality, ownership, and access control.

Data Lakehouse

Dough & Delight now has an operational transactional database, its analytics and reporting needs sorted, and a way to store structured and unstructured data together; but at the end of the year, they want to answer more specific questions:

- Which recipe videos do customers like the most?

- Are website reviews affecting sales?
- Is there a link between positive reviews and more purchases?

To answer these questions, they need data from both their data lake and data warehouse. A storage solution that combines these two to give a single, unified view is called a *data lakehouse*. A data lakehouse is a modern data architecture that combines the best features of a data lake and a data warehouse, making it easier to store, manage, and analyze all types of data within a single system.

Features of a Data Lakehouse

- **Unified storage**: Just like a data lake and data warehouse, a data lakehouse can store massive amounts of raw, unstructured, and semi-structured data and also organize structured data for fast queries. You get the scalability of a data lake and the organization of a warehouse in one place.

- **Transactional support**: A data lakehouse supports ACID (Atomicity, Consistency, Isolation, Durability) transactions, ensuring data consistency when multiple users or processes are accessing and modifying the data.

- **Performance**: Data lakehouses deliver query speeds similar to traditional data warehouses, with indexing, caching, and optimization techniques.

- **Flexibility**: Whether you're running dashboards for executives or building machine learning models, a lakehouse can handle both, so there's no need to copy data between tools.

- **Cost-effectiveness**: Since you don't need to maintain separate systems for raw storage and analytics, you cut down on infrastructure and ETL costs.

Data Lakehouse Architecture

A data Lakehouse architecture, shown in Figure 6-6, outlines the flow of data as it moves through different stages in a unified framework. In the first stage, data is ingested from diverse sources such as transactional systems, IoT devices, streaming platforms, or external APIs using an *Extract and Load* process. This raw, unprocessed data is stored in a data lake.

The architecture in Figure 6-6 consists of the following layers:

Storage layer: The storage layer is the data lake layer for all of your raw data.

Metadata layer: The Lakehouse extracts all the metadata and stores it in a separate catalog in a structured format. It provides a detailed catalog of all the data objects in the data lake.

Consumption layer: The consumption layer exposes all your data for use, using a query engine that connects to the data lake and data catalog.

For example, if a data analyst needs to access the data warehouse, the system would fetch structured records from the catalog like videos, images, and reviews and apply necessary transformations like dates, addresses, and prices to build separate tables. The data analyst can then apply a star schema to arrange these tables into fact and dimension tables. This can now be connected to visualization applications to create dashboards for the business.

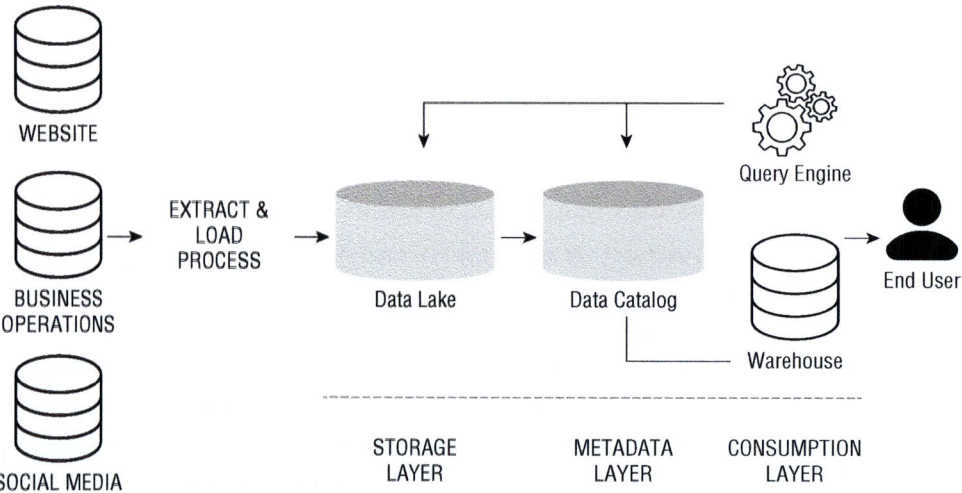

Figure 6-6: Data lakehouse architecture

The Key Differences Between a Database, Data Warehouse, Data Lake, and Data Lakehouse

- A database stores real-time transactional data that supports day-to-day application operations.

- A data warehouse stores both current and historical data from one or more systems, organized in a predefined and structured schema, making it easy for business analysts and data scientists to analyze the data.

- A data lake stores both current and historical data from one or more systems in its raw, unprocessed form.

- A data lakehouse combines the features of both data lakes and data warehouses, offering the flexibility of raw data storage with the structure and performance optimization for analytics, allowing for more efficient data analysis. Table 6-1, compares these storage designs under various key factors.

Table 6-1: Comparison Between a Database, a Data Warehouse, and a Data Lake

ARCHI-TECTURE	WORKLOADS	DATA STRUCTURE	USE CASE	PERFOR-MANCE	STORAGE FORMAT
Database	Operational and Transactional	Structured data with predefined schema	Real-time applications, transactional processing	Fast read/ write for transactional workloads	Row-based format (ideal for fast, record-level transactions)
Data Lake	Analytical	Structured, semi-structured, and unstructured	Storing large volumes of raw data for future analysis	Scalable for large data but not real-time optimized	Flexible format (e.g., Parquet, ORC, JSON, CSV)
Data Warehouse	Analytical	Structured data with optimized schemas	Reporting, business intelligence, complex querying	Optimized for read-heavy and complex analytical queries	Columnar format (ideal for aggregations and analytical processing)

Summary

- A data warehouse is a special type of database optimized for analytics, and it consolidates all the data into one table and provides a unified view.

- An integral part of a data warehouse architecture is the Extract, Transform, and Load (ETL) process, where data is cleaned, standardized, and enriched before being loaded into the warehouse.

- The transformation step involves data enrichment, reformatting, cleaning, standardization, and aggregation.

- Data is loaded into a data warehouse, using two loading strategies: full or incremental load. A full load is the best choice if the data volume is small and the frequency of updates is low, while an incremental load is often used for regular updates and when dealing with large datasets that grow over time.

- Data warehouses are optimized for OLAP systems, they're built to handle large volumes of historical data and perform complex queries. On the other hand, traditional databases are optimized for OLTP systems, they're designed for fast, reliable transaction processing.

- A data warehouse supports two types of schema designs, the star and snowflake schema.

- A star schema organizes data into a central fact table, which stores quantitative metrics, and multiple surrounding dimension tables, which contain descriptive attributes.

- A snowflake schema is a variation of the star schema, where the central fact table is connected to multiple dimension tables.

- Slowly changing dimensions (SCD) is a framework for updating and maintaining data stored in dimension tables, as dimensions change. There are 3 types: Type 1, Type 2, and Type 3.

- Type 1 Slowly Changing Dimensions are suitable for situations where historical tracking is unnecessary, and only the latest data matters.

- Type 2 Slowly Changing Dimensions preserves history by adding a new row, such as metadata—start and end dates or a flag for the current version.

- Type 3 Slowly Changing Dimensions stores limited historical information by adding new columns for previous values.

- A data mart is a subset of a data warehouse designed to focus on a specific business area or department within an organization.

- A data lake is a centralized repository that stores large volumes of structured, semi-structured, and unstructured data at any scale.

- The storage layer of a data lake contains three zones: the raw zone, which contains unprocessed data; the cleansed zone, where cleaned data is stored; and the curated zone, where the transformed data is kept.

- In a data lake architecture, data cataloging is the process of organizing and indexing metadata (information about data) to make it easier for users to find, understand, and access the data stored in a data lake.

- Data lakes operate on a schema-on-read principle, where the data structure is applied only when the data is accessed or queried, not when it's stored.

- A data lakehouse is a modern data architecture that combines the best features of a data lake and a data warehouse. Its architecture consists of a storage, a metadata, and a consumption layer.

Data Pipelines

The data engineering life cycle consists of various stages, but how does data flow between these stages? It flows through *data pipelines*. Data pipelines power data systems and are a foundational component of data engineering. A data pipeline simply moves data between systems, applies transformations to make it analysis-ready, or does both concurrently.

It's a structured system that controls the flow of data from one or more sources to one or more destinations. Along the way, it can perform operations like cleaning, filtering, joining, or aggregating data. Data pipelines can run in real time or in batches, depending on the needs of the business, and it usually follows a series of stages: collect, ingest, process, store, and serve.

IN THIS CHAPTER, YOU WILL LEARN THE FOLLOWING:

- Popular ingestion methods in data engineering
- How batch and streaming pipelines work
- Publish and subscribe patterns in message queues
- Windowing in stream processing
- The Lambda architecture
- Data orchestration and its key components

- Scheduling and automation in data pipelines
- Best practices for designing directed acyclic graphs (DAGs)
- How to build an ETL pipeline and automate with Apache Airflow

At the end of this chapter, you will have a good understanding of various types of data pipeline architectures, their use cases, and the techniques needed to design, build, and manage them effectively.

Batch Pipelines

Imagine a fintech (financial-technology) company that offers loan services. At the end of each month, the company must generate detailed financial reports that include metrics such as total loans issued, interest accrued, and customer payment trends. To support this, a data pipeline is designed to run automatically at midnight on the last day of the month. It collects all relevant transaction data from the database, processes it in bulk, and stores the results in a data warehouse for reporting. This is a classic example of batch processing. Batch processing involves processing large volumes of historical data at scheduled intervals, and this makes it ideal for tasks where the data does not need to be processed in real time, such as generating monthly reports, performing data backups, or processing payroll.

Batch pipelines can ingest data in two ways, time or size intervals. In time-based intervals, data is ingested into the pipeline at fixed time intervals. This method is ideal when data needs to be processed regularly (e.g., every hour, day, or week), especially in data warehousing. In size-based intervals, data is ingested into the pipeline once a certain volume threshold is reached, irrespective of the time taken to accumulate the data. For example, processing can begin when a specific data size, such as 1 GB or 10,000 records, is reached. This method is suitable when there are significant fluctuations in the rate of data generation, and it also helps with efficient resource utilization by ensuring sufficient data volume is available before triggering processing.

Components of a Batch Pipeline

To understand how batch processing works in practice, it's helpful to understand the key components involved. As shown in Figure 7-1, a typical batch pipeline has the following stages, each playing an important role in the movement and transformation of data:

- Data Sources
- Staging Area

- Data Transformation
- Data Storage
- Data Consumption
- Job Scheduler

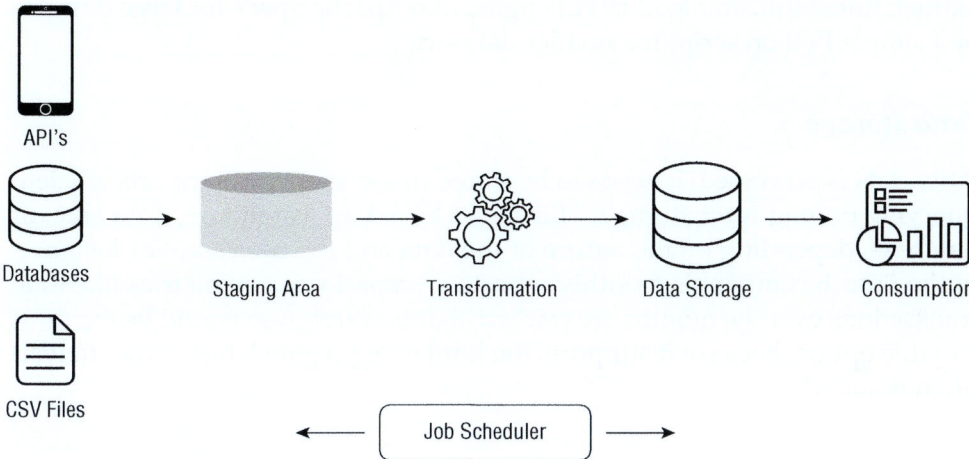

Figure 7-1: Batch pipeline

Data Sources

Data sources are the starting point of any pipeline. The first step is collecting raw data from various sources. In the fintech company scenario, this could include the following:

- Transactional databases storing daily records of customer transfers, card payments, or mobile deposits
- CSV/JSON exports from customer support logs
- APIs from payment gateways or third-party services that provide exchange rates

Staging Area

Once collected, the raw data is temporarily stored in a staging area, a safe place where data lands for a short duration before it's cleaned or transformed. A staging area could be a cloud storage or even a staging table in a database. This staging area is also important for backups and acts as a safeguard for data that might be missed if your batch job fails. For example, if the batch job that generates the monthly report fails, you don't need to re-pull everything—you just fetch the data from the staging area.

Data Transformation

The transformation layer is where the actual business logic and data transformations happen. As discussed in the previous chapter, transformation involves cleansing, filtering, aggregating, joining, and enriching data. In a batch pipeline, these transformations usually happen in bulk. The process could be done on an extract, transform, and load (ETL) engine like Apache Spark for large datasets or a simple Python script for smaller datasets.

Data Storage

After data is processed, it needs to be stored in a system that supports efficient querying or long-term storage. This could be a data warehouse, data lake, or database, depending on the nature of the data and the use case. For instance, in the fintech company's monthly reporting scenario, where metrics like total transactions over the months are tracked, a data warehouse would be the most suitable option, because it supports the kind of aggregated, historical analysis often required.

Data Consumption

This is where the processed data is made available for upstream and downstream users. A batch data pipeline can feed data directly into dashboards, reporting tools, or internal business systems. In the context of our fintech company, analysts might use the monthly aggregated data to populate dashboards tracking key metrics. Data scientists could use historical transaction trends to train models. Internal systems like alerting tools may consume this batch data daily to flag unusual behavior.

Job Scheduler

Once a pipeline has been designed, it needs a trigger to start running. This is where we use a job scheduler. A job is a specific unit of work within the pipeline. In batch processing, these jobs are triggered on a regular schedule by a scheduler. A scheduler ensures that tasks run at the right time, daily, weekly, or monthly, without manual intervention. For simple cases, this could be a cron job, which is a time-based command scheduler in Unix-like systems, that can be configured to run a script every evening. In more complex pipelines, tools like Apache Airflow are used to provide more control, such as handling dependencies between jobs and retrying failed steps.

In the fintech scenario, the job scheduler might trigger a sequence every month, which may look like this:

- Pull the past month's transactions
- Run transformation logic to compute the total transaction value and active users
- Load the cleaned data into the data warehouse
- Notify the analytics team or automatically refresh business dashboards

ETL Pipelines vs. ELT Pipelines

In the previous chapter, we discussed ETL and ELT processes. ETL and ELT are two methods that enable batch processing. Each method is suited for different use cases depending on the system's infrastructure and data requirements.

Extract, Transform, and Load (ETL)

ETL supports batch processing by extracting data from source systems, transforming it according to business rules, and then loading it into a target system. This process is often used in traditional data workflows where jobs are scheduled during off-peak hours to reduce the strain on source systems. For example, pulling customer data from a CRM, normalizing and aggregating it, and storing it in a centralized data warehouse. While ETL is effective in many scenarios, it has some challenges. In ETL, transformation happens before loading, which can slow down various processes, especially for large datasets.

Extract, Load, and Transform (ELT)

The ELT process was introduced as a modern data integration process, particularly for organizations working with big data and cloud-based architectures. Instead of transforming data before loading it, as in traditional ETL, ELT loads raw data directly into the target system, such as a cloud data warehouse or lakehouse, and applies transformations in place. This design significantly reduces performance bottlenecks because it leverages the distributed computing and parallel processing capabilities of modern data warehouse platforms. It's also effective for evolving analytical needs, as it allows data to remain accessible and reusable for multiple transformation workflows.

In the fintech monthly report example, the company might prefer ELT since it uses a modern data warehouse and deals with large volumes of data.

The workflow could look like this: extract data from CRMs, transaction systems, and marketing tools; load it in raw form directly into a cloud data warehouse; and then transform it using SQL scripts to calculate metrics.

Stream Pipelines

We've solved one of the data processing needs for the fintech company, but there are more requirements. The same fintech company wants to monitor transactions to detect fraudulent activities, which requires immediate action like freezing an account or blocking a transaction, to prevent further damage. Here is why a batch pipeline wouldn't work. In this scenario, every millisecond matters, and a batch pipeline cannot analyze individual transactions in real time, so it is not appropriate for a fraud detection system, which needs to be able to analyze each transaction as it occurs. If the fintech company waits to process transactions in bulk, fraudulent activity might go unnoticed until the next processing cycle. With these limitations, the fintech company can implement a streaming pipeline.

How Would This Work?

The bank's payment gateway continuously generates transaction data, which is streamed in real time to a stream processing system. The system analyzes each transaction against a set of predefined fraud detection rules to identify suspicious patterns. If a transaction is flagged as potentially fraudulent, the system triggers an alert. The alert is sent to the customer for confirmation, and the transaction is temporarily held. Also, a dashboard for fraud analysts is updated in real time with the flagged transactions for further investigation. The benefit of using stream processing is that fraudulent transactions are identified and mitigated in real time, reducing potential losses.

Stream processing is the continuous processing of events as data streams are generated in real time or near real time. In stream processing, an event is a single unit of data, or a record representing an occurrence or change of state in a system. When a user transfers money between accounts, this action generates an event with details like the transfer amount, source, destination, and timestamp.

Streaming pipelines have three major characteristics:

- **Event-driven:** Streaming pipelines are triggered by individual events, such as a user swiping a card or clicking a button. This means the system doesn't wait for a scheduled batch; instead, it responds as events occur.
- **Continuous data processing:** Unlike batch systems that work on fixed intervals, streaming pipelines ingest and process data continuously.

As soon as data enters the pipeline, it's processed right away, without waiting for a collection of other data points.

- **Low latency:** This refers to the speed at which the system responds. A low-latency system ensures that from the moment an event occurs to when it is processed and responded to, only a minimal amount of time passes (often milliseconds to seconds).

Other common use cases for streaming pipelines include real-time analysis of stock market data to identify price fluctuations, as well as monitoring social media feeds to track sentiment and user behavior.

Components of a Streaming Data Pipeline

A streaming data pipeline has various components that work together to process, analyze, and deliver data in real time. In Figure 7-2, each component in a streaming data pipeline serves a specific purpose, and a proper understanding of these components would be useful while designing and maintaining a streaming pipeline. Let's look at each of them in detail.

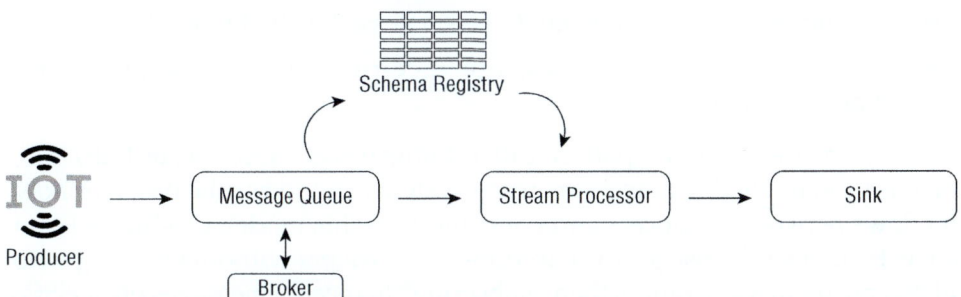

Figure 7-2: A streaming pipeline architecture

Producers

Producers are the origin points of data in a streaming pipeline that constantly generates data streams to be processed. Depending on the application, producers can take many forms. For example, in an industrial setting, IoT sensors on machinery might produce data about temperature, pressure, and vibrations in real time. In financial systems, stock trades, deposits, and withdrawals are examples of continuous data production. Social media platforms are another classic example, where every post, comment, like, or share constitutes an event in the data stream.

Producers are critical because they form the starting point for the entire pipeline. They must be reliable and consistent, as any failure or downtime can disrupt the flow of data through the pipeline, leading to gaps in analysis. The format of the data emitted by producers is often semi-structured, like JSON or XML, which makes it easier to handle and transform in subsequent pipeline stages.

Message Queue

A message queue sits between the data producers and the processing framework, and its primary role is to ensure that data is reliably collected, ordered, and passed along for further processing, ensuring no message is lost even if the consumer is temporarily unavailable. This component decouples the producers from the downstream systems, enabling the pipeline to scale independently at both ends. However, a message queue is typically managed by a message broker. A message broker is the system that orchestrates how messages are handled within the queue. It handles the following:

- It temporarily saves messages until they're processed.
- It ensures messages get delivered at least once, exactly once, or at most once.
- It resends messages if they fail to be processed (called retries).
- It confirms successful message receipt and processing (called acknowledgments).

Message brokers follow a pattern called Publish and Subscribe, or Pub/Sub, which is fundamental to many streaming systems and forms the basis for how data flows between producers and consumers. In this model, producers (data sources) "publish" messages to an intermediary system without knowing who will receive them. Consumers then "subscribe" to receive messages on specific topics of interest.

HOW DOES A PUB/SUB WORK?

Imagine we have an e-commerce platform that implements a notification system to keep customers, warehouse staff, and delivery partners updated about orders. The order management system, *producer*, produces events as orders are placed, shipped, or delivered. The message broker organizes these events into what we call *topics* like order/placed, order/shipped, and order/delivered. We have multiple consumers like the customer app and warehouse management system, also known as *subscribers*, subscribing to these topics.

The customer app subscribes to the order/placed, order/shipped, and order/delivered topic to send real-time updates to customers about their orders. The warehouse management system subscribes to orders/placed to prepare for packaging and shipping. Then the delivery partner system subscribes to orders/shipped to plan delivery routes.

In Pub/Sub patterns, *topics* serve as categories to which messages are published. They act as a sorting mechanism, allowing producers to tag messages and consumers to subscribe only to messages that relate to their specific interests. Messages published to a topic are typically immutable (unable to be changed), and consumers subscribing to that topic receive copies of the messages. Topics enable the streaming system to handle multiple data streams independently, allowing for better organization and filtering of information.

If an event arrives and it doesn't match any of the defined topics, our pipeline may crash or simply ignore the event. A common technique to manage such errors is using a dead letter queue (DLQ). A DLQ is a special storage mechanism where problematic or unprocessable events are sent instead of being discarded. When an invalid event arrives, the system redirects this event to the DLQ and these events in the DLQ are stored along with their metadata for further investigation. Engineers can later review the DLQ to analyze why the event was not processed, which makes error-handling and maintaining integrity important.

Schema Registry

A *schema registry* is a centralized place where the structure (schema) of these event messages is stored and managed. For example, an event for a placed order might look like this:

```
{
  "order_id": 123,
  "customer_name": "Jane Doe",
  "delivery_address": "123 Maple St",
  "order_time": "2025-01-15T10:00:00Z"
}
```

Later, the development team decides to add a new field to the schema, such as `preferred_delivery_time`, to include more information about the order. Now, the event looks like this:

```
{
  "order_id": 123,
  "customer_name": "Jane Doe",
  "delivery_address": "123 Maple St",
  "order_time": "2025-01-15T10:00:00Z",
  "preferred_delivery_time": "2025-01-15T12:00:00Z"
}
```

If the consumer doesn't know about this new field, it will crash or throw errors when subscribing to the event. A schema registry is useful here, because it helps coordinate these changes smoothly. By using a schema registry:

- Schema evolution is centrally managed, allowing producers to register new versions of message schemas. This ensures that changes to the data structure, such as adding, removing, or modifying fields, are tracked and controlled over time.

▪ Both producers and consumers can query the registry to access current and historical schema versions. This helps them validate and interpret data correctly, even when operating on different schema versions.

▪ Backward and forward compatibility is maintained, meaning updated schemas can coexist with older versions. This allows changes like adding optional fields without breaking existing consumers, or reading older messages using newer consumers. This compatibility promotes seamless feature integration, enabling data engineers to introduce updates to data formats while maintaining the stability and functionality of existing systems.

Stream Processor

A stream processor is the engine that processes, transforms, and analyzes data in real time. Once the message broker delivers data, the stream processing framework handles various operations such as filtering, aggregation, transformation, and enrichment. For example, in an e-commerce application, the framework might calculate the real-time total sales for each product as they occur. Stream processors have several key features that make them efficient these operations:

▪ Windowing
▪ Checkpointing
▪ Watermarks
▪ Stateful processing

Windowing

In streaming pipelines, windowing groups events into time-based snapshots to aggregate and process data over defined periods. Streaming windows can be divided based on different criteria. This could be time-based, for instance, 5-minute intervals, or count-based, grouping every 1,000 messages or grouping changes in data value. We can also apply mathematical computations to streaming windows. These could be aggregations such as sum, count, and average, or transformations like joins and maps to streaming windows. Examples of these computations include the following:

▪ Finding the total number of vehicles passing through a toll booth every *15 minutes* to detect congestion patterns.

- Tracking the frequency of a hashtag every *30 seconds* to identify viral trends in real time.

- Aggregating energy consumption data from smart meters every *hour* for billing purposes

- Tracking the number of viewers watching a live stream in *1-minute* intervals to monitor engagements

Without windowing, data streams are infinite, and the event system would need to process and store all incoming data indefinitely, but by limiting the data volume that needs to be processed at any given time, streaming windows help reduce computational load and the use of system resources.

In streaming windows, the concept of time is important to ensure accuracy, because this determines how data is ordered, grouped, and analyzed. When working with streaming data, time is viewed in three different ways:

- **Event time:** Event time is the timestamp indicating when the event occurred in the real world, as recorded by the event producer.

- **Ingestion time:** Ingestion time refers to when an event is received and recorded by the streaming system.

- **Processing time:** Processing time is when the streaming system processes an event, based on the system clock of the machine performing the computation.

For example, if a sensor records a temperature reading at 10:00:00 a.m., that's the event time. If, due to network delays, the data doesn't reach the system until 10:00:05 a.m., that's the ingestion time. And, assuming there is a delay before the system analyzes that event, which might happen at 10:00:10, making this the processing time.

The choice between event time, ingestion time, and processing time depends on what your application needs. Event time is best when you need accuracy based on when an event happened, like in IoT or finance. Ingestion time is simpler and works well when you need quick data, like for social media tracking or logging, especially when event timestamps aren't reliable. Processing time focuses on speed, making it ideal for real-time applications like dashboards, alerts, or gaming leaderboards. Choosing the right time type ensures your system meets the accuracy, complexity, and speed needed for your task.

Types of Streaming Windows

In stream processing, various types of streaming windows define how windows are grouped. We will describe each of them, their specific use case, and how they work. In this section we will be using the following terms commonly, so let's define them:

- **Window:** A window segments a continuous data stream into manageable chunks.

- **Contiguous:** This means that there are no gaps or interruptions between items in a data stream.

- **Non-overlapping:** This means that there is no shared content between intervals. Each segment is independent and does not include elements or data points from another segment.

Tumbling Window

Tumbling windows process streaming data in fixed-size, contiguous, and non-overlapping chunks. In Figure 7-3, where we defined a tumbling window of 30 seconds, the stream would be divided as follows: 0–30 seconds, 30–60 seconds, 60–90 seconds, and so on. All tumbling windows are of the same size and are nonoverlapping, meaning that each event is uniquely assigned to a single tumbling window and processed only once.

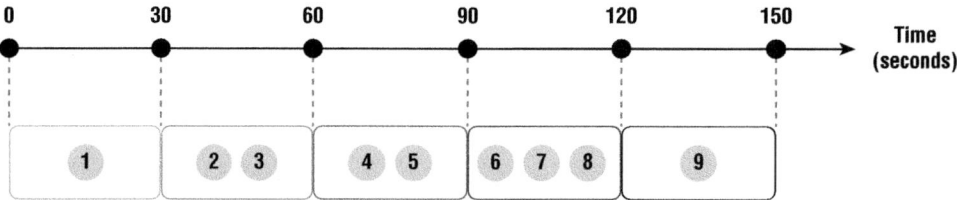

Figure 7-3: 30-second tumbling window

   Tumbling windows are useful when you need to analyze data in equal, separate chunks, making it easier to compare results over time. For example, you could use tumbling windows to measure e-commerce transactions minute by minute, giving you clear insights into how users are purchasing products. They're also helpful in finance for tasks like calculating moving averages for stock prices over fixed periods.

   However, choosing the right window size can be tricky. If the window is too big, you might miss smaller details in the data. On the other hand, if it's too small, you'll end up with too many windows, each having just a little data and this can make it hard to spot important trends or patterns.

Hopping Window

Hopping windows let you process data in fixed-size chunks that overlap and move forward at a set interval. In Figure 7-4, each window lasts 60 seconds, and it moves forward and "hops" every 30 seconds. This means each new window overlaps with the previous one.

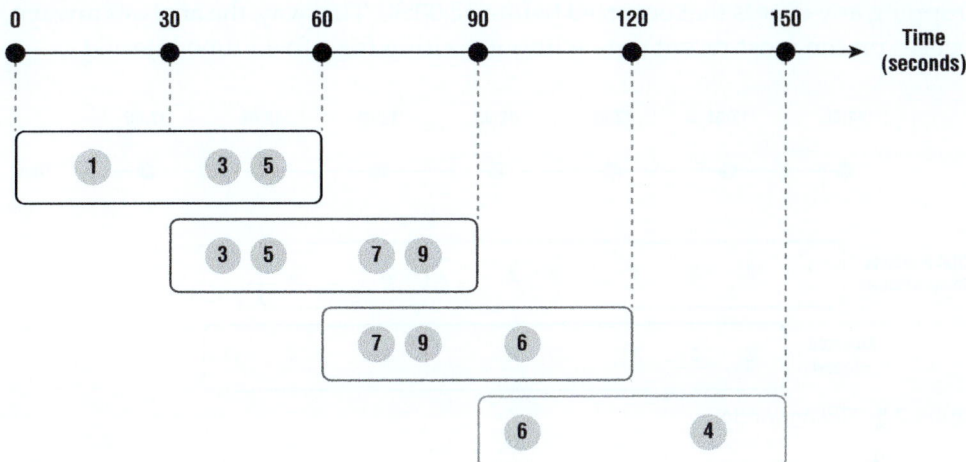

Figure 7-4: Hopping window

Unlike tumbling windows, where each event belongs to only one window, an event in a hopping window can appear in multiple windows. This overlap is useful because it ensures that no data is missed. It's important to note that the hop interval (how much the window moves forward) should be smaller than the window duration; otherwise, there could be gaps between windows, leaving some data unprocessed.

Hopping windows are great for continuous, detailed analysis where you need to track changes over time and catch sudden spikes or drops in data. For example, if a sudden spike in network traffic happens at the edge of one window, it may not be fully captured by that window, but because the windows overlap, the spike will likely be included in the next window as well. This overlap ensures that any important changes or unusual events are analyzed across multiple intervals and reduces the chance of missing critical events that might be overlooked with nonoverlapping windows like tumbling windows.

While implementing hopping windows, you might face a few challenges like computational overhead, because the same data might be processed multiple times in different windows, making it difficult to find the right balance between window size and hop interval.

Sliding Window

Sliding windows in stream processing allow you to group events within a moving time interval that updates as new events arrive. Unlike other windows, sliding windows change based on the arrival of data.

In Figure 7-5, we have a sliding window that lasts 5 minutes. If the window starts at 12:00:00 and ends at 12:05:00, and a new event arrives at 12:05:30, the window slides forward. It will now cover the time from 12:00:30 to 12:05:30, dropping any events that occurred before 12:00:30. This way, the analysis always focuses on the most recent data without waiting for a fixed time interval.

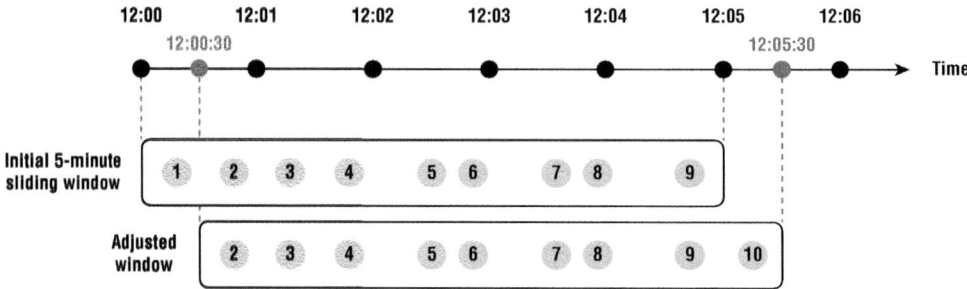

Figure 7-5: Sliding window

Sliding windows are great for continuous, real-time analysis. For instance, they can be used to monitor data from sensors on machines, such as temperature or pressure, because the window constantly slides and updates, so you're always working with the most up-to-date information. This continuous monitoring helps you to spot patterns or issues that might lead to equipment failure.

However, working with sliding windows has some challenges. First, they require more computational power because the window adjusts every time a new event arrives. Second, finding the right balance between the window size and the slide interval is important and can be tricky. It needs to be tuned based on what you're analyzing.

Session Window

A session window is a way to group events based on activity. It creates a time block that starts when an event happens. As long as more events keep coming within a set amount of time, the session stays open. If no events come during that time, the session closes, and a new session starts with the next event. You can see this illustrated in Figure 7-6, where there is an inactivity gap.

Session windows are useful for studying activity patterns. For example, in a video game, session windows can track how long someone plays and how engaged they are.

Working with session windows can be challenging when you need to decide the right inactivity timeout. If the timeout is too short, events that should be in the same session might get split into different ones. If it's too long, unrelated events could end up in the same session.

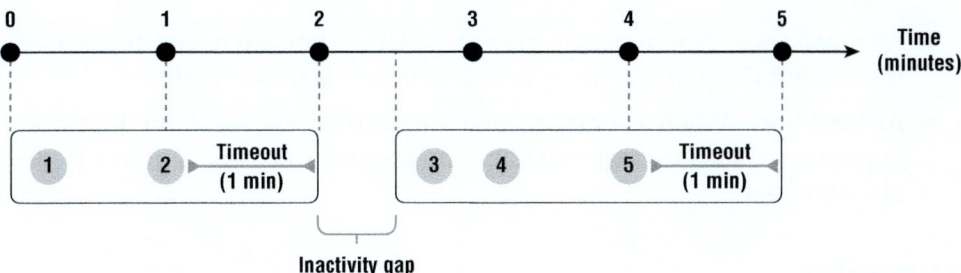

Figure 7-6: Session window

Also, session windows can stay open for different lengths of time, which means they need more memory and careful management, especially when there's a lot of data. With session windows, events don't always arrive in order or on time because of delays, like network issues, which can mess up the session boundaries, so it's important to make sure events are processed in the right order.

Checkpointing

Checkpointing is the process of periodically saving an application's state to persistent storage. It enables fault tolerance by allowing the system to recover from failures without restarting the processing from scratch. Here, fault tolerance refers to the ability of a system to recover (to continue functioning correctly) even when unexpected failures (or faults) occur. A checkpoint typically includes data such as the position of consumed data in the stream called *offsets* and the current state of any stateful operations or aggregations called *snapshots*.

Let's imagine this scenario. A fintech company manages a real-time fraud detection system for credit card transactions. The system uses a stream processing engine to analyze transaction streams and flag suspicious activity. Midway through the processing, the stream processor crashes due to a network issue.

Without checkpointing, the system restarts from the beginning of the transaction stream, reprocessing all transactions and possibly generating duplicate fraud alerts. But with checkpointing, the stream processor periodically saves its progress, including the data it has already processed, using an offset. An *offset* is a marker or pointer that indicates how far a stream processor or consumer has read through a stream of data. If the system crashes or restarts, it resumes from the last saved offset instead of starting over.

This mechanism helps ensure what's called *exactly once* processing, meaning each event is processed only once, even in the event of a failure, and is neither lost nor duplicated, offering the most robust guarantee in stream processing systems. It's important in use cases like fraud detection or billing, where duplicate or missing events can lead to serious errors. The other alternatives are as follows:

- **At-most-once:** Where events may be lost, but they are never duplicated. It's fast but risky in scenarios where data loss is unacceptable.

- **At-least-once:** Where events are guaranteed to be processed but duplicates might occur. This is more reliable than at-most-once but requires deduplication logic.

Watermarking

Imagine a fintech company operating a real-time stock trading platform that analyzes and aggregates stock trades from various exchanges. The system calculates the total traded volume for each stock symbol in one-minute windows (a tumbling window), based on the event time, the actual time when the trade occurred, not when it was processed.

Some trades might arrive out of order due to latency differences in data sources and network delays. If a trade for a stock arrives after the system has already closed the one-minute window, it may be dropped or incorrectly ignored without proper handling, which could result in incomplete or inaccurate metrics. Here, we use watermarking.

Watermarking is a technique in stream processing used to handle out-of-order events or late-arriving events by tracking the progress of event time. It serves as a marker that indicates up to which point in the event timeline the system has processed all events, including late-arriving ones up to a specified threshold. Watermarking ensures accurate results in scenarios where events may not arrive in order due to network delays or system latencies.

With watermarking, we can define a lateness threshold, such as 5 seconds. This ensures that trades arriving within 5 seconds after the end of a window are still included in the window's calculations. Once the watermark advances past the end of the window plus the lateness threshold, the system finalizes and emits the results. This helps balance timeliness and completeness, because the system doesn't wait forever for late events, but still tolerates a small delay.

PICKING THE RIGHT WATERMARK THRESHOLD

When you're designing a streaming pipeline, here are ways you can determine the best watermark threshold for your stream processor:

Understand Your Data Characteristics

The first step in determining the threshold for a watermark is to analyze the characteristics of your data. Observe how events arrive in the stream, whether they are mostly in order or prone to delays, and measure the typical time lag between when an event occurs and when it is received. For instance, you might discover that most events arrive within 2 seconds, but outliers can take up to 8 seconds. To ensure accuracy, you want your system to include these late-arriving events.

To handle this, you set a watermark threshold of 10 seconds, allowing the system to wait for late events within that window. If a fraudulent transaction from an international gateway arrives 6 seconds late, it's still processed and flagged within the same analysis window. However, events arriving later than 10 seconds are marked as "too late" and logged for separate processing. Visual tools like histograms can help you spot trends and guide your initial decision on setting a reasonable threshold.

Create a Balance Between Application Needs and Trade-offs

The ideal watermark threshold strikes a balance between the accuracy of your results and the latency of your application. Shorter thresholds improve responsiveness but risk excluding late events, whereas longer thresholds capture more late data at the cost of delayed results. Consider your application's requirements; if you're building a real-time stock trading platform, you may need low latency, but for regulatory compliance or financial reporting, you might prioritize completeness and accuracy.

Iteratively Monitor and Refine

Once you set an initial threshold based on application requirements, use monitoring tools to evaluate its effectiveness. Most stream processing frameworks, like Apache Flink or Spark Structured Streaming, provide metrics on late events and watermark progression. Regularly review these metrics and adjust the threshold iteratively based on your observations to achieve the best balance between data completeness and system performance.

Stateful Processing

Stateful processing is another important feature of stream processors. A state refers to the information the system needs to remember and track as new data comes in, and stateful processing is when the system keeps track of information (called state) across multiple events in a data stream.

For example, imagine you want to detect suspicious behavior by tracking a user's spending habits, such as making several large purchases in a short period. To do this, the system needs to maintain a state, a running record of the user's recent transactions. For instance, it will keep track of

- How much the user has spent in the last 60 minutes
- How many transactions they've made in that time frame

If a user normally makes small purchases of $20 and $30 but suddenly buys something for $1,000 in the same time frame, say 60 minutes, the system can compare this with the user's previous spending and flag it as suspicious because it's an anomaly in their behavior.

Stateful processing is like having a memory, where the system doesn't just look at one transaction at a time but remembers what happened before to make smarter decisions. This is useful when you want to detect fraud or abnormal patterns in real time. In contrast, stateless processing handles events independently, with no memory of previous events. This works well for simple tasks like filtering or format conversion.

Sinks

Sinks are the destination for data in a streaming pipeline. Once data is ingested, processed, and transformed, it needs to be either stored for future use or consumed immediately to drive actions. Sinks typically fall into two categories: storage systems and consumers.

Storage systems act as long-term or temporary destinations where processed data is saved. This allows organizations to retain, query, and reuse data after it flows through the pipeline. It could be *temporary* storage—which are fast, in-memory systems that hold data briefly for real-time access and that are useful for caching intermediate results or storing session-level data used for immediate decision-making—or *permanent* storage, designed to hold large volumes of data over time and which store processed or raw data that can be used for future analysis. This is often where a data lake or data warehouse comes in. For more on the types of storage systems, refer to the previous chapter.

Consumers, on the other hand, are systems or applications that act on the processed streaming data in real time. It could be dashboards and visualization tools that display live metrics. This is also common in monitoring applications where fast feedback is essential. Consumers drive real-time actions that bring value from the data as it flows.

Lambda Architecture

You're a data engineer at an e-commerce company tasked with building a real-time analytics dashboard. Executives want to track live sales trends as they happen, while also generating detailed reports on historical customer behavior. You can design either a streaming or a batch pipeline, but they would struggle to meet both needs simultaneously because a streaming pipeline lacks historical depth and batch pipelines are too slow for live insights. This is where the Lambda architecture shines.

The Lambda architecture is a robust data processing design architecture that combines both batch and stream processing. It was created to address the challenges of processing massive volumes of real-time data and the fetching of historical data, while ensuring low-latency updates, fault tolerance, and accuracy.

Components of the Lambda Architecture

As shown in Figure 7-7, there are three main layers in the Lambda architecture: the batch, the speed, and the serving layer.

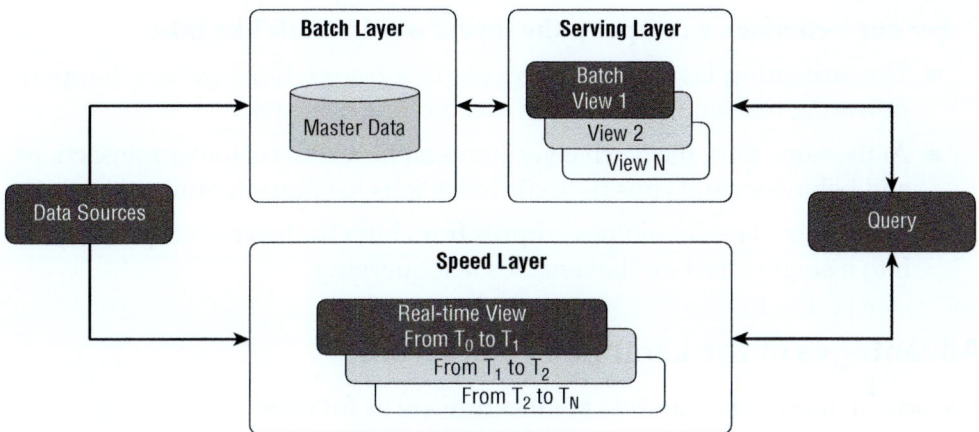

Figure 7-7: Components of the Lambda architecture

The Batch Layer

As data flows continuously from the data sources, it is sent to two layers: the batch layer and the speed layer. The batch layer stores the full, immutable raw data, called the master data, and processes it on a set schedule to ensure everything is accurate and complete. This area is also where traditional data tools like ETL processes and data warehouses are used. The batch layer plays two important roles: keeping the main dataset organized and preparing summaries or precomputed results (called batch views) for easier access later.

The Speed Layer

The speed layer handles data processing. It works in parallel with the batch layer to provide up-to-the-minute results. Here, data is processed as it arrives, in small increments, creating views over smaller time intervals (T_0 to T_1, T_1 to T_2, etc.) to provide low-latency insights. The speed layer helps to fill in the gaps in batch processing, providing a complete view of the data to the user by creating real-time views.

The Serving Layer

The serving layer is where the results from both the batch and the speed layers are merged. The serving layer stores batch views and real-time views in a way that facilitates querying. It allows end users or applications to access the final, combined data, which gives them a comprehensive view of both historical and recent data. After processing both historical data and real-time user activity, the serving layer can allow users to query the data and get insights like "How many people visited the website today?" and "How does this compare to last week?"

For our e-commerce company, the layers would work like this:

- The streaming layer would process live transactions as they happen, powering real-time dashboards and alerting systems.

- At the same time, the batch layer stores all historical customer transactions and behaviors and runs periodic batch jobs to compute summaries.

- The serving layer combines outputs from both the batch and speed layers into a single interface that enables fast querying.

Advantages of the Lambda Architecture

The advantages of the Lambda architecture are as follows:

- **Fault tolerance:** The Lambda architecture is fault-tolerant because it has both batch and speed layers. If the real-time system crashes due to an issue, the batch layer ensures all data is eventually processed and the system remains accurate. This way, no data is lost.

- **Scalability:** The Lambda architecture is designed to scale easily as data grows because it distributes the workload across multiple machines.

- **Flexibility:** The Lambda architecture allows experimentation with different methods of real-time or batch processing and change of architecture as needed.

Challenges and Trade-offs

While the Lambda Architecture offers several benefits, there are also some challenges:

- **Complexity:** The architecture can become complex to maintain, as it requires both batch and real-time processing pipelines, which makes debugging difficult.

- **Data duplication:** Sometimes, duplicate data exists between the batch and speed layers, requiring deduplication logic.

- **Latency:** Although it's fast, there is some inherent latency in the system, especially in the batch layer.

In summary, the Lambda architecture is a powerful approach to processing and analyzing large datasets in both real time and batch modes. It is useful in scenarios where we need to balance speed with accuracy, ensuring we get both fast insights and comprehensive data analysis.

Data Orchestration

To understand orchestration in data engineering, we can use an actual orchestra as an analogy. In an orchestra, we have various instrumentalists and a conductor. The conductor doesn't just lead, they ensure that every note aligns to create a masterpiece. The instrumentalists must play at an exact time with the correct tempo. Now, imagine that orchestra as your data pipeline. Each instrument could represent a stage of the data engineering life cycle, and like an orchestra, a data pipeline has numerous moving parts. To achieve harmony, these parts need to work together seamlessly.

As a data engineer, you are the conductor. It's your responsibility to coordinate these processes and workflows to ensure they run smoothly. Let's explore what this might look like in practice. Picture yourself working at a small startup. You've just built your first ETL pipeline to run daily batch jobs, and the pipeline has several key components such as a data ingestion script that pulls raw data from source systems, another script that runs transformations, and a service that loads this data into a storage system.

Initially, you run each of these components manually by testing the ingestion process, confirming the transformations work as expected, and checking if the data lands in the correct storage destination. This is good for testing, but the process is not sustainable, because each time your downstream users request batch data, you have to manually execute each task. In situations where you're not available, how would someone else figure out the order to run these tasks?

This is where orchestration comes in. Orchestration in data engineering refers to the process of managing and coordinating workflows across different tools and systems to ensure seamless data movement and processing. Various building blocks make orchestration possible; it relies on the following:

- Directed Acyclic Graphs (DAGs) to define task dependencies
- Automation to reduce manual triggers
- Scheduling to run workflows at specific times or intervals
- Monitoring to track progress and performance
- Alerting to notify teams when something goes wrong

Let's discuss each of these topics in detail.

Directed Acyclic Graphs (DAGs)

In data engineering, pipelines and workflows involve many interdependent tasks. To ensure these tasks run in the correct order, we use directed acyclic graphs (DAGs), a key building block of orchestration. A DAG organizes tasks in a sequence where each one depends on the successful completion of previous steps.

In orchestration tools like Apache Airflow, a DAG defines the structure of your workflow, such as which task runs first, what follows next, and what must wait. This kind of coordination is a must-have when you're managing complex data workflows where the failure or delay of one step can impact others.

As shown in Figures 7-8 and 7-9, DAGs are a type of graph, a nonlinear data structure made up of nodes (representing tasks) and edges (representing dependencies). While similar to general graphs in computer science, DAGs are specifically designed to ensure a one-way, cycle-free flow, making them ideal for orchestrating reliable and repeatable data pipelines.

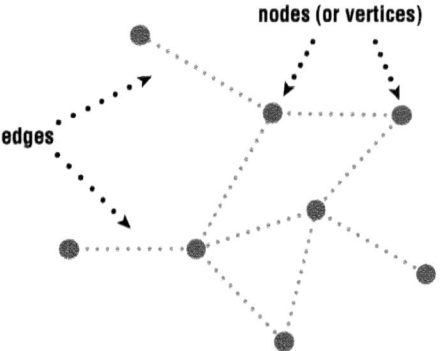

Figure 7-8: A graph structure

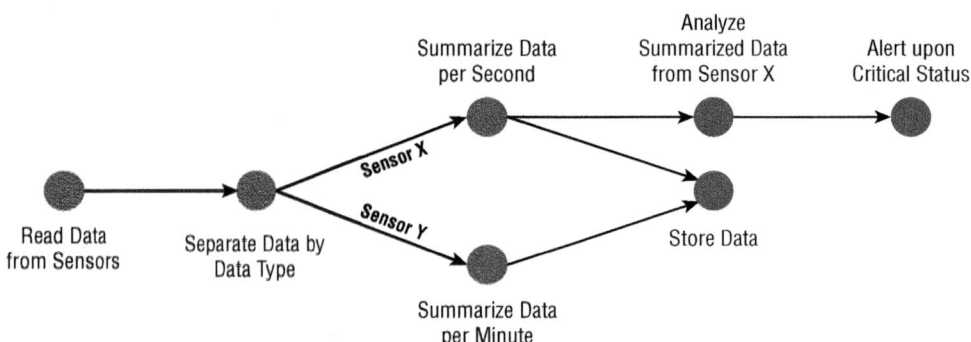

Figure 7-9: A directed acyclic graph

In a graph, nodes represent individual objects and edges represent relationships between them. In a directed graph, the edges have a direction. This means the connection goes from one node to another in a specific way. For example, if there is an edge from node A to node B, it shows a connection from A to B, but not necessarily from B to A. A path is a sequence of nodes connected by edges in the graph. In a directed graph, the path must follow the direction of the edges. It starts at one node and moves through the connected edges to reach another node.

The term *directed acyclic graph* implies two key properties. *Directed* means the graph has edges with a specific direction. The direction shows how one task leads to another or the sequence in which tasks need to be executed. *Acyclic* means the graph has no cycles. A cycle occurs when you can start at one task, follow the directed edges, and eventually return to the starting task. In an acyclic graph, this is not possible, which ensures there is no repetition or looping of tasks.

In a DAG, tasks are represented by nodes, where each node corresponds to a specific task or unit of work that needs to be completed. Dependencies are represented by edges. A dependency shows that one task depends on the completion of another task before it can proceed. The direction of the edge indicates the order of execution. For example, if there is an edge from node A to node B, it means that task A must be completed before task B can start.

While all data pipelines, whether batch or streaming, require tasks to be performed in a particular order, DAGs are required for this orchestration because they make these dependencies explicit. In batch processing, DAGs are widely used to schedule and coordinate workflows like data ingestion, transformation, and loading. For example, you might have a DAG where a file must be downloaded before it can be cleaned and then stored in a data warehouse.

In contrast, streaming frameworks don't typically expose a user-defined DAG, even though under the hood, the engine constructs one to manage flow between operations like windowing, aggregations, and joins. When we discussed concepts like windows or checkpoints, those fit into a streaming engine's internal DAG to ensure correct processing, but they're not about orchestration—they're about computation and state.

BEST PRACTICES FOR DESIGNING DAGs

Here are some best practices for designing DAGs:

Set clear dependencies.   When you're designing a DAG for data pipelines, it's essential to define dependencies explicitly. This ensures that tasks are executed in the correct order. For example, if Task B depends on the output of Task A, this relationship must be represented in the DAG structure. This clarity prevents unexpected execution sequences and ensures data consistency.

Keep it simple.   Simplicity is key to creating effective DAGs. Avoid adding unnecessary nodes or introducing overly complex structures. Simpler DAGs are not only easier to understand but also quicker to debug and maintain. A clean, straightforward design minimizes errors and reduces onboarding time for new team members.

Use modular workflows.   Large DAGs can become difficult to manage. Breaking them into smaller, reusable sub-DAGs or modular workflows enhances clarity and makes testing more manageable. For instance, a sub-DAG handling data extraction can be reused across multiple pipelines, saving development time.

Implement error handling.   Always set up alerts to notify stakeholders of failures, and design mechanisms to skip or rerun failed tasks without restarting the entire pipeline. This approach ensures reliable workflows.

Use version control.   Use version control systems like Git to manage your DAG definitions. This practice helps track changes, enables collaboration among team members, and allows you to revert to earlier versions if needed. Version control also promotes transparency in pipeline development.

Use monitoring and logging.   Effective monitoring and logging are critical for maintaining healthy pipelines. Continuously monitor the DAG's execution to ensure tasks run as expected. Log errors, successes, and performance metrics for each task. These logs come in handy for troubleshooting and optimizing pipeline performance.

Scheduling and Automation

In orchestration, automation refers to building workflows that run without manual intervention. This helps reduce human error and ensure consistency across repetitive tasks. An example is automatically running an ETL pipeline to pull, transform, and load data without anyone pushing a button.

At the heart of automation is scheduling, which defines when these automated tasks should run. Scheduling ensures tasks are triggered at optimal times based on predefined rules, helping teams align workflows with business needs or system usage patterns. For instance, a backup job might run daily at midnight when system activity is low, and a batch processing pipeline could be scheduled hourly to deliver near real-time insights. Automation uses the following triggers to initiate workflows:

- **Time-based triggers:** These run tasks at fixed intervals or specific times (e.g., every day at 8:00 a.m.).

- **Dependency-based triggers:** These ensure tasks run only after certain other tasks are complete.

- **Event-driven triggers:** These respond to real-world signals, like a new file landing in an S3 bucket or an API call from an app.

To better understand these terms, *scheduling* is like setting the coffee machine to brew every morning at 7:00 a.m. and *automation* is what makes the machine start brewing without you pressing a button. Scheduling is just one way it can be automated. So, scheduling is a form of automation, but automation also includes event-driven and manual workflows, giving you much more flexibility. Together, they allow data pipelines to operate smoothly and reduce manual effort.

Monitoring

Monitoring is an important aspect of the data engineering life cycle. It involves continuous observation of workflows to ensure they're running as expected. Monitoring helps detect issues early and provides insights into performance, usage, and resource consumption. These insights are provided through metrics. Metrics are numerical values that are collected at regular intervals to describe some aspect of a system at a particular time. Let's examine a few metrics you should look out for.

Performance Metrics

Performance metrics ensure your pipeline operates at its peak and meets service-level agreements (SLAs). SLAs are formal agreements between a service provider and a customer that define the level of service expected. In terms of performance, we track three major things:

- **Latency:** This is the time it takes for data to move through the pipeline, especially for real-time applications. For example, an SLA for a real-time pipeline could be a latency of ≤100 ms.

- **Throughput:** This is the rate of data ingestion and processing to ensure the pipeline handles the required load. A pipeline's throughput can be 500 MB/s.

- **Error rates:** This is the frequency of errors in data ingestion, transformation, or loading stages. For example, in an ETL pipeline, out of 1,000,000 records ingested, only 2,000 records fail due to schema mismatches, resulting in an error rate of 0.2 percent.

Resource Metrics

Monitoring resource utilization ensures your pipeline operates efficiently, using resources effectively while minimizing costs. By tracking key metrics, you can identify when to scale resources up or down to match workload demands. These resource metrics are as follows:

- **CPU and memory usage:** This metric tracks how much CPU and memory your pipeline consumes to identify overloading or underutilization. For instance, a data processing pipeline running on a Spark cluster shows

80 percent CPU usage and 65 percent memory usage during peak hours, which is normal, but if the CPU usage frequently exceeds 90 percent, this may signal the need for scaling up.

- **Disk input/output (I/O):** This metric measures the speed and volume of read/write operations on storage devices. If a pipeline's read speed exceeds 500 MB/s, ensure the storage infrastructure can handle the load without delays.

- **Network bandwidth:** This metric tracks the capacity and utilization of network resources to ensure data transfer. A data ingestion pipeline transferring 5 GB/min between systems operates within the network bandwidth limit of 10 Gbps. If data transfer consistently reaches 9 Gbps, consider upgrading network capacity.

Data Quality Metrics

Data quality metrics ensure that as data moves through each stage of the pipelines, it is complete, accurate, and consistent. Let's look at a few data quality metrics:

- **Data completeness:** This is the percentage of missing or incomplete data. This value measures how much data is missing or incomplete in the pipeline. A drop in completeness could indicate some failures in data collection, transformation, or ingestion processes. To check completeness, you can set up rules in your monitoring tool to compare the actual record count with the expected count from the source system.

- **Data accuracy:** This metric is the percentage of records that match expected values or business rules. This ensures that data is correct and conforms to business requirements. An example of this is using SQL queries to validate data at each stage of the pipeline.

- **Data consistency:** This metric tracks the percentage of records that are the same across different datasets or stages of the pipeline. It ensures that data doesn't contradict itself between multiple sources or stages.

Alerts

A typical data pipeline is prone to failure for various reasons, but how can we detect when these failures happen? We use alerts. *Alerts* are notifications triggered when a certain condition is met, ensuring immediate action when issues occur. For example, an alert might notify a team when a data pipeline fails to ingest data within a given time. Depending on the alerting tool used, alerts can be delivered through various channels such as emails or by SMS. Alerts are important, especially for critical pipelines.

Best Practices for Setting Alerts

While alerts are great, they can also be misused. Let's discuss some best practices for setting up alerts for your data pipeline.

- **Define critical thresholds:** Always define critical thresholds to avoid excessive noise from noncritical alerts. You might set a critical alert if a job fails to run for two consecutive hours, as this could delay financial reporting. However, setting an alert for every 5-minute delay in processing may overwhelm your team with noise. Without critical thresholds, your team might get bombarded with alerts at midnight about minor delays, making them likely to ignore alerts

- **Use context-rich messages:** When an alert is triggered, ensure it provides sufficient details to help the team resolve the issue quickly. Be sure to include the pipeline name, issue details, and resolution steps, especially for other employees on other teams who might be on call.
  If you receive an alert that just says "Pipeline failed," you'd have to dig through logs to find the root cause. Instead, if the alert says: "Pipeline daily_sales_aggregator failed at step 3. Error: Database connection timeout. Suggested action: Check the database server's health and retry the job," your team can respond more effectively.

- **Set severity levels:** Not all alerts are created equal, and prioritizing them helps the team respond to the most critical ones first. Severity levels could be high, medium, or low. High severity could mean a major business impact, like production pipelines. Medium severity could mean minimal business impact but needs resolution. Low severity might just be informational alerts for monitoring purposes.

- **Set appropriate channels:** Ensure alerts are directed to the right team via appropriate channels like email, Slack, or incident management tools. This is designed to elicit a quick response.

Lab: Building an ETL Pipeline and Automating with Apache Airflow

In this lab, you will build an ETL (extract, transform, load) pipeline to process customer data from a bakery. The pipeline will extract raw data, apply necessary transformations, and load the processed data into a PostgreSQL database using Python. Additionally, you will automate the ETL process by integrating it with Apache Airflow, a widely used orchestration framework.

Requirements

Hardware:

- Laptop or desktop computer (macOS, Windows, or Linux): Any modern system with at least 8 GB of RAM and sufficient storage (SSD preferred) to run development tools and data processing tasks.

Software:

- Python (version 3.8 or higher)
- Jupyter Notebooks
- Visual Studio Code (VS Code)
- Apache Airflow
- Railway

Codebase:

- All the code for this chapter is available in this GitHub repository: `https://github.com/Sommie09/data_pipelines`.

Python libraries:

- Pandas (Data manipulation library)
- psycopg2 or SQLAlchemy (PostgreSQL database connector)

Project files:

- `Bakery_Customer_Data.CSV`

Set Up Your Development Environment

Install Python

1. Ensure Python is installed on your computer. If not, you can download it from `www.python.org/downloads`. After installation, verify Python by running it on your terminal:

   ```
   python --version
   ```

Install VS Code and Other Extensions

1. If you don't have VS Code installed, download it from `https://code.visualstudio.com`.
2. Open VS Code.
3. Go to the Extensions view by clicking the square icon on the sidebar or by pressing Ctrl+Shift+X (Windows/Linux) or Cmd+Shift+X (macOS).

4. Search for **Python** and install the extension provided by Microsoft.

5. Search for **Jupyter** and install the Jupyter extension in VS Code.

Set Up Your Project Folder

1. Download the file `Bakery_Customer_Data.csv` to your computer.

2. Create a new folder on your desktop called `Customer_ETL`.

3. Move the CSV file into the `Customer_ETL` folder.

4. Open the folder in VS Code by choosing File ⇨ Open Folder and navigating to `Customer_ETL`.

Set Up a Virtual Python Environment (Inside Your Project Folder)

1. Open the terminal in VS Code (Ctrl+ or Cmd+).

2. From the root of the `Customer_ETL` folder, create a virtual environment:

```
python -m venv env
```

3. Activate the virtual environment:

   Windows:

```
.\env\Scripts\activate
```

   macOS/Linux:

```
source env/bin/activate
```

4. Press Ctrl+Shift+P (Windows/Linux) or Cmd+Shift+P (macOS) to open the Command palette.

5. Type **Python: Select Interpreter** and choose it.

6. Select the Python interpreter from your virtual environment (`env`).

Install Pandas, Jupyter, and SQLAlchemy in Your Python Environment

In the terminal (still within the `Customer_ETL` folder), run the following:

```
pip install pandas
pip install notebook jupyter
pip install psycopg2 sqlalchemy
```

Create a New Python File to Test Python

1. Create a new file with a `.py` extension (e.g., `test.py`).

2. Write a sample script to test pandas:

```
import pandas as pd
data = {'Name': ['Alice', 'Bob', 'Charlie'], 'Age': [25, 30, 35]}
```

```
customer_data = pd.DataFrame(data)
print(customer_data)
```

Right-click the editor and select Run Python File In Terminal.

3. View the output in the terminal.

Create a Jupyter Notebook

In VS Code, inside the `Customer_ETL` folder, create a new file named `Customer_Notebook.ipynb`. Doing so creates a new Jupyter notebook.

Extracting Data from CSV

Importing the Data

To import our customer data, we're going to be using a built-in function in the Pandas Library. With this function, we can import CSV, JSON, or Excel files. Hover on the function to view other options.

1. In the Jupyter Notebook cell, type

```
import pandas as pd
#Import the CSV file
customer_data = pd.read_csv("customer_data.csv")
```

Exploring the Data

It's best practice in data engineering to explore your data before applying any transformations. One common way to do this in pandas is by using the `.head()` function, which returns the first five rows of a DataFrame.

1. Click the plus sign to create a new cell and paste the following command:

```
customer_data.head()
```

2. Run the cell by clicking the play/run button next to it or by pressing Shift+Enter. This will display a snapshot of your dataset, as seen in Figure 7-10, helping you understand its structure and contents before proceeding with any data cleansing or transformation steps.

Check for Duplicates

We also need to check for duplicates in our data because duplicates can skew analysis and lead to incorrect insights.

1. Check the shape of the dataset to see how many rows and columns it has:

```
customer_data.shape #Get the number of rows and columns
```

2. Identify duplicate rows:

```
customer_data.duplicated() #Shows the rows with duplicates as
true and false
customer_data.head()#Do this after each block of code to see the
output before moving on.
```

3. Run the cell using Shift+Enter or by clicking the Run button in your notebook.

	customerID	name	email	gender	birthday	phone	delivery_address	last_delivery	status
0	99ba8a24-a8aa-4d7d-90a7-0bf666ce7ce0	Mark Scott	natalie49@yahoo.com	male	1947-01-04	+1 804-290-1984	PSC 3882, Box 3516, APO AE 35342	2024-04-29,00:11:10	gold
1	99ba8a24-a8aa-4d7d-90a7-0bf666ce7ce0	Melanie Morgan	muellervalerie@marks-acosta.biz	male	1999-10-14	+1 806-254-6441	819 Joshua Fall Suite 215, New James, KY 13038	2020-06-09,12:53:20	bronze
2	49b24041-be7f-4cc4-860b-fef1808253b3	Robert Chung	jackie38@gmail.com	female	1952-05-08	+1 107-962-8106	848 Harris Islands, North Tiffany, WA 63998	2020-12-15,17:07:56	silver
3	65ab9ea7-7153-437c-aaa2-cfc9f2a5053c	Linda Holmes	robert88@mata-mejia.com	female	1945-04-11	+1 443-237-8961	069 Martin Roads, Morganmouth, AZ 47045	2021-06-26,18:37:18	gold
4	ef366876-76f8-40a0-a952-209e0985ef53	Amanda Woodard	zkemp@merritt.info	female	1954-12-11	+1 283-487-5386	284 Hooper Corners, Jamesburgh, TX 20864	2023-01-10,23:38:50	gold

Figure 7-10: The first 5 rows of our customer data

Transforming the Data

We need to prepare our data to be suitable for analysis. The preparation process will include removing null values, validating and correcting phone number formats, and eliminating duplicate rows to ensure data quality, integrity, and consistency.

Check for Duplicates and Drop Them

To ensure consistency, we want to identify and remove rows where both the customerID and email fields are duplicated, as these indicate repeated entries of the same customer.

```
# Remove any rows where both customerID and email are duplicated
customer_data = customer_data.drop_duplicates(subset=['customerID',
'email'])
```

Rename Null Values

In order to handle incomplete data without discarding potentially valuable records, we will address missing values in the phone number and email address columns. Rather than dropping rows with null entries, we replace missing values with a placeholder. This approach ensures that the dataset remains intact while clearly indicating which entries originally lacked this information.

```
# Fill missing phone numbers and emails with 'Unknown' to prevent
loss of data
customer_data['phone'].fillna('Unknown', inplace=True)
customer_data.head()
```

Run the cell using Shift+Enter or by clicking the Run button in your notebook.

Split the *delivery_address* into Separate Components: Address, Country Code, and Zip Code

To make the delivery address data more structured and easier to analyze, it is helpful to split the delivery_address field into separate components: the address, the country code, and the zip code. This separation enables more precise filtering, validation, and geographic analysis in downstream processes.

```
# Extract the first part of the address before the first comma
(street address)
customer_data['address'] = customer_data['delivery_address'].str.
split(pat=',').str[0]
# Extract the second part after the first comma (country code)
customer_data['country_code'] = customer_data['delivery_address'].
str.split(pat=',').str[1]
# Extract the third part (zipcode)
customer_data['zipcode'] = customer_data['delivery_address'].str.
split(pat=',').str[2]
customer_data.head()
```

Run the cell using Shift+Enter or by clicking the Run button in your notebook. The output would display the table, as shown in Figure 7-11.

customerID	name	email	gender	birthday	phone	delivery_address	last_delivery	status	address	country_code	zipcode
99ba8a24-a8aa-4d7d-90a7-bf666ce7ce0	Mark Scott	natalie49@yahoo.com	male	1947-01-04	+1 804-290-1984	PSC 3882, Box 3516, APO AE 35342	2024-04-29,00:11:10	gold	PSC 3882	Box 3516	APO AE 35342
99ba8a24-a8aa-4d7d-90a7-bf666ce7ce0	Melanie Morgan	muellervalerie@marks-acosta.biz	male	1999-10-14	+1 806-254-6441	819 Joshua Fall Suite 215, New James, KY 13038	2020-06-09,12:53:20	bronze	819 Joshua Fall Suite 215	New James	KY 13038
49b24041-be7f-4cc4-860b-ef1808253b3	Robert Chung	jackie38@gmail.com	female	1952-05-08	+1 107-962-8106	848 Harris Islands, North Tiffany, WA 63998	2020-12-15,17:07:56	silver	848 Harris Islands	North Tiffany	WA 63998
65ab9ea7-7153-437c-aaa2-fc9f2a5053c	Linda Holmes	robert88@mata-mejia.com	female	1945-04-11	+1 443-237-8961	069 Martin Roads, Morganmouth, AZ 47045	2021-06-26,18:37:18	gold	069 Martin Roads	Morganmouth	AZ 47045
ef366876-76f8-40a0-a952-9e0985ef53	Amanda Woodard	zkemp@merritt.info	female	1954-12-11	+1 283-487-5386	284 Hooper Corners, Jamesburgh, TX 20864	2023-01-10,23:38:50	gold	284 Hooper Corners	Jamesburgh	TX 20864

Figure 7-11: The delivery address column split into separate columns

Split the Last Delivery Time Column into Separate Columns

To clean and organize our data, let's split the `last_delivery` column into two separate columns: one for the date and one for the time. The original column contains both values separated by a comma (e.g., 2025-05-01, 14:30), so we'll use the `.str.split()` function.

1. Paste the following code into a new cell:

```
#Extract the first and second string
customer_data['last_delivery_date'] = customer_data['last_
delivery'].str.split(pat=',').str[0]
customer_data['last_delivery_time'] = customer_data['last_
delivery'].str.split(pat=',').str[1]
customer_data = customer_data.drop(['last_delivery'],
axis = 1)
#View the data frame
customer_data.head()
```

Run the cell using Shift+Enter or by clicking the Run button in your notebook. The output would display the table shown in Figure 7-12.

email	gender	birthday	phone	delivery_address	status	address	country_code	zipcode	last_delivery_date	last_delivery_time
natalie49@yahoo.com	male	1947-01-04	+1 804-290-1984	PSC 3882, Box 3516, APO AE 35342	gold	PSC 3882	Box 3516	APO AE 35342	2024-04-29	00:11:10
muellervalerie@marks-acosta.biz	male	1999-10-14	+1 806-254-6441	819 Joshua Fall Suite 215, New James, KY 13038	bronze	819 Joshua Fall Suite 215	New James	KY 13038	2020-06-09	12:53:20
jackie38@gmail.com	female	1952-05-08	+1 107-962-8106	848 Harris Islands, North Tiffany, WA 63998	silver	848 Harris Islands	North Tiffany	WA 63998	2020-12-15	17:07:56
robert88@mata-mejia.com	female	1945-04-11	+1 443-237-8961	069 Martin Roads, Morganmouth, AZ 47045	gold	069 Martin Roads	Morganmouth	AZ 47045	2021-06-26	18:37:18
zkemp@merritt.info	female	1954-12-11	+1 283-487-5386	284 Hooper Corners, Jamesburgh, TX 20864	gold	284 Hooper Corners	Jamesburgh	TX 20864	2023-01-10	23:38:50

Figure 7-12: The last delivery column split into date and time columns

Drop Original Address

Now that we've split `delivery_address` into `address`, `country_code`, and `zipcode`, we no longer need the original column.

Run this cell using Shift+Enter.

```
# Drop the original 'delivery_address' column as the data is now split
customer_data = customer_data.drop(['delivery_address'], axis = 1)
customer_data.head() #Inspect the updated DataFrame, this helps This
verify that the new columns are present and delivery_address has been
successfully removed.
```

Run the cell using Shift+Enter or by clicking the Run button in your notebook. The output would give the table shown in Figure 7-13.

	customerID	name	email	gender	birthday	phone	status	address	country_code	zipcode	last_delivery_date
0	99ba8a24-a8aa-4d7d-90a7-0bf666ce7ce0	Mark Scott	natalie49@yahoo.com	male	1947-01-04	+1 804-290-1984	gold	PSC 3882	Box 3516	APO AE 35342	2024-04-29
1	99ba8a24-a8aa-4d7d-90a7-0bf666ce7ce0	Melanie Morgan	muellervalerie@marks-acosta.biz	male	1999-10-14	+1 806-254-6441	bronze	819 Joshua Fall Suite 215	New James	KY 13038	2020-06-09
2	49b24041-be7f-4cc4-860b-fef1808253b3	Robert Chung	jackie38@gmail.com	female	1952-05-08	+1 107-962-8106	silver	848 Harris Islands	North Tiffany	WA 63998	2020-12-15
3	65ab9ea7-7153-437c-aaa2-cfc9f2a5053c	Linda Holmes	robert88@mata-mejia.com	female	1945-04-11	+1 443-237-8961	gold	069 Martin Roads	Morganmouth	AZ 47045	2021-06-26
4	ef366876-76f8-40a0-a952-209e0985ef53	Amanda Woodard	zkemp@merritt.info	female	1954-12-11	+1 283-487-5386	gold	284 Hooper Corners	Jamesburgh	TX 20864	2023-01-10

Figure 7-13: The delivery address column has been dropped

Rename Birthday Column

To maintain consistent naming conventions across the dataset, we will rename the Birthday column to a more descriptive label. This helps ensure that the column name clearly conveys its contents and aligns with naming practices used throughout the project.

```
# Rename the 'birthday' column to 'birth_date' for better clarity
customer_data = customer_data.rename(columns={'birthday':' birth_date'})
# View the updated DataFrame
customer_data.head()
```

Run this cell using Shift + Enter to see the effect of the renaming and to preview the updated data. The output would give the table shown in Figure 7-14.

	customerID	name	email	gender	birth_date	phone	status	address	country_code	zipcode	last_delivery_date
0	99ba8a24-a8aa-4d7d-90a7-0bf666ce7ce0	Mark Scott	natalie49@yahoo.com	male	1947-01-04	+1 804-290-1984	gold	PSC 3882	Box 3516	APO AE 35342	2024-04-29
1	99ba8a24-a8aa-4d7d-90a7-0bf666ce7ce0	Melanie Morgan	muellervalerie@marks-acosta.biz	male	1999-10-14	+1 806-254-6441	bronze	819 Joshua Fall Suite 215	New James	KY 13038	2020-06-09
2	49b24041-be7f-4cc4-860b-fef1808253b3	Robert Chung	jackie38@gmail.com	female	1952-05-08	+1 107-962-8106	silver	848 Harris Islands	North Tiffany	WA 63998	2020-12-15
3	65ab9ea7-7153-437c-aaa2-cfc9f2a5053c	Linda Holmes	robert88@mata-mejia.com	female	1945-04-11	+1 443-237-8961	gold	069 Martin Roads	Morganmouth	AZ 47045	2021-06-26
4	ef366876-76f8-40a0-a952-209e0985ef53	Amanda Woodard	zkemp@merritt.info	female	1954-12-11	+1 283-487-5386	gold	284 Hooper Corners	Jamesburgh	TX 20864	2023-01-10

Figure 7-14: The birthday column has been renamed to birth_date

Save the Cleaned DataFrame to a New CSV File

After completing all necessary cleaning steps, the final version of the dataset is saved to a new CSV file. This ensures that the cleaned data is preserved for future analysis or use without altering the original source.

```
customer_data.to_csv("customer_data_cleaned.csv", index=False)
```

Load the New CSV File into a Postgres Database Instance

Once your data has been cleaned and transformed, the next step is to load it into a PostgreSQL database so that it can be queried efficiently and integrated into downstream systems.

Set Up Railway

To set up a PostgreSQL instance with Railway, follow these steps:

1. Visit Railway at `https://railway.app`.
2. Sign up using your GitHub, Google, or email account.
3. After logging in, click the New Project button on the dashboard.
4. Select Provision PostgreSQL from the templates offered.
5. Once the PostgreSQL instance is provisioned, Railway will automatically set it up.
6. You will be redirected to the project dashboard, where you'll see the details of your PostgreSQL instance.
7. Click the PostgreSQL service in your project.
8. Select the Connect tab.
9. Copy the provided Connection URI.

Connect Railway to Jupyter Notebook

To connect a Railway PostgreSQL instance to your Jupyter Notebook, follow these steps:

1. Create a new code tab in your Jupyter Notebook by clicking the + (plus) icon in the Jupyter Notebook toolbar.
2. Set up the database engine to connect to Railway:

```
# Replace with your Supabase connection details
connection_uri = "postgresql://postgres:[YOUR-PASSWORD]@
db.******.supabase.co:*****/postgres"
```

```
# Create a database engine
engine = db.create_engine (connection_uri)
```

3. Click Run, and the engine shows up in the output.

Load the Data into Railway

The customer data that has been transformed would be loaded to a customer table in Railway. On the railway dashboard, you can view the Customer table that has just been created:

```
customer_data_cleaned.to_sql("customers", engine, if_exists=
'replace', index=False)
```

Schedule ETL Pipeline with Apache Airflow

Set Up Apache Airflow

1. Make sure you're still in your project's virtual environment. If it's not active, activate it:

   ```
   # For Windows:
   .\env\Scripts\activate

   #For macOS:
   source env/bin/activate
   ```

2. Once your virtual environment is active, run the following commands in the VS Code Terminal:

   ```
   # Installing Airflow
   pip install apache-airflow
   # Initialise the airflow database
   airflow db init
   ```

Configure the User Credentials

With these commands, Airflow would require a username and password:

1. From your computer's terminal, run the following to locate and open the airflow.cfg file:
   $AIRFLOW_HOME/airflow.cfg

2. Search for **webserver** in the file.

3. Add the following lines:

```
authenticate = True
auth_backend = airflow.contrib.auth.backends.password_auth
```

4. Save and close the file.

5. On the terminal, run:

```
airflow users create  -u USERNAME  -p PASSWORD -e EMAIL -r
ROLE -f FIRSTNAME -l LASTNAME
```

Start Airflow

1. Start the web server:

```
airflow webserver --port 8080
```

2. Open a new tab on your terminal and start the scheduler:

```
airflow scheduler
```

3. Run the local host link on your browser and view the Airflow UI:

```
http://localhost:8080:453
```

Creating a DAG

Setting Up the ETL Python Script

1. Navigate to $AIRFLOW_HOME/airflow.cfg on your computer terminal.

2. Open the dag folder in that directory on your Visual Studio Code.

3. In the dag folder on Visual Studio Code, create a customer_etl.py file.

4. Copy and paste the import and engine code:

```
import pandas as pd
import re
import sqlalchemy as db
customer_csv = "/your_path /customer_data.csv"
# Replace with your Supabase connection details
connection_uri = "postgresql://postgres:[YOUR-PASSWORD]@
db.******.supabase.co:*****/postgres"
# Creates a database engine
engine = db.create_engine (connection_uri)
```

5. Copy and paste the transformation logic under def main():

```
def main():
customer_data = pd.read_csv(customer_data)
```

```
        customer_data = customer_data.drop_duplicates(subset=['customerID',
'email'])
        customer_data['phone_number'].fillna('Unknown', inplace=True)


        # Split delivery address
        customer_data['address'] = customer_data['delivery_address'].str
.split(pat=',').str[0]
        customer_data['country_code'] = customer_data['delivery_address']
.str.split(pat=',').str[1]
        customer_data['zipcode'] = customer_data['delivery_address'].str
.split(pat=',').str[2]
        #Split delivery date
        customer_data['last_delivery_date'] = customer_data['last_delivery']
.str.split(pat=',').str[0]
        customer_data['last_delivery_time'] = customer_data['last_delivery']
.str.split(pat=',').str[1]
        customer_data = customer_data.drop(['last_delivery'], axis = 1)
        # Drop the original 'delivery_address' column as the data is
now split
        customer_data = customer_data.drop(['delivery_address'], axis = 1)
        # Rename the 'birthday' column to 'birthday_date' for better clarity
        customer_data = customer_data.rename(columns={'status':'loyalty_
status'})
        customer_data.to_sql("customers_2", engine, if_exists='replace',
index=False)
        print("ETL successful!")
```

Setting Up the DAG Script

1. Create a new file, `customers_dag.py`.

2. Import the following libraries. The last line is the name of the `customer_etl.py` file.

```
from datetime import datetime, timedelta
from airflow import DAG
from airflow.operators.python_operator import PythonOperator
from orders_etl_logic import main
```

3. Paste this code block in the next line to define default arguments for the DAG:

```
default_args = {
    'owner': 'airflow',  # Owner of the DAG
    'depends_on_past': False,  # Does not depend on the success of
previous DAG runs
    'start_date': datetime(2024, 1, 1),  # Start date for the DAG
schedule
    'email_on_failure': False,  # Disable email alerts on failure
    'email_on_retry': False,  # Disable email alerts on retries
```

```
            'retries': 1,   # Number of retries for failed tasks
            'retry_delay': timedelta(minutes=5),   # Delay between retries
        }
```

4. Define the DAG:

```
        dag = DAG( 'customer_full_load', # Unique identifier for the DAG
        default_args=default_args,
        description='Customer Table ETL DAG', # Description of the DAG's
    purpose
        schedule_interval='@daily', # Schedule the DAG to run daily
```

5. Define the task to run the ETL process:

```
        run_etl = PythonOperator(
        task_id=run_customer_etl, # Unique identifier for the task
        python_callable=main, # Function to execute in the customer_ETL
    script
        dag=dag, # The DAG to which this task belongs
```

6. Finally, call the `run_etl` task at the end of the editor and run the script:

```
        run_etl
```

Running the DAG on Airflow

Once the DAG has been defined and scheduled in Airflow, you can manually trigger and monitor its execution through the Airflow web interface. Follow these steps to run the DAG and verify the results:

1. Go back to your browser and refresh the Airflow tab.
2. View the task `run_etl` or search for it in the search bar.
3. Click Auto Refresh.
4. When the DAG is done running, view the new table customer2 created on Railway.

Summary

- Batch processing involves processing large volumes of data at scheduled intervals, while stream processing involves processing data in real time or near real time as it arrives.
- A batch pipeline consists of six stages: data sources, staging area, data transformation, data storage, consumption layer, and job scheduler.
- A staging area is important in batch pipelines for data backup in case of job failures.

- An ELT process addresses the limitations of an ETL by loading data into the storage system before transformations.

- Streaming pipelines process data continuously; they are event-driven and have a low latency.

- A streaming pipeline has four main components: Producers, Message Queues, Schema Registry, and Stream Processors.

- Stream processors consist of four key features that make them function efficiently: windowing, checkpointing, watermarking, and stateful processing.

- In stream processing, there are four different types of windowing patterns: Tumbling, Session, Sliding, and Session Window.

- A Lambda architecture in data engineering is a combination of both batch and streaming solutions. It consists of the batch, streaming, and serving layers.

- Orchestration in data engineering relies on directed acyclic graphs (DAGs) to define task dependencies, automation to reduce manual triggers, scheduling to run workflows at specific times or intervals, monitoring to track progress and performance, and alerting to notify teams when something goes wrong.

- A directed acyclic graph (DAG) in data orchestration is a collection of tasks arranged in a specific order to ensure that they are executed in the correct sequence.

- Three important metrics to look out for when monitoring a pipeline are performance, resource, and data quality metrics.

Data Quality

So far, we've discussed the fundamentals of databases, data storage systems, and data pipelines. While these are essential components of the data engineering process, even the best designs or storage solutions are meaningless if the data delivered to downstream users is bad. So, how do we ensure quality data in our data engineering process?

IN THIS CHAPTER, YOU WILL LEARN ABOUT THE FOLLOWING:

- Causes of bad data and the impact
- Understanding what data quality means and the importance
- Various data quality dimensions
- How to identify data quality issues
- Common data quality checks
- Your role in ensuring data quality in your organization using best practices

Data quality is an important aspect of the data engineering process, but let's step back and look at the broader picture. Data engineering serves multiple business needs in an organization across various departments. To truly understand the impact of bad data or why we need to ensure data quality, we can examine how it affects the overall business performance and decision-making process.

The truth is a lot of organizations don't care about the quality of their data. Although quality data is an important part of their process, it is still overlooked. Most organizations want to start initiatives that can impact their business positively, but since they have bad data, they rather build walk-arounds or create makeshift solutions.

In this era of innovation, poor data quality is a major roadblock for businesses looking to innovate—especially with the rise of artificial intelligence. These technologies rely on accurate, high-quality data to function effectively, as these AI systems learn from data to make predictions and optimize processes. When the data is inconsistent or flawed, the potential of AI is significantly limited if the foundation it relies on is unreliable.

Additionally, with poor data quality, a business doesn't have a competitive edge. Companies that rely on poor data cannot adapt quickly to market changes at the scale of their competitors. In summary, addressing data quality isn't just a technical task, it is a strategic decision that affects the entire organization.

Bad Data

Before we describe what quality data truly means, you should understand what bad data is. Organizations define certain thresholds that deem data to be of good quality. Subject to several requirements, bad data is any data that doesn't meet these requirements.

Data is bad when it fails to meet the standards needed for meaningful analysis. Bad data is incomplete, with missing values that leave gaps in understanding. It is also poorly formatted, where data fields like dates are inconsistent or text appears in numerical columns. Sometimes, it's outdated, reflecting conditions that are no longer relevant. All these issues combined make it harder to derive insights. For example, imagine a sales department trying to generate a monthly revenue report, only to find that several entries are missing or some sales are recorded in the wrong month or maybe duplicated. This leads to multiple inconsistencies in the reports.

Bad data is both a cultural and a technical problem. From a cultural perspective, it starts with how data is perceived, handled, and prioritized within an organization. If employees are not trained to enter accurate and consistent data, or if there's a lack of accountability for maintaining data quality, there will be errors. On the technical side, inadequate tools contribute significantly. Legacy databases or source systems that are poorly integrated can introduce errors and inconsistencies.

To truly address bad data, organizations need a combination of a strong data culture that promotes ownership and accountability, along with the right technical systems for data validation and integration. But where does this bad data come from?

- Human error is one of the most common causes of poor data quality. This occurs especially during data entry processes. Imagine an employee manually entering customer information into a CRM system. Due to a lack of standardization, the employee might enter the same data in different formats. For example, the phone number could be entered as "555-1234" in one record and "5551234" in another.

- Another cause of bad data is when organizations store data across multiple systems, which are sometimes separate from each other. When creating a dataset, data integration from these systems can lead to problems such as duplicated data, missing fields, or inconsistent labels. Also, different systems may use different terminology for the same concept, creating further complications.

- Consider an organization with sales data stored in one system and inventory data stored in a separate system. When trying to combine data from both sources to generate a report on product performance, duplicates could arise. For example, the same product listed under different names in each system or important fields might be missing. Additionally, the data labels for the same concept may differ, such as "customer ID" in one system being labeled "client number" in another system.

The key distinction between high-quality and low-quality data lies in how well the data serves its intended purpose. In other words, the distinction tells us if data is reliable and suitable for use in making decisions, running operations, or powering analytics. Without high-quality data, even the best systems and tools can produce inaccurate insights or fail to function efficiently.

When we're talking about data quality, we're looking at how well the data serves the organization's needs. For example, if a company's data is accurate, they can confidently use it to guide strategic decisions. This also ties into operational efficiency. Imagine a supply-chain company relying on incorrect inventory data. This could result in production delays or overstocking, which is both time-consuming and costly. If a business has clean and reliable data, it can ensure smooth workflows, reduce errors in systems, and avoid costly rework.

Additionally, one of the main goals of any business is to offer an exceptional customer experience whether directly or indirectly. If the quality of your data is high, you can create personalized services and interactions with your customers. For example, a company like Amazon relies on high-quality data to suggest products tailored to each individual, which is a huge part of why they have such a strong customer base.

Finally, in industries where regulatory compliance is crucial, maintaining data quality is not optional. Accurate data ensures that organizations meet legal requirements and avoid hefty fines. Legal requirements refer to the laws, regulations, and standards that organizations must follow to ensure their operations are compliant with local, national, or international rules. These requirements are typically set by governing bodies or regulatory agencies to ensure fairness and protect consumer rights. For instance, in healthcare, legal requirements often focus on the protection of personal health information with strict standards for how health data should be stored, processed, and shared. In this instance, poor data quality such as incomplete or incorrect patient information can lead to violations of these laws, and this could result in patient harm, fines, and significant reputational damage for healthcare providers.

Maintaining good data quality isn't just about preventing errors—it's about ensuring that the data available is fit for its intended purpose, enabling the organization to operate efficiently and, most importantly, prioritize good data quality practices.

Dimensions of Data Quality

Let's explain the various dimensions of data quality. Think of these dimensions as different lenses through which we evaluate the fitness of data. When we encounter bad data, these dimensions help us assess its suitability for its intended use and pinpoint areas where transformation or improvement is needed. These dimensions are also important when discussing service level agreement (SLA) requirements with stakeholders. SLA requirements are the specific standards and performance metrics outlined in a contract between a service provider and a customer, defining the expected quality, availability, and response time of the service provided, including consequences for not meeting those standards.

In this section, we will go over these dimensions, explore their significance, and discuss how they can be measured effectively. Each dimension gives us a unique perspective on how well the data is serving its purpose. At the end of this section, you'll be able to identify data quality issues and know the necessary steps to take to ensure data meets each dimension. The dimensions are as follows:

- Accuracy
- Completeness
- Consistency
- Validity
- Uniqueness
- Timeliness
- Accessibility
- Relevance

Accuracy

Accuracy is one of the fundamental aspects of data quality. It measures how closely data matches the real-world entities it represents and ensures that data is free from errors that could mislead decision-making.

Consider this example. A customer database ingests data from a form. The email column contains incorrect values, such as "jaen_doe@mail.com" instead of "jane_doe@mail.com." Imagine you're part of the marketing team and you're sending out a promotional email campaign. With the incorrect values, the mail would be sent to the wrong recipient. Similarly, if the delivery address on the form is stored incorrectly, packages could be routed to the wrong person or locations that don't exist in the real world. Accurate data is critical in maintaining the credibility of data-driven operations. The SLA for accuracy could be that data values must be correct with an error rate below 0.1% per reporting period.

CUSTOMER FORM

Name: Jane Doe
Email: jane_doe@mail.com
Birth Date: 02-10-1997
Delivery Address: 23 Elm Marker Street
City: London
Postal code: E1 BA2

NAME	EMAIL	BIRTH DATE	DELIVERY ADDRESS	CITY	POSTAL CODE
Jane Doe	jaen_doe@ mail.com	02-10-1997	23 Elm Marker Street	London	E1 BA2
Gabriel Johnson	gjohnson@ gmail.com	09-01-1996	221B Baker Street	London	NW1 6XE

Completeness

Completeness evaluates whether all required data is present in a dataset. It is the degree to which all expected records are populated and ensures that no important pieces of information are missing.

For instance, in the following example data, we have a database for a banking application. If we have missing data like First Name, Last Name, or Social Security Number (SSN), this could halt the registration process. If the system expects these fields and they are missing, it may not allow the user to proceed with onboarding. Analytics relies heavily on the completeness of datasets. If critical data is missing, the analysis will be skewed, which could lead to incorrect conclusions.

Completeness also refers to maintaining the same number of records between systems. This ensures that data transfer processes have correctly captured all records without omission. This is important because, if one system contains 10,000 customer records but the target system only shows 9,950 after migration, this inconsistency can result in data gaps.

CUSTOMER ID	FIRST NAME	LAST NAME	SSN	EMAIL	ADDRESS	ACCOUNT CREATION DATE
101	John	Doe	555-12-3456	john.doe@email.com	123 Elm St, NY	01-01-2025
102	Null	Smith	987-65-7432	Null	456 Maple Ave, TX	01-10-2025
103	Jane	Null	Null	janef@gmail.com	789 Oak Blvd, CA	01-15-2025
190	Daniella	Peters	678-01-2678	daniellapet@yahoo.com	12, Oklahoma Street, DC	01-25-2025

Let's explore some effective ways to perform a completeness check.

Checking for NULL Values

NULL value checks are a way of identifying whether certain fields in your data contain missing or undefined values. In a database, a NULL value represents the absence of any data in a column for a particular record. However, it's not the same as 0, an empty string, or a blank space; it just means "no value."

Mathematical operations or joins involving NULLs can produce unexpected results, so catching them early helps avoid issues. Also, identifying NULLs helps you assess whether your data meets completeness requirements or if critical data is missing.

The following SQL query retrieves all rows from a table where a specific column contains NULL values. The NULL keyword was discussed in detail in Chapter 4, "SQL Fundamentals."

```
SELECT * #This selects all columns from the table for each row where the
condition is met.
FROM table_name
WHERE column_name IS NULL; #This filters the rows to include only those
where the value in the specified column (column_name) is NULL.
```

To handle NULL values, you can either fill in missing values with a default value, like 0 for numeric fields or Unknown for strings, or remove rows if the missing data is insignificant.

Checking the Completeness Score

A *completeness score* is expressed as a percentage that reflects the proportion of data that is complete compared to the total expected data. To calculate the completeness score of a table, use this formula:

$$\text{Completeness Score} = \left(\frac{\text{Total Records / Total Records Without}}{\text{Missing Values}} \right) \times 100$$

Assume we're checking completeness by field. Let's say you have the following columns and the number of missing records for each:

FIELD NAME	TOTAL RECORDS	MISSING RECORDS	COMPLETENESS SCORE
First Name	1,000	50	95%
Last Name	1,000	30	97%
SSN	1,000	100	90%

The completeness score for each field is calculated as

Completeness for First Name = (1,000 − 50 / 1,000) × 100 = 95%

Completeness for Last Name = (1,000 − 30 / 1,000) × 100 = 97%

Completeness for SSN = (1,000 − 100 / 1,000) × 100 = 90%

To get the overall completeness score for the entire dataset, you can average the individual field completeness scores. This is particularly useful when comparing the completeness of different columns or datasets.

Overall Completeness Score = Number of Fields / Sum of Completeness Scores

The overall completeness score would be

Overall Completeness Score = 95 + 97 + 90 / 3 = 94%

This means that, on average, 94 percent of the expected data across these fields is complete.

The completeness score provides you with a quick overview of how much of the dataset is ready for use in reports or models. A low completeness score indicates that there may be issues with missing data that need to be addressed before the data can be reliably used for decision-making or analysis.

Checking the Volume of Data

Data volume checks ensure that the data volume (the size of the data) is within its expected limit. This check also helps to detect missing data to ensure no data is lost during ingestion or transformation processes. We can manually compare the volume of current data with historical baselines. For example, if a batch pipeline normally outputs 200 rows but suddenly jumps to 1,500, this should flag an issue in the query.

Automated min/max threshold alerts can be set for data volume. A common way to monitor data volume is to validate that the number of records ingested from source systems matches the number stored in your destination. A completeness SLA might specify that at least 99.9 percent of all required fields must be filled in for each dataset.

Consistency

Consistency refers to the uniformity and accuracy of data across different systems and datasets. Inconsistencies arise when errors occur during data entry, such as one system recording "John Doe" while another captures "J. Doe." They can also occur when updates in one database are not sent to other systems, causing synchronization issues. Additionally, inconsistencies happen when merging data from diverse sources with conflicting formats or values.

For example, a customer's email address should match across multiple tables and remain consistent throughout the data life cycle. Inconsistent data, such as differing values for the same customer in separate systems, can lead to errors in reporting. Consistency is also important when integrating data from multiple sources, as it ensures that analysis and decisions are based on reliable information.

Also, consistency involves maintaining referential integrity within and across datasets. In relational databases, referential integrity ensures that the relationships between primary keys and foreign keys are valid. This means that every foreign key in a child table must reference a valid primary key in a parent table. If this rule is violated, the data becomes inconsistent, leading to potential errors in reporting, analytics, and operations.

Referential integrity is a concept that ensures the consistency of relationships between tables by guaranteeing that foreign key values in one table always correspond to valid primary key values in another table.

Suppose you have two tables, Orders and Customers. The CustomerID in the Orders table (a foreign key) must always match an existing CustomerID in the Customers table (a primary key). If OrderID=1001 is referencing a CustomerID=9999 but CustomerID=9999 does not exist in the Customers table, this violates referential integrity and creates inconsistent data.

The following SQL query checks referential integrity between the Orders and Customers tables, ensuring that every CustomerID in the Orders table exists in the Customers table:

```
SELECT orders.customer_id
FROM orders
LEFT JOIN customers ON orders.customer_id = customers.customer_id
WHERE customers.customer_id IS NULL;
```

In this query, the LEFT JOIN combines all records from the orders table with matching records from the customers table. WHERE customers.customer_id IS NULL filters for cases where there is no matching customer_id in the customers table, indicating a referential integrity violation. This query will return any orphaned orders with missing corresponding customer records.

Ensuring referential integrity is a consistency check because it maintains the logical structure and prevents contradictions within the database. Without it, you might end up with orphaned records—that is, orders without a corresponding customer or duplicate relationships, leading to unreliable and inconsistent data representations.

Validity

Validity measures the degree to which the values in a data element are valid. Validity ensures that data conforms to expected formats, types, and ranges, such as ensuring dates are logical, numerical values are within defined ranges, and text fields match predefined formats. Validity also ensures that data adheres to business rules and industry requirements. Data that fails validation can cause a lot of system errors because applications expect data in a certain format.

Let's look at the following table to identify some validity issues:

STUDENT ID	NAME	AGE	BIRTH DATE	GRADE
101	Alice Green	18	12-05-2006	A
102	Bob White	−3	01-15-2029	B
103	Jane Doe	20	09-10-2004	X

Some issues found:

- Bob's age is −3; age values cannot be negative.
- Bob's birth date is in the future; birth dates must be in the past.
- Jane's grade is X, and X is not a grade in the school's curriculum.

To validate data within relational databases, one approach is using the CHECK constraint in SQL, as discussed in Chapter 4. This constraint allows us to enforce rules directly at the database level, ensuring that only data meeting predefined conditions is accepted. By embedding these validation rules within the database schema, organizations can maintain data integrity and reduce the risk of errors downstream.

Let's walk through some SQL query examples designed to assess the validity of data in each of these columns.

Checking birthdays: This query enforces the rule that all birth dates should always be in the past.

```
CREATE TABLE Student (
  student_id INT PRIMARY KEY,
  name VARCHAR(50) NOT NULL,
  birthdate DATE NOT NULL,
  CHECK (birthdate <= CURRENT_DATE)#This ensures that the birthdate
cannot be in the future.
);
```

Checking grades: This query ensures that all grades should only be within a predefined range (e.g., A, B, C, D, F).

```
CREATE TABLE StudentGrades (
  student_id INT PRIMARY KEY,
  subject VARCHAR(50) NOT NULL,
  grade CHAR(1) NOT NULL,
  CHECK (grade IN ('A', 'B', 'C', 'D', 'F'))
);
```

Checking ages: This query ensures that the field Age is always a positive integer and within a reasonable range (e.g., between 1 and 120).

```
CREATE TABLE AgeValidation (
  student_id INT PRIMARY KEY,
  name VARCHAR(50) NOT NULL,
  age INT NOT NULL,
  CHECK (age BETWEEN 1 AND 120)
);
```

These completeness checks are implemented as constraints within the database schema. Rather than correcting invalid data, they prevent it from being inserted into the database in the first place. If someone tries to insert or update a row that violates any of these checks, the database will reject the operation and return an error. A validity SLA could specify that 100 percent of data entries must conform to defined formats and business rules.

Uniqueness

Uniqueness is an important part of data quality. It measures the degree to which the records in a dataset are not duplicated. Duplicate data can lead to errors in processing and incorrect reporting, and it can also increase storage requirements or slow down processing and querying.

Consider a banking application where customers are registered. If a customer's data is entered more than once, it could lead to multiple accounts being created for the same individual. This can cause errors in transactions, orders, or even fraud detection. A unique constraint ensures that every customer has only one record in the system.

In this table, the customer John Doe appears twice in the database.

CUSTOMER ID	FIRST NAME	LAST NAME	SSN	EMAIL	ADDRESS	ACCOUNT CREATION DATE
101	John	Doe	555-12-3456	john.doe@email.com	123 Elm St, NY	01-01-2025
102	Null	Smith	987-65-7432	Null	456 Maple Ave, TX	01-01-2025
103	Jane	Null	111-220-3333	janef@gmail.com	789 Oak Blvd, CA	2025-01-15
104	Michael	Johnson	222-33-4444	michael.j@email.com	321 Birch Ave, TX	2025-01-20
105	John	Doe	555-123-456	john.doe@email.com	123 Elm St, NY	2025-01-01

Data uniqueness checks are used to ensure that data in a dataset are distinct and that no duplicate records exist. To ensure data uniqueness, a common approach is the *duplicate record check*. This check identifies and removes or resolves duplicate entries based on key fields.

```
SELECT customer_id, COUNT(*) AS record_count
FROM sales
GROUP BY customer_id
HAVING COUNT(*) > 1;
```

In this query, GROUP BY customer_id groups records by the unique identifier (customer_id). COUNT(*) > 1 identifies cases where the same customer_id appears more than once, indicating duplicates.

In addition to querying for duplicates, data uniqueness can also be enforced at the schema level by using the SQL UNIQUE constraint, as seen in the following SQL query. This ensures that certain fields, like email addresses or student IDs, remain unique across all records, and that any attempt to insert a duplicate value will be rejected by the database.

```
CREATE TABLE sales (
  customer_id INT UNIQUE
);
```

Timeliness

Timeliness refers to the degree to which data is available and up-to-date, especially when meeting SLA requirements. For example, in the banking application database, the customer dataset must be loaded at 9:00 a.m. Some records in the following database table do not meet those requirements.

CUSTOMER ID	CUSTOMER NAME	TRANSACTION AMOUNT ($)	EXPECTED UPDATE TIME	EXPECTED UPDATE TIME	SLA MET
101	Jane Doe	500.00	9:00 a.m.	9:10 a.m.	No
102	John Smith	200.00	9:00 a.m.	8:55 a.m.	Yes
103	Alice Brown	750.00	9:00 a.m.	9:30 a.m.	No

Accessibility

Accessibility refers to the ease with which users can locate, retrieve, and use data when needed. This dimension ensures that data is accessible and made available to the right people at the right time and in the right format. Without accessibility, even high-quality data becomes useless because it cannot serve its intended purpose. Consider an e-commerce company, where sales and inventory teams need access to real-time product stock data to avoid overselling. If this data is only available to IT administrators or is stored in an outdated system requiring multiple steps to access, although the data is of good quality it is not accessible. An accessibility SLA could require that authorized users must have 99.9 percent uptime access to data platforms during business hours.

Relevance

Relevance is the degree to which data meets the specific needs of its users. It addresses whether the data is meaningful and applicable to the context in which it is used. Data needs to align with the specific questions or goals of the business, it needs to be captured at the right level of detail, and most importantly, it has to be filtered to remove data that does not contribute to insights. Say a marketing team is preparing a targeted campaign for Valentine's Day and they need recent customer purchase behavior data. Providing customer data from two years ago is irrelevant to their current objective. They would most likely need timely data from the last three months.

Data Quality Hierarchy

Data quality is perceived differently depending on who is using the data. The *data quality hierarchy* is a conceptual framework that outlines the various levels at which data quality is evaluated, depending on the user's perspective. As engineers, our focus is primarily on cleaning, transforming, and maintaining the accuracy of data throughout its life cycle. However, stakeholders view data through a different lens, often prioritizing its usability, relevance, and reliability for decision-making. Figure 8-1 represents the different layers stakeholders go through to get the right data.

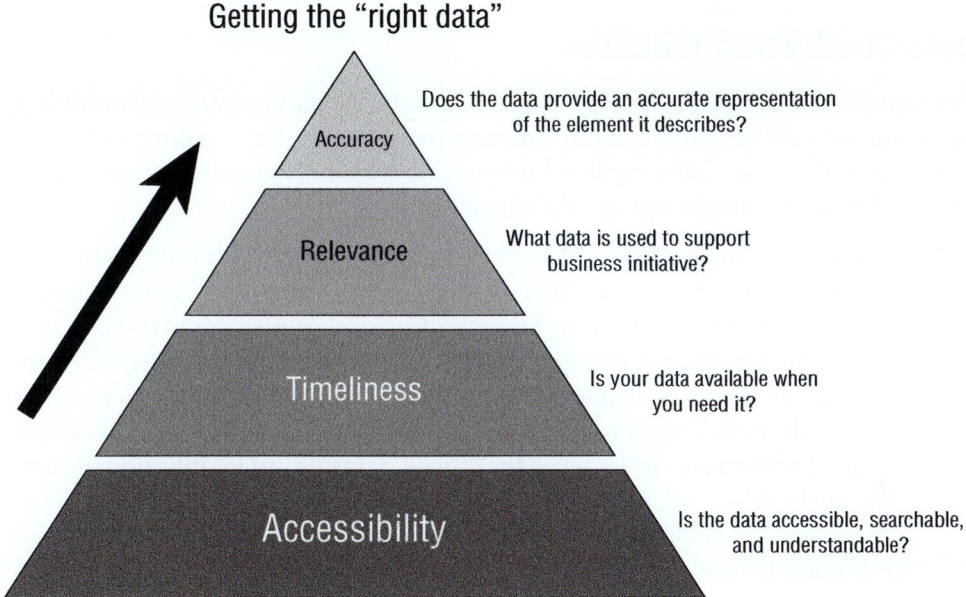

Getting the "right data"

Accuracy — Does the data provide an accurate representation of the element it describes?

Relevance — What data is used to support business initiative?

Timeliness — Is your data available when you need it?

Accessibility — Is the data accessible, searchable, and understandable?

Figure 8-1: Data quality hierarchy

In the accessibility layer in Figure 8-1, stakeholders, whether downstream or upstream, simply want to know if data can be easily accessed, searched, and understood. At this stage, they are concerned with whether they can find and retrieve the data they need without jumping through a lot of hoops.

In the timeliness layer, they want to know if the data is available when needed. Timeliness is crucial for stakeholders like business managers who rely on up-to-date data for reporting and making time-sensitive decisions. Delays in data availability reduce its value.

In the relevance layer, they check if the data supports the current business initiatives and decisions. Executives and decision-makers look for data that is directly relevant to solving business problems or answering key questions. In this layer, data that isn't aligned with business goals is often ignored.

At the accuracy layer, they check if the data is an accurate representation of the element it describes. As this is the final level, stakeholders such as data scientists or auditors need assurance that the data accurately reflects reality. Any inaccuracies can lead to flawed insights and costly errors.

In summary, the pyramid structure implies that each layer builds on the previous one. Moving beyond accuracy, data engineers and stakeholders can decide on more granular requirements for specific projects.

Data Quality Best Practices

Data quality is not just about having clean data. Achieving and maintaining high data quality requires a comprehensive approach that combines cultural and technical efforts. Let's explore best practices that organizations can implement to safeguard the integrity of their data.

Establishing a data quality culture: The change starts with you. To build a strong data quality culture, the first step is leadership involvement. Senior leaders need to set the tone and demonstrate a commitment to data quality by allocating necessary resources and prioritizing them across teams. However, it's not just up to leadership; every department should own the data they work with. This is where data stewards come in; they're responsible for specific datasets and ensure that those datasets are maintained to high standards. Also, encouraging cross-department collaboration allows for a more comprehensive approach to data quality, making sure everyone understands data quality best practices. When everyone in the organization knows that data quality is a shared responsibility, it becomes part of the organizational culture.

Building a data quality framework: A data quality framework sets the rules for what good data looks like. These rules focus on six key dimensions; accuracy, completeness, consistency, timeliness, uniqueness, and validity. It's important to define quality thresholds for each of these dimensions so that everyone knows what good data means in the organization. Once these standards are in place, tools like Monte Carlo—a data observability platform that helps organizations monitor, detect, and resolve data quality issues across their data pipelines—can help operationalize the framework by continuously monitoring data for issues related to those dimensions. This ensures that the framework is not just theoretical, but actively enforced in real time.

Data profiling: To truly understand the quality of your data, you need to profile it. Data profiling helps identify patterns, errors, and inconsistencies in your data. It's like taking a deep dive into your data to see how it looks, and this will help you spot issues like missing values, duplicates, or inconsistent formatting. Once you've profiled the data, data cleansing comes into play. Here you can use Great Expectations, an open source data validation tool that allows you to create, manage, and test data quality rules throughout your data pipelines. It can be used as a tool to automatically validate data quality at ingestion or transformation time.

Effective monitoring and reporting: Data quality requires constant monitoring. Real-time systems allow you to keep an eye on the quality of data as it flows through your pipelines, allowing you to spot issues like missing records or invalid values before they impact your analysis or decision-making.

Dashboarding tools like Looker, Tableau, and PowerBI are great tools for this purpose, as they allow you to design dashboards that visualize key metrics such as completeness, consistency, and error rates. Reports generated from these dashboards provide insights that help teams stay on top of potential data quality issues. Having this ongoing visibility enables them to act proactively rather than reactively, preventing bigger issues down the road.

Summary

- Data quality measures how well data aligns with its intended purpose, showing us if data is reliable and suitable for use in making decisions.

- Bad data is data that fails to meet the standards needed for meaningful analysis. It is usually incomplete, with missing values and poorly formatted.

- Two common causes of bad data are human error and synchronizing data across multiple systems.

- Service level agreements (SLAs) are the specific standards and performance metrics outlined in a contract between a service provider and a customer.

- Data quality dimensions are the different lenses through which we evaluate the fitness of data. These dimensions are accuracy, completeness, consistency, validity, uniqueness, timeliness, accessibility, and relevance.

- Accuracy measures how closely data matches the real-world entities it represents.

- Completeness evaluates whether all required data is present in a dataset. A completeness score is expressed as a percentage that reflects the proportion of data that is complete compared to the total expected data.

- Consistency refers to the uniformity and accuracy of data across different systems and datasets.

- Referential integrity is a concept that ensures the consistency of relationships between tables by guaranteeing that foreign key values in one table always correspond to valid primary key values in another table.

- Validity measures the degree to which the values in a data element are valid. To validate data within relational databases, one approach is using the CHECK constraint in SQL.

- Uniqueness measures the degree to which the records in a dataset are not duplicated. A common approach to ensure this is by carrying out a duplicate record check.

- Other dimensions are timeliness, which refers to the degree to which data is available and up-to-date; accessibility, which refers to the ease with which users can locate, retrieve, and use data when needed; and relevance, which refers to the degree to which data meets the specific needs of its users.

- The data quality hierarchy is a conceptual framework that outlines the various levels at which data quality is evaluated, depending on the user's perspective.

- Data quality best practices include establishing a data quality culture, building a data quality framework, effective monitoring and data profiling, and most importantly, utilizing the right tools.

CHAPTER

9

Data Security

In 2017, Uber Technologies, one of the world's leading ride-hailing companies, disclosed a massive data breach that had occurred a year earlier in 2016. Hackers accessed Uber's AWS cloud storage, stealing personal information of 57 million users and drivers globally. The stolen information included names, email addresses, phone numbers, and in some cases, trip details.

The attackers gained access by obtaining API credentials that had been published in a private GitHub repository. Using these keys, they accessed Uber's cloud environment and downloaded the data. The breach went undetected for nearly a year. When it was discovered in late 2017, Uber chose not to disclose it publicly. Instead, the company paid the hackers $100,000 to delete the data, disguising the payment as part of a bug bounty program. The breach raised concerns about the broader state of cybersecurity in the tech industry.

What could they have done differently? The hackers gained access to Uber's AWS systems because API keys were exposed. This shows that Uber might not have followed adequate security practices for protecting sensitive credentials, and it also suggests their access controls might have been too weak or set up incorrectly. Uber didn't detect the breach for over a year, which suggests that their monitoring systems were either insufficient or not appropriately configured, and there wasn't any real-time monitoring setup to quickly detect unauthorized access.

The Uber data breach was a wake-up call for tech companies about the importance of securing sensitive data. Data engineers, in particular, have a role in ensuring that data is protected from unauthorized access and that best practices are followed in storing and processing sensitive information.

It's perfectly fine if some of the terminologies in this story aren't clear to you yet. As we learn more about the fundamentals of data security, you'll gain a better understanding of these concepts and see how they play a crucial role in safeguarding data. Data security is the backbone of modern data systems, ensuring that data stays private and accessible only to the right people. Knowing how to secure your data is a must for any data engineer. In this chapter, we'll explore the following:

- Why data security matters
- The principles of data security
- How to protect data at rest and in transit
- The concepts of authentication and authorization
- Data encryption and masking basics
- The principle of least privilege
- Access control models
- Understanding network security

By the end of this chapter, you'll not only understand the basics of securing your data, but you'll also be confident enough to make smart decisions to protect your data systems from threats.

What Is Data Security?

Data security refers to the measures and processes used to protect data from unauthorized access, corruption, or loss. In the context of data engineering, it focuses on ensuring the confidentiality of data throughout its life cycle, from when it's generated, stored, processed, and finally consumed by different systems or users.

When data is properly secured it has multiple benefits. Looking at the Uber data breach, we can see that data breaches can expose sensitive information such as personal details, financial data, or proprietary business information, which can result in a lot of damages. Implementing data security practices ensures that only authorized individuals can access sensitive data, significantly reducing the risk of breaches.

Data security also maintains the integrity of our data. Integrity refers to the accuracy and consistency of data. If data is not properly secured, it can be altered, corrupted, or tampered with, affecting the quality of the data. Data security ensures that the data remains intact and trustworthy, especially when being processed or transferred across various systems.

A proper data security framework helps organizations that handle sensitive data, like healthcare and finance companies, build trust because they must prove that they can securely manage the data. Also, businesses must comply with data protection laws and regulations, like the GDPR (General Data Protection Regulation) in Europe or CCPA (California Consumer Privacy Act) in the United States. These are regulatory bodies that we will be exploring in the next chapter. These regulations mandate that data is stored securely and that individuals' privacy is protected. Noncompliance can lead to heavy fines and legal consequences.

In the era of big data, many organizations rely on large datasets for competitive advantage. Poor data security practices can result in intellectual property theft, where competitors steal valuable data. In summary, data security is a critical aspect of data engineering. Even the most advanced systems and architectures are ineffective if the data they handle can be easily accessed or compromised.

Common Threats to Data Security

Data breaches make sensational news stories, but there are other common data security threats with unique challenges, particularly in environments where data storage and processing systems manage large volumes of sensitive information. By understanding these potential threats, you gradually build a security-conscious mindset while designing your data infrastructure.

- **Malware:** This is like a poison that gets into your water system and spreads everywhere. Malware is software that can infect your cloud storage, databases, or data processing tools. The worst kind is ransomware, which locks up your data and demands money to unlock it. If this happens, your entire data pipeline can shut down, and all your work is stuck until you fix it. Suppose you have a data pipeline that moves customer transactions from an app to a database. If ransomware attacks your database, all transaction records become unreadable, and your company can't process payments or refunds.

- **Phishing attacks:** Phishing is when a hacker pretends to be someone you trust like your boss or a coworker, tricks you into giving them your keys, and reveals your login details for cloud storage or databases. Once they have access, they can steal, delete, or change important data. For instance, say you get an email that looks like it's from your company's IT team, asking you to reset your database password. But it's fake—once you enter your password, the hacker now has access to your company's customer data and can do whatever they want with it.

- **Insider threats:** Sometimes, the biggest danger isn't from outside; it's from someone *inside* the company. An employee with the right privileges and access to databases might leak or manipulate data, either by accident or on purpose.

- **SQL injection:** Many data ingestion pipelines interact with SQL-based databases. If an API endpoint or data ingestion process accepts unsanitized inputs, an attacker could sneak a bad command into a system that isn't properly protected. For instance, if a website or app allows users to enter text, like a search bar or a login form, but doesn't check it properly, hackers can insert a command that makes the database spill out information or delete records.

- **Lack of encryption**: Data engineers often work with sensitive data in transit and at rest. Without proper encryption, data can be intercepted or stolen during transfer or accessed by unauthorized individuals once stored.

Core Principles of Data Security

To handle these numerous threats, there are core principles that act as a framework that guides data security and forms the foundation for protecting data in any organization. As shown in Figure 9-1, the core principles of data security are confidentiality, integrity, and availability, often referred to as the CIA Triad.

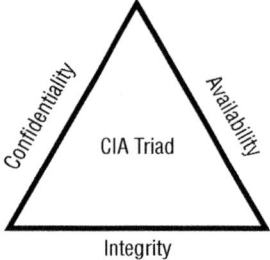

Figure 9-1: The CIA Triad

Confidentiality

Confidentiality ensures that data is kept private and is accessible only to those who are authorized to view it. It's important for sensitive data, especially personal information. It is also a requirement for legal compliance. Companies have strict regulations around protecting personal data, such as HIPAA in healthcare or

GDPR in the EU. If confidentiality isn't maintained, the company can face data breaches and reputational damage. Confidentiality is often maintained through the following practices:

- **Encryption:** This is a process where we transform data into an unreadable format using an encryption algorithm. Only those with the correct key can decrypt it and make sense of it.

- **Data masking:** This is a technique that protects sensitive information by replacing it with fake or randomized data.

- **Access control:** We can define who can access data and what level of access they have. For example, only certain team members might be able to modify data, while others can only view it.

- **Network security:** When transferring data over the Internet, we need to secure protocols (like HTTPS) to prevent unauthorized interception. We will be discussing these in detail in this chapter.

Integrity

Integrity involves ensuring that data is accurate, consistent, and not altered or corrupted in any unauthorized manner. This principle helps maintain the trustworthiness of data throughout its life cycle and ensures that unauthorized changes, whether accidental or malicious, don't occur in the system. For instance, if a hospital sends patient records across a network, it needs to ensure that the data isn't tampered with during transmission. To do this, data engineers often use techniques like checksums or data auditing.

- **Checksums:** A checksum is a unique value or code generated by applying a mathematical algorithm (usually a hashing function) to a set of data, such as a file, database row, or network packet at the time it's sent. The checksum acts as a digital fingerprint of the data; when it reaches the destination, the code is checked again. If the codes match, we know the data hasn't been altered. According to Figure 9-2, we have three columns:

  - The input text, which contains original data or messages
  - A checksum function that takes the text and generates a checksum
  - The checksum output, the output of the checksum function, shown as a sequence of values

We notice that "The red fox jumps **over** the blue dog" has a checksum of 92 33 86 37 92 31 33 and "The red fox jumps **ouer** the blue dog," with a typo of *ouer* instead of *over*, has a checksum of 93 33 86 33 88 03 89. This shows that even a small change like switching letters produces a very different checksum.

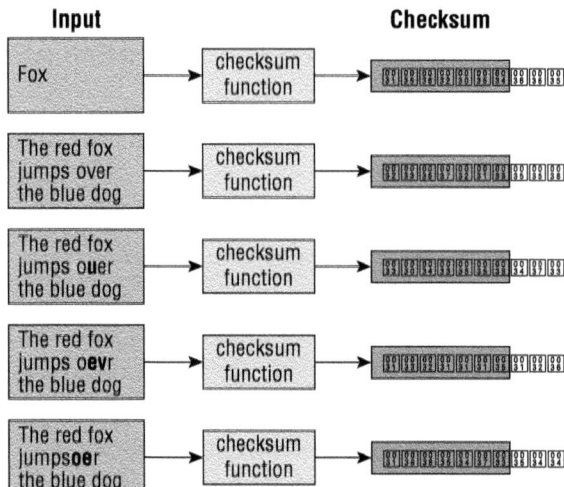

Figure 9-2: How a checksum works

Checksums are used to ensure data integrity by verifying that data has not been altered, corrupted, or tampered with during storage or transmission.

- **Data auditing:** Another way to preserve the integrity of our data is auditing. Data auditing helps us keep track of all data modifications, access, and actions, using audit logs. Audit logs are used to track who accessed data and what changes were made, and this helps detect unexpected alterations. They also provide a compliance trail to prove that sensitive data is handled properly. Additionally, version control systems are used to keep a history of changes, allowing you to revert to previous states if needed.

Availability

This principle ensures that data is accessible and usable when needed. It's not enough for data to be secure and accurate; it also needs to be accessible when users or systems require it. We ensure availability through redundancy, setting up backup systems, and using failover mechanisms.

- **Redundancy:** One of the most effective ways to ensure availability is through redundancy. Your system is redundant when multiple copies of the same information are stored in more than one place at a time. By replicating data across multiple systems or locations, you ensure that there is always an accessible copy available in case one system fails. This can be done at the database level or by using distributed filesystems. In case of a failure in one location, another replica can take over. The key lesson here is to never rely on a single point of failure.

- **Failover mechanisms:** Failover is switching to a backup system automatically when the primary system fails. This ensures that services remain available even in the event of system crashes or hardware failures. Automated systems that can detect failures are set up, ready to jump into action the moment an issue occurs.

- **Backups and disaster recovery:** Regular backups ensure that data can be restored in case of any loss or system failure. These backups can be incremental or full. In incremental backups, only changes to data since the last backup are saved, making the process faster and using less storage, while full backups restore the complete copy of the data. Without availability, systems can't function properly. If an e-commerce website crashes during a sale, customers can't make purchases, which would result in lost revenue. Data systems need to be running continuously to support day-to-day operations.

We've discussed techniques that support the core principles of data security. In the following sections, our focus will shift more specifically toward practices that ensure confidentiality.

Data Encryption

In the CIA Triad, *encryption* is one of the practices under Confidentiality and a fundamental component of security. It converts readable data (plaintext) into an unreadable format (ciphertext) to prevent unauthorized access. This transformation is achieved using encryption algorithms and keys, ensuring that only those with the correct decryption key and algorithm can restore the data to its original form.

We can see encryption in action in online banking. When a customer logs in to their bank's website, their username, password, and financial data are encrypted before transmission to prevent interception by hackers. Messaging applications like WhatsApp use end-to-end encryption to ensure that only the sender and recipient can read the messages, even if someone gains access to the network.

Two major techniques are used to encrypt data using a key: symmetric and asymmetric encryption. In encryption, a key is a string of bits used to encrypt and decrypt data; it acts as a secret code that ensures only authorized parties can access the information. They both have different ways of handling this key, serving different use cases in security.

Symmetric Encryption

In *symmetric encryption*, as seen in Figure 9-3, the same key is used for both encrypting and decrypting data. This means that both the sender and the receiver must have access to the same secret key, which makes the process fast and efficient. The advantage of symmetric encryption is its speed and efficiency, making it ideal for encrypting large amounts of data. However, symmetric encryption has a significant drawback: key management. Since the same key is used for both encryption and decryption, securely sharing the key between parties becomes a challenge. If an attacker gains access to the key, they can decrypt all encrypted data.

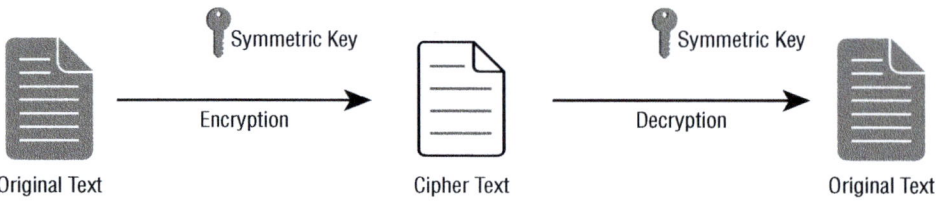

Figure 9-3: Symmetric key encryption

Asymmetric Encryption

Unlike symmetric encryption, *asymmetric encryption* (see Figure 9-4) uses two separate keys: a public key for encryption and a private key for decryption. This approach eliminates the need to share a secret key between parties, reducing the risk of interception and making it especially suitable for secure communication over untrusted networks. The main advantage of asymmetric encryption lies in enhanced security. Since the private key is never shared, the risk of key compromise is significantly reduced, even if the public key is widely available. Without the private key, decryption is practically impossible. However, it is computationally slower than symmetric encryption due to the complexity of its algorithm.

Figure 9-4 illustrates the concept of asymmetric encryption. The process begins with a readable message or data (plain text) that needs to be secured. A public key (depicted on the left) is used to encrypt the plain text. This key is freely distributed and can be shared with anyone. After encryption, the plain text becomes cipher text (unreadable to unauthorized parties). The cipher text is the scrambled version of the original message, which ensures that even if intercepted, it cannot be read without the correct decryption key.

After this, a different but mathematically related key, called the private key, is used to decrypt the cipher text back into plain text. The private key is kept secret and only known to the intended recipient. After decryption using the private key, the original message is restored.

A key differentiator between these two methods is key management. In symmetric encryption, both parties must securely share and store the same secret key. In contrast, asymmetric encryption simplifies this process by enabling public key distribution while keeping the private key secure. This distinction makes key management not just an important concept, but a central factor in determining the practicality and security of each encryption method in different use cases.

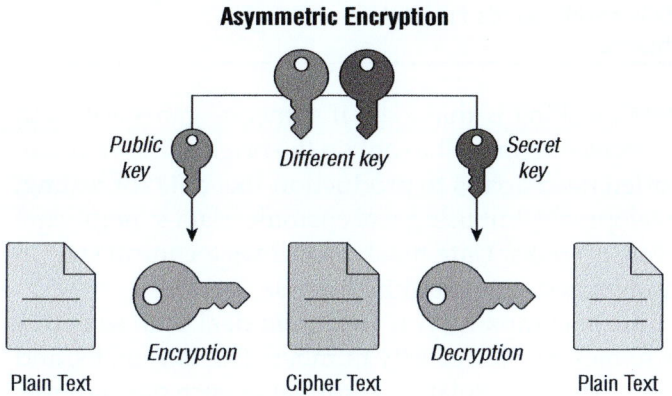

Figure 9-4: Asymmetric key encryption

Source: Generated using Scaler Topics

Data Masking

Let's look at another data protection technique under confidentiality called data masking. *Data masking* involves altering sensitive data to make it unreadable or unusable for unauthorized users while maintaining its integrity for applications and workflows. It is commonly used to protect personally identifiable information (PII) and other sensitive data.

Personally Identifiable Information (PII) refers to any data that can be used to identify, locate, or contact an individual. According to Table 9-1, personally identifiable information (PII) can be categorized into direct identifiers and indirect identifiers, with different risk levels. In cases where PII is exposed, it can lead to identity theft, fraud, and reputational damage for both individuals and organizations.

Table 9-1: Personally Identifiable Information (PII) and Respective Risk Levels

CATEGORY	EXAMPLES	RISK LEVELS
Direct Identifiers	Full name, Social Security Number (SSNs), passport number, driver's license, biometric data	High
Indirect Identifiers	Date of birth, gender, zip code, phone number, IP address	Medium
Sensitive PII	Credit card numbers, bank account details, health records, financial transactions	Very High

The key idea behind data masking is that even if someone gains access to masked data, they cannot reverse-engineer it to obtain the original information. Developers and analysts often need access to production-like data for testing, analytics, and software development, but using real customer data in nonsecure environments increases security risks. Data masking allows technical staff to work with realistic but anonymized data, minimizing risk.

If you're working in a fintech company, you will often deal with sensitive customer information like names, Social Security numbers (SSNs), emails, and credit card numbers. However, due to regulatory compliance such data is never stored or processed in raw form. Instead, it is masked to protect customer privacy while still allowing necessary business operations.

In this table, storing information like this violates data protection laws. To ensure security, you implement a masking policy.

FULL NAME	SOCIAL SECURITY NUMBER (SSN)	EMAIL	CREDIT CARD NUMBER
John Doe	123-45-6789	johndoe@email.com	9876-5432-1234-5678
Jane Smith	234-56-7890	janesmith@email.com	8765-4321-5678-1234

After implementing your data masking logic, the transformed dataset looks like this:

FULL NAME	SOCIAL SECURITY NUMBER (SSN)	EMAIL	CREDIT CARD NUMBER
John Doe	XXX-XX-6789	johndoe@email.com	–****-5678
Jane Smith	XXX-XX-6789	janesmith@email.com	–****-1234

This approach allows customer service agents to verify users without exposing their full personal details.

DATA AT REST vs. DATA IN TRANSIT

In data engineering, data exists in two primary states: at rest and in transit. Each requires different security measures.

Data at rest refers to any data that is stored on a physical or cloud-based storage system, such as hard drives, databases, or cloud storage platforms, and not actively moving across a network but is instead stored for later retrieval. Since stored data is a common target for cybercriminals, data-at-rest encryption is critical for preventing unauthorized access.

We typically use symmetric encryption for this purpose, because it is efficient for encrypting large amounts of data. Encryption methods for data at rest include full-disk encryption (FDE), which secures all the contents of a storage device, and database encryption, which protects sensitive records within databases. For example, Microsoft SQL Server and Oracle databases offer Transparent Data Encryption (TDE), ensuring that even if someone gains access to the database files, the data remains unreadable without the encryption key.

A real-life example of data at rest encryption is in cloud storage services like Google Drive and Dropbox, which encrypt user files on their servers to prevent unauthorized access by hackers or employees. The advantage of encrypting data at rest is that even if a device is lost, stolen, or accessed by an unauthorized person, the encrypted files remain protected.

On the other hand, data in transit refers to data actively being transferred between devices, networks, or systems. This includes data sent over the Internet, corporate networks, or mobile communications. Data in transit is more vulnerable to interception through attacks, where a hacker intercepts and alters communication between two parties.

One of the most common methods for protecting data in transit is Transport Layer Security (TLS), which encrypts data between a user's device and a web server. When you enter your credit card details on an e-commerce website, TLS ensures that your sensitive information is encrypted before being transmitted to the payment processor.

Another example of data in transit encryption is the use of Virtual Private Networks (VPNs). A VPN encrypts Internet traffic between a user's device and a remote server, preventing ISPs, hackers, or governments from monitoring online activity. This is particularly useful for remote workers accessing company systems securely. The advantage of encrypting data in transit is that it prevents eavesdropping and unauthorized access, ensuring secure communication over the Internet and private networks. These are key concepts in networking fundamentals, which we'll explore in detail in the next section.

Understanding Network Security

Network security is the practice of protecting data as it travels across or is accessed through computer networks. As a data engineer, you will work with various tools and services such as APIs, data pipelines, and cloud storage systems that exchange data over networks. Data doesn't just move freely; protocols are in place to ensure that it remains secure at every stage, preventing tampering and unauthorized access. One of the most commonly used protocols to secure data during transmission (data in transit) is *Transport Layer Security (TLS)*, which encrypts data in transit between systems, so that even if intercepted, the data remains unreadable. But TLS evolved from an older protocol known as Secure Sockets Layer (SSL).

SSL was the original protocol designed to secure communications over a network, specifically between a client (like a web browser) and a server (like a web server or database). SSL provided key security services, it ensured that the data being transmitted is scrambled so that only the intended recipient can read it, it also ensured that the data has not been altered during transmission, and it verified the server's identity, ensuring you're communicating with the correct system. However, SSL had several vulnerabilities, leading to its deprecation in favor of TLS.

TLS is the successor to SSL and offers stronger encryption and better security features. It is designed to address the weaknesses in SSL and provide more robust security measures. TLS is what is actually in use today, even though many systems still refer to it as SSL due to historical reasons. TLS supports more modern and secure encryption algorithms, and it has an improved handshake process that establishes a secure connection, reducing the risk of attacks.

For example, when you're fetching customer data from a third-party API, TLS ensures no one alters the data before it reaches your system. It ensures that the data is encrypted during transmission and also encrypts database connections to prevent attackers from sniffing credentials or queries. PostgreSQL, MySQL, and Snowflake DB allow connections over TLS to ensure secure query execution.

We mentioned that TLS has an improved handshake process, so if you're wondering what goes on behind the scenes, let's see how that handshake works using a web browser as an example. This process is shown in Figure 9-5.

Step 1: When you type a website address (like `https://snowflake.com`), your browser sends a "Hello" message to the website's server, as shown in Figure 9-5. This message means, "Hey, I want to connect securely! What security options do you support?"

Step 2: The website's server replies with its own "Hello" and says, "Great! I support TLS. Here's my security certificate!" This certificate is like an ID card that proves the website is legitimate.

Step 3: Your browser looks at the certificate to make sure it's valid and trustworthy. It checks things like whether the certificate is from a trusted authority, expired, does it match the website you're visiting. If everything looks good, the HTTP request is sent for the website above. If not, you get a security warning.

Step 4: The request is received and the HTTP response is sent to the client. Now, your browser and the server agree on a secret key. This key will be used to encrypt the information sent between them so no one else can read it.

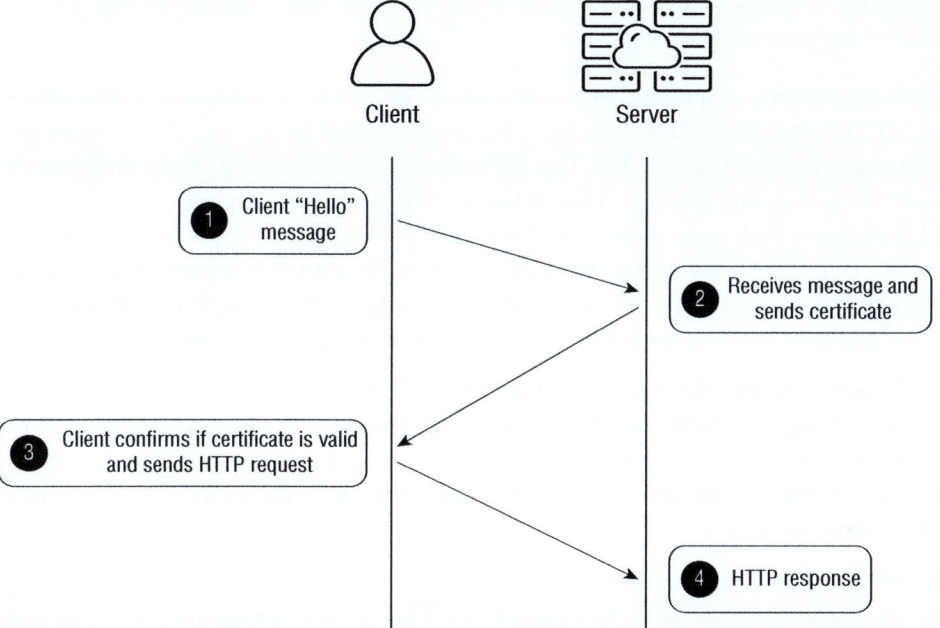

Figure 9-5: TLS handshake

Once the key is shared, all the data between your browser and the website is locked with encryption. Even if a hacker intercepts the data, they won't be able to read it without the secret key. At this moment, you will notice a padlock icon in your browser's address bar. This means your connection is secure, and you can safely send sensitive information like passwords or credit card details.

Now that you grasp the fundamentals, let's explore the role TLS plays in a typical data engineering task. Suppose you've been tasked with building a data pipeline that pulls data from a third-party API, processes the data, and writes it to an Amazon Relational Database Service (RDS) instance. The key requirement is that all communications between your services should be encrypted using TLS to ensure the data is secure during transmission. Let's look at all the steps.

1. **Pulling data from the API:**

When your data pipeline calls an external API, it often communicates over HTTPS. APIs typically expose HTTPS endpoints, which use TLS encryption to ensure confidentiality and integrity of the data in transit.

For example, consider a scenario where you're using Python's requests library to retrieve data from an external API. The following code sends a secure HTTP (HTTPS) GET request:

```
import requests
url = "https://api.example.com/data"
response = requests.get(url)#This sends an HTTP GET request to the API.
data = response.json()
```

In this example, `requests.get(url)` sends an HTTP GET request to the specified HTTPS endpoint. Because the URL begins with `https://`, the communication is encrypted using **TLS**. The data received is securely transferred over the network, helping protect it from tampering or eavesdropping.

TLS ensures that your system and the API provider authenticate each other. The data being sent is encrypted during transit to prevent it from being intercepted by unauthorized parties and the integrity of the data is maintained so that no one can tamper with the API response during transmission.

2. **Processing the data on your local machine:**

After pulling the data, you may process or transform it before sending it to the Amazon RDS database. In this step, TLS doesn't apply, as you're handling data locally. However, the next step of writing the data to RDS will require secure transmission.

3. **Writing data to Amazon RDS:**

When writing the data to Amazon RDS, TLS is used to secure the database connection and prevent unauthorized access or tampering of data while it's in transit.

Access Control

Access control refers to the processes put in place to ensure that only authorized users, systems, or applications can access specific data within a system. It involves defining who can access what data, under which conditions, and for what purposes, to maintain data privacy, integrity, and security.

Access control is important because it ensures that sensitive data is protected from unauthorized access and misuse, especially in environments that handle large-scale data, such as data lakes, data warehouses, and distributed databases and where multiple users need to interact with the data. Let's discuss some core concepts that ensure access control:

- Authentication and authorization
- Access control models
- The principle of least privilege
- Access levels

Authentication

Imagine you arrive at a hotel to check in. The first thing the receptionist does is ask for your passport, driver's license, or booking confirmation to verify your identity. If your credentials match the hotel's records, you are authenticated, and they proceed with assigning you a room.

Authentication is the process of verifying the identity of a user or system before granting access. It answers the question, "Are you who you say you are?" Before granting access to a system, the system needs to confirm that the person or application trying to log in is legitimate. In data engineering, authentication happens when a user logs into a system, database, or cloud platform. A user must prove their identity using one or more authentication methods:

- Username and password
- Multifactor authentication
- Biometrics authentication
- OAuth authentication

Username and Password Authentication

This is the most common and fundamental form of user authentication. It involves two pieces of information: a unique username that identifies the user and a password known only to the user, which acts as a secret key to access their account. When a user attempts to log in to a system, they input their username and the corresponding password. If both match what the system has stored, access is granted. This method is simple and widely used; however, its simplicity is also a weakness. If someone gains access to both the username and password, they can impersonate the legitimate user. Passwords can also be weak, reused across sites, or forgotten.

Multifactor Authentication (MFA)

Multifactor authentication (MFA) is a security method that requires users to present multiple forms of identification before being granted access. As shown in

Figure 9-6, it involves two or more factors, something you know (a password or PIN), something you have (a phone, security token, or smart card), or something you are (biometric factors like fingerprints or facial recognition).

For example, when logging in to your online banking app, after entering your password, you might be required to enter a one-time code sent to your phone via SMS or use an authentication app like Google Authenticator to generate a code. This method provides an extra layer of security, as even if an attacker gains access to the username and password, they will also need access to the

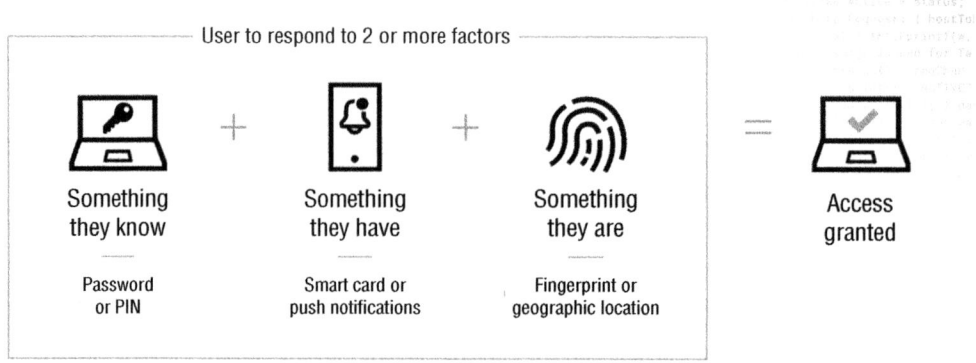

User to respond to 2 or more factors

Something they know	Something they have	Something they are	Access granted
Password or PIN	Smart card or push notifications	Fingerprint or geographic location	

Figure 9-6: How multifactor authentication works

second factor (e.g., your phone) to successfully authenticate. MFA makes it significantly more difficult for unauthorized users to break into an account, thus enhancing overall security.

Biometric Authentication

Biometric authentication uses unique physical or behavioral characteristics of a user to verify their identity. These characteristics include things like fingerprints, facial recognition, and voice patterns. Biometric systems work by comparing the captured data to a pre-enrolled template stored in a database. If there's a match, access is granted. Using Face ID on an iPhone or unlocking your laptop with a fingerprint sensor are both forms of biometric authentication. Biometrics are also unique to individuals, making them harder to spoof than traditional passwords. However, while biometric authentication is more secure than passwords, it's not entirely immune to attacks, especially if the database storing the biometric data is compromised.

OAuth Authentication

OAuth, which stands for *Open Authorization*, is an open standard for authentication that allows users to share their private resources stored on one site with another site without exposing their credentials. OAuth enables third-party applications to access user data on a service on behalf of the user, using tokens instead of the user's password. OAuth is commonly used in scenarios where users want to grant limited access to their accounts on one platform without sharing their passwords. For example, using your Google account to log into a third-party website allows that website to access your Google account information, without needing to know your Google password. The service asking for access receives a token that can only be used for specific actions and a limited time.

OAuth authentication is important because it improves security by limiting the exposure of passwords. It also enhances user experience by reducing the number of login credentials users need to remember while maintaining control over the information they share.

In summary, most cloud platforms support OAuth for API access and MFA for securing accounts, and some also integrate biometric options for securing personal devices or mobile access. The choice of method can be influenced by the resources you're using, the level of security needed, and the user experience you want to create.

Authorization

Authentication and authorization are two fundamental concepts that determine how users access systems and what they can do once inside. Though they are often confused, they serve distinct purposes. Now, think of them as two gates in a security process, one verifying who you are and the other deciding what you're allowed to do.

Authentication is the first step in access control. But just because someone successfully logs in doesn't mean they should have unrestricted access. This is where authorization comes in. *Authorization* determines what actions an authenticated user can perform and what resources they can access. It answers the question, "Now that we know who you are, what are you allowed to do?"

Let's go back to the hotel scenario. After confirming your identity, the receptionist doesn't just give you access to any room in the hotel. Instead, they issue you a key card that only opens your assigned room. If you booked a standard room, you cannot enter the presidential suite or any other standard room other than the one assigned to you. Similarly, hotel staff like housekeeping or managers have different levels of access; housekeeping can enter guest rooms for cleaning, but they can't access the hotel's financial records.

In cloud databases, once a user logs into a data system, authorization determines what actions they can perform. The marketing team might only have read access to query datasets but not modify them, a data engineer might have write access to modify tables but not delete them, and a database administrator (DBA) might have full access, including deleting databases and modifying

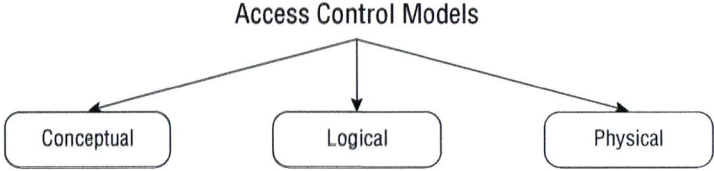

Figure 9-7: Access control models

access policies. Without proper authorization controls, a company risks data leaks, breaches, or accidental modifications that could lead to a lot of issues. Authorization is usually implemented using different access control models, as shown in Figure 9-7.

- Role-based access control (RBAC)
- Attribute-based access control (ABAC)
- Access control lists (ACLs)

Role-Based Access Control (RBAC)

Role-based access control (RBAC) is a widely used method of managing user permissions based on roles within an organization. In this principle, access to resources is granted based on the user's role within an organization rather than individual permissions. A role represents a collection of permissions that define what actions a user can perform on a resource. Users are assigned roles, and roles are linked to specific permissions.

In RBAC, permissions are grouped by role, and users are assigned one or more roles depending on their job function. For example, in a company's internal system, you may have roles like Admin, Manager, and Employee. An Admin can create and delete accounts, a Manager can access certain reports and manage teams, and an Employee might only be able to view their data or submit requests. Each role has a predefined set of permissions. This arrangement simplifies the assignment and management of access rights, because rather than assigning individual permissions to each user, roles can be assigned to users, and permissions are automatically granted based on those roles.

RBAC also reduces the complexity of managing permissions at a granular level. It ensures users only have the permissions necessary for their role, improving both security and efficiency.

Attribute-Based Access Control (ABAC)

Attribute-based access control (ABAC) is a more flexible and dynamic approach to managing access than RBAC. In ABAC, access is granted based on the attributes/characteristics of the user, the resource, and the environment. These attributes can include things like the user's department, location, time of access, or even the classification of the resource being accessed.

ABAC uses a policy engine, which is a tool that applies rules to each access request. This tool evaluates various attributes to make an access decision. For example, a policy might specify that only users who are part of the human resources department and are accessing employee records during business hours can have access to those records. The access decision would depend not just on the user's role but also on attributes like time of day, the department, and the sensitivity of the data being accessed. ABAC policies are highly customizable and can incorporate a wide range of factors, which makes it a good choice for complex systems where roles alone are insufficient.

Access Control Lists (ACLs)

An *access control list (ACL)* is a more direct and fine-grained way of defining permissions for specific resources, especially in cloud resources. ACLs are typically attached to objects such as files, databases, or network devices and specify which users or groups can perform which actions (e.g., read, write, delete) on those objects. Each entry in the ACL lists a user or group and the actions they are allowed to perform on a particular resource.

Unlike RBAC and ABAC, which work by grouping users or permissions into roles or policies, ACLs specify exactly what access a specific user or group has to a particular resource. Each resource has its own ACL, and each ACL entry typically grants or denies specific permissions to individual users or groups.

Let's say you're managing a cloud-based data lake stored in Amazon S3 or Google Cloud Storage and you have multiple teams, including Marketing, Analytics, and Engineering, who need access to different datasets. However, you don't want to give every user full access; instead, you want to restrict access at a granular level.

If you have the following datasets stored in your cloud storage, and each dataset is stored in a separate folder in Amazon S3:

```
s3://company-data/raw/raw_sales_data.csv
s3://company-data/processed/cleaned_sales_data.csv
s3://company-data/sensitive/customer_sensitive_data.csv
```

Amazon S3 Bucket

We can use ACLs to define permissions at the file level. Here, we set up ACLs for each file to control exactly who can access what.

RESOURCE	USER/GROUP	PERMISSIONS
`raw_sales_data.csv`	audit_compliance_team	Read
`raw_sales_data.csv`	analytics-team	Read
`cleaned_sales_data.csv`	analytics-team	Read, Write
`cleaned_sales_data.csv`	marketing-team	Read
`customer_sensitive_data.csv`	security-team	Read, Write
`customer_sensitive_data.csv`	analytics-team	Deny

The analytics team has read and write access to cleaned sales data since they are responsible for generating business insights. The audit and compliance team, however, can read the raw data but cannot modify it. Meanwhile, access to sensitive customer data is restricted for the analytics team, ensuring privacy, while the security team has full read and write permissions to manage and protect it. ACLs provide detailed access control at the object level, which is ideal for managing data security and governance in cloud-based environments. However, managing ACLs can become cumbersome in large systems with many users and resources. ACLs are typically used in more static environments where access control rules are not as dynamic or complex.

In summary, RBAC is ideal for simpler, more static systems where access can be grouped based on roles. ABAC is a more flexible system that evaluates a variety of attributes to make complex access decisions. Access control lists (ACLs) provide granular, resource-specific control over who can do what with specific objects, offering precise control at the object level.

The Principle of Least Privilege

A key concept in access control is the principle of least privilege, which means users should only be given the minimum level of access necessary to perform their tasks. This principle guides the design of many access control systems, including models like RBAC and ABAC.

Let's assume you're working in a company and a junior engineer is given full access to a company's entire cloud storage. One wrong command and they could accidentally delete a critical database. This is exactly why the principle of least privilege (PoLP) exists. It's the practice of giving users, applications, and systems only the access they need, nothing more, nothing less. Figure 9-8 clearly shows a good intersection of what should be accessible to the employee. Additionally, if an attacker gets hold of an employee's credentials, PoLP ensures they can't access everything. They're limited to only what the employee was allowed to do, reducing the damage they can cause.

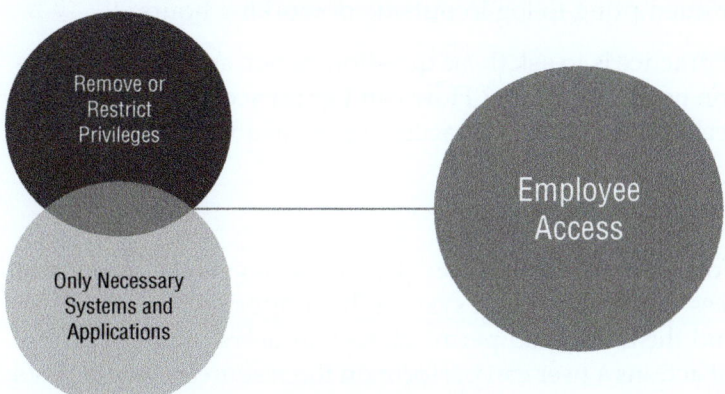

Figure 9-8: The principle of least privilege

Here are a few ways organizations implement these principles effectively:

- **Use role-based access control (RBAC):** Rather than assigning permissions to individuals directly, organizations define roles, and each role should come with predefined access rights tailored to specific job functions. For example, as a data engineer, I might not need access to financial reports, but I do need access to raw datasets and ETL workflows. With RBAC, I'm assigned only the permissions required for my work, nothing more.

- **Apply just-in-time (JIT) access:** Permanent access increases security risks, especially in highly regulated environments. Instead, organizations should implement just-in-time (JIT) access, granting permissions only when needed and for a limited duration. In my role, I often need access to specific datasets, and I must request permission each time. When approved, I typically receive temporary, read-only access, which is automatically revoked once the assigned timeframe expires. This approach enforces security best practices while ensuring I can still perform my tasks efficiently.

- **Regularly audit and revoke unused privileges:** Employees switch teams, change projects, or leave the company altogether, yet their access privileges often remain unchanged. Over time, this creates a security risk, as dormant accounts with excessive permissions become potential vulnerabilities. Regular access audits help identify unnecessary privileges and revoke them proactively. I've seen cases where former employees still had database access months after leaving a project. Routine audits ensure that only the right people have access at any given time.

- **Monitor access logs and set alerts:** Monitoring access logs allows security teams to track who accessed what and when. Automated alerts can flag unusual behavior, such as a user accessing a dataset they don't typically interact with or attempting to log in outside of working hours.

In summary, a best practice is to ask these questions when assigning permissions: Does this person need this access? How can I grant access with the least risk possible? Are there ways to automate access removal after use?

Access Levels

There are typically four standard access levels. Access levels are important when managing access to resources in a system. It's important to define different access levels and the associated permissions that users can have. These levels determine what actions a user can perform on the resources, whether it's reading data, modifying it, or managing the system. The levels are as follows:

Reader: Users with this access level can read data, view reports, or examine content, but they cannot modify or delete anything. This access level is ideal for users who need to view information but should not have the ability to alter it. It is often assigned to employees or stakeholders who require visibility into the data or operations but are not responsible for maintaining or updating them. Examples include nontechnical staff or clients who need to access reports or analytics, or executives who need to view data or business metrics. This level minimizes the risk of accidental changes or data corruption, which makes it low-risk.

Writer: This level allows users to make changes to the content or data. With this level of access, users can create, update, or modify resources such as documents, database entries, or records. Write access is typically granted to users who need to update, edit, or contribute to a resource but do not need full administrative control. However, granting it without proper controls can result in unauthorized changes or errors, so it's better to limit it to trusted individuals with specific roles.

Administrator: This level provides users with full control over a system or resource. This includes the ability to manage settings, add or remove users, and modify system configurations. Admins can also delete or modify permissions for other users. Typically, admin access is granted to system administrators, security officers, or managers who need to manage the system's infrastructure, install software, or configure servers. Admin access is powerful and can potentially harm the system if misused, so it must be tightly controlled.

Superuser: The superuser, also known as the owner, is the highest level of access and grants full control over all aspects of a system or resource.

In addition to the permissions of an admin, a superuser can typically make irreversible changes to the system, including deleting entire databases, shutting down servers, or transferring ownership. Superusers should be reserved for individuals with the highest level of trust and responsibility. This level is usually granted to founders or executives who own the system or resource and need complete control over it, and to system architects or other professionals responsible for the foundational setup and operation of large systems. The superuser carries the highest risk of misuse or error.

Secrets Management

We've talked a lot about keys and passwords, but how do we securely manage them? Secrets management refers to the secure storage, handling, and access control of sensitive credentials such as database passwords, API keys, encryption keys, and authentication tokens. Secrets are used at multiple stages when connecting to data sources, cloud platforms, and third-party services—for example, when an ETL job needs to authenticate with a cloud storage service, or a connection is set up between a data warehouse and a business intelligence tool.

Secrets management is important because exposed credentials can be a significant security risk. If an API key or database password is accidentally committed to a public repository or stored in an insecure location, unauthorized users could gain access to sensitive data or security breaches (like the Uber Technologies breach). To effectively manage secrets, organizations should follow these best practices:

- Never store passwords, API keys, or tokens directly in code or configuration files. Instead, use secure vaults or environment variables to avoid hardcoding secrets.

- Implement secret management tools like AWS Secrets Manager, HashiCorp Vault, Azure Key Vault, or Google Secret Manager to store and manage your secrets securely.

- Apply role-based access control (RBAC) to ensure that only authorized users and services can retrieve secrets.

- Change passwords, API keys, and tokens periodically to reduce the risk of compromised credentials being exploited.

Data Security and Data Privacy

We've discussed various concepts related to data security. Now let's look at the difference between data security and privacy. Data security and data privacy both involve protecting data, but they focus on different aspects. A lot of people often confuse them because both fields overlap, but while security focuses on preventing unauthorized access and breaches, privacy is about ensuring that personal data is handled lawfully and transparently.

Think of a house. Data security is like locking the doors and installing an alarm system to keep burglars out. It protects the house itself from being broken into. Data privacy is like deciding who gets invited inside, which rooms they can enter, and what they're allowed to see or know about your personal life. It's about controlling access. So while security keeps the house safe, privacy manages the rules for the people inside.

The goal of data security is to ensure that data is protected from breaches, attacks, and any form of unauthorized access or modification. Key aspects of data security include encrypting data so that only authorized parties can read it, defining who can access this data and what they can do with it, and protecting data as it travels across networks. The focus of data security is on ensuring data integrity and confidentiality from a technical standpoint.

Data privacy, on the other hand, is about the rights and expectations regarding the collection, storage, and sharing of personal information. It focuses on how individuals' data is handled. It ensures individuals must permit their data to be collected only when necessary for a specific purpose, being transparent in the process, and most importantly, giving users the right to access, correct, or delete their data. The main concern here is respecting individuals' personal autonomy and legal rights regarding their data.

Data security often relies on technological tools like encryption, firewalls, and so forth, whereas data privacy focuses more on policies, consent, and compliance with laws like the General Data Protection Regulation (GDPR).

In the next chapter, we will explore data governance, a broad framework that encompasses both data quality and data security. This chapter will explain the policies, regulations, and best practices that guide how data is managed and protected within an organization.

Summary

- Data security refers to the measures and processes used to protect data from unauthorized access, corruption, or loss.

- Aside from data breaches, there are other common threats to data security such as malware, phishing attacks, SQL injections, and insider threats.

- Data security focuses on preventing unauthorized access and breaches, while data privacy ensures that personal data is handled lawfully and transparently.

- The core principles of data security are confidentiality, which protects sensitive data, integrity, which ensures data is accurate and unaltered, and availability, which ensures data is accessible when needed.

- Encryption is converting readable data (plain text) into an unreadable format (cipher text) to prevent unauthorized access. We have two main types of encryption: symmetric and asymmetric encryption.

- Data at rest refers to any data that is stored on a physical or cloud-based storage system; data in transit refers to data actively being transferred between devices, networks, or systems.

- Data Masking is a technique that protects sensitive information by replacing it with fake or randomized data.

- Transport Layer Security encrypts data in transit using an improved handshake process that establishes a secure connection.

- A checksum is a unique value or code generated by applying a mathematical algorithm (usually a hashing function) to a set of data, to ensure integrity.

- Audit logs are used to track who accessed data and what changes were made, and this helps detect unexpected alterations.

- Availability ensures that data is accessible and usable when needed. We ensure availability through redundancy, setting up backup systems, and using failover mechanisms.

- Network security is the practice of protecting data as it travels across or is accessed through computer networks.

- TLS (Transport Layer Security) encrypts data in transit between systems so that even if intercepted, the data remains unreadable.

- Access control refers to the processes put in place to ensure that only authorized users, systems, or applications can access specific data within a system.

- We have three major access control methods: role-based access control (RBAC), attribute-based access control (ABAC), and access control lists (ACLs).

- Authentication is the process of verifying the identity of a user or system, whereas authorization determines what actions an authenticated user can perform and what resources they can access.

- The principle of least privilege is giving users, applications, and systems only the access they need, nothing more, nothing less.

- There are four access levels with different levels of permissions:, Reader, Writer, Admin, and Superuser.

- Secrets management refers to the secure storage, handling, and access control of sensitive credentials such as database passwords, API keys, and encryption keys.

- The goal of data security is to ensure that data is protected from breaches, attacks, and any form of unauthorized access or modification, while data privacy is about the rights and expectations regarding the collection, storage, and sharing of personal information.

Data Governance

In the early days of technology, data was much simpler, mostly on paper records or small digital files stored on local computers. Fast-forward to today: Organizations generate massive amounts of data every second. With that growth, regulations and frameworks are needed to ensure that data is managed responsibly. This is where data governance comes in. I know data governance might sound like a dry, bureaucratic concept, but it plays an important role in any organization. Think of it as a rulebook that ensures data is high-quality, well organized, secure, and accessible to the right people. It also ensures that everyone interacting with data knows their responsibilities and follows best practices.

The two major pillars of data governance are security and quality, both of which were covered extensively in earlier chapters. But governance goes beyond just protecting data and keeping it clean; it's about creating a structured approach and a template to manage data across an organization ethically and efficiently.

IN THIS CHAPTER, WE'LL EXPLORE:

- A simple analogy to explain data governance
- The key components of data governance
- Policies and processes that guide data governance
- Common regulatory policies and their guidelines

- How data is classified and disposed of in an organization
- Metadata management and why it matters
- The roles and responsibilities involved in governance and their impact on an organization

By the end of this chapter, you'll have a comprehensive understanding of how data governance frameworks establish control, maintain trust, and ensure the reliability of data across an organization. You'll also learn how these frameworks help enforce data quality, security, and compliance.

How to Think About Data Governance

Imagine you've just bought a hotel that's been abandoned for over five years. Everything inside the hotel, including the furniture, artwork, and appliances, comes with the building, but you have no clue of what's valuable or what's junk. The first thing you'd probably do is take a tour around the hotel to figure out what's inside. That step is what we call *discovery* in data governance, which involves understanding all the data assets your company has across different systems, even the ones no one remembers are there.

After the tour, the next step is figuring out how to organize the items you've seen. You start sorting items into large boxes, things to keep, things to throw out, and things you might want to donate. This is *classification*, grouping data into different categories based on what it is, how valuable it is, or how sensitive it might be.

But imagine trying to organize hundreds of items without writing anything down. You'd probably forget what's inside each box. You don't just throw items in boxes—you label them, list what's inside, and maybe even add extra details like where the item was found or how valuable it is. In data governance, *metadata* acts like those labels, giving information about the data itself, such as when it was created, who owns it, or whether it contains sensitive information.

Before you start sorting or labeling, you need some rules to guide your decisions. How do you know what's worth keeping, what needs to be locked away, or what should be discarded? Those rules are your *policies*, and policies help set guidelines for how data should be handled, especially when it comes to sensitive information like personally identifiable information (PII). For example, any document in the hotel with people's private details should be locked away, not tossed out or left lying around.

Let's move on to delegation. Since running everything alone isn't feasible, you hire staff and assign them specific roles, entrusting them with key responsibilities in different areas of the hotel to ensure smooth operations. With these roles and responsibilities, processes should be put in place to make sure that the rules you set are followed by your staff. In data governance, we have *Roles and Responsibilities* given to people in the organization and *processes* to follow these rules.

While you're sorting through the hotel, you stumble on some valuable paintings and hidden safes you had no idea were there. Maybe you're not interested in keeping them, but you could sell them for a good price. That's the hidden value data governance can unlock, helping companies discover insights buried in their data that could drive growth or even create new business opportunities. This analogy gives a good understanding of how data governance works, but don't worry about the terms mentioned, as we will be explaining them in more detail in this chapter.

Data governance is simply the way organizations set rules and processes to manage their data properly. It's like creating a playbook that guides how data should be handled, who can access it, how it should be stored, and what it can be used for. At its core, data governance is not just about tools and tech—it's about setting the right rules, assigning responsibilities, and making sure everyone follows them.

Imagine a company where everyone stores data however they want: on their laptops, in random spreadsheets, or with different cloud storage platforms. Some data might be duplicated, some might be outdated, and some might be completely wrong. Without some rules in place, the company would have no way of knowing which version of the data is accurate or whether sensitive customer information is being handled securely.

If you've ever called someone from customer service to fill in your information and a few days later, you're talking to someone else from another department asking for the same information, that's a red flag. This highlights how poor data governance negatively impacts the business. In this situation, data silos start to form when different departments keep their separate versions of the same data without talking to each other.

There have been many high-profile cases where poor data governance cost companies millions of dollars in fines and damaged their reputation. In 2018, Facebook faced backlash for mishandling user data in the Cambridge Analytica scandal, where third parties accessed personal information without proper consent. This incident showed the world how dangerous it can be when there are no clear rules for managing data.

We've talked about data security and data quality in the previous chapters, and they're both important. Data governance is what ties everything together. Think of it like an umbrella that covers both security and quality. Let's break it down. While data security ensures that only the right people can access data and that sensitive information stays protected, data quality makes sure data is accurate, consistent, and reliable, data governance is a big-picture framework that sets the rules and processes for how security and quality should be applied across the entire organization.

Without governance, different teams might do things their own way, some following best practices, others not so much. Governance creates a clear blueprint, ensuring that data quality and security measures are applied consistently, so data is managed the right way across the board.

Data Governance Framework

In every organization, there is a central repository for data, and this data could come from websites, customer forms, and multiple sources. This data can be a mix of nonconfidential and confidential information like customer name, address, SSN, or account number.

Imagine you're working in a company where different teams are storing the same customer information in different ways. For example, one team might save a customer's name as FirstName LastName, while another team stores it as LastName FirstName. It might not seem like a big deal at first, but when you're trying to merge data or generate reports, these small inconsistencies can cause major headaches.

In terms of security, what happens when unauthorized employees access sensitive customer data, like account details or personal information? Not only does that put customer privacy at risk, but the company could also face serious legal penalties for not protecting that data properly.

Without clear rules on who owns what data, things can get even messier. If something is wrong in the system, who is responsible for fixing it? Is it the finance or customer service team? This lack of accountability can slow down operations.

Additionally, if there are no rules on how long data should be kept, companies can end up storing unnecessary information for years. This not only clutters systems but also leads to higher storage costs.

Lastly, tracking where data comes from and how it moves through different systems is called data lineage. This becomes almost impossible without proper governance, and this makes it harder to troubleshoot issues or prove compliance with regulations.

Now, the question is how we control the flow of this data within the organization, making sure all these issues are prevented. Organizations do this by designing a data governance framework. A *data governance framework* is a structured set of policies, processes, roles, and tools that guide how an organization manages its data. It's like a blueprint for handling data across the entire company. A good data governance framework answers the question of what data the company has; who owns the data; who is responsible for its accuracy and usage; what regulations and internal guidelines govern how the data should be stored, protected, and managed; who can access the data; and how long should it should be retained. To answer these questions, according to Figure 10-1, a comprehensive data governance framework is typically built on three key components, which play an important role in ensuring an effective data governance strategy:

- Policies
- Processes
- Roles and Responsibilities

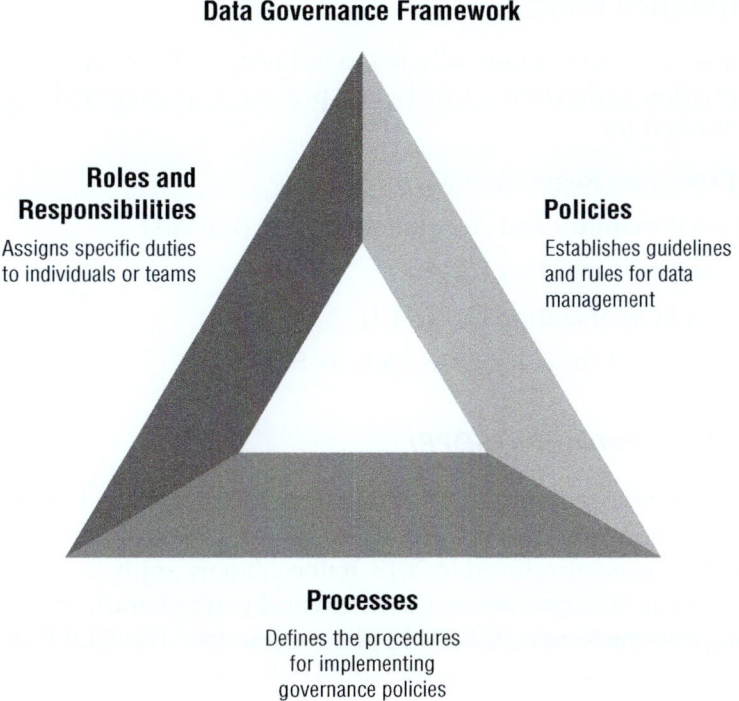

Data Governance Framework

Roles and Responsibilities
Assigns specific duties to individuals or teams

Policies
Establishes guidelines and rules for data management

Processes
Defines the procedures for implementing governance policies

Figure 10-1: Data governance framework

Policies

Policies are formal rules and guidelines that dictate how data should be handled across an organization. They guide what you're allowed to do, what you're not allowed to do, and how things should be done when it comes to managing data. Policies aren't just internal rules; they align with legal requirements that companies must follow to protect individuals' rights and avoid legal penalties. Think of them as the foundation of data governance, setting the standards for collecting, storing, and sharing data. While there are many data policies, this book will focus on six common ones.

- Regulatory compliance policies
- Data classification policies
- Data retention and disposal policies
- Data quality policies
- Data security policies
- Data sharing policies

Regulatory Compliance Policy

This policy ensures that an organization adheres to industry and government regulations that govern data protection, security, and privacy. These regulations include, but are not limited to:

- General Data Protection Regulation (GDPR)
- Health Insurance Portability and Accountability Act (HIPAA)
- CCPA (California Consumer Privacy Act)
- SOC 2 (System and Organization Control 2)
- PCI DSS (Payment Card Industry Data Security Standard)

General Data Protection Regulation (GDPR)

The General Data Protection Regulation (GDPR) is one of the biggest and most famous regulatory policies in data governance. It's a data privacy law from the European Union (EU) that was introduced in 2018. It doesn't only apply to companies inside Europe. If you're anywhere in the world and you're handling the personal data of European customers, GDPR applies to you too. The GDPR is built on seven key principles that guide how personal data should be handled:

- **Principle 1—Lawfulness, Transparency, and Fairness:** This triad forms the cornerstone of GDPR. It ensures that data is collected for legitimate reasons, processed in a way that individuals understand, and handled fairly without misleading or harming them.
- **Principle 2—Data Minimization:** This means collecting only the necessary data for a specific purpose and nothing extra. It prevents businesses from gathering excessive or irrelevant information.
- **Principle 3—Accuracy:** This principle requires data to be correct and regularly updated.
- **Principle 4—Storage Limitation:** This principle mandates that data should not be kept longer than necessary, with unused data promptly deleted.

- **Principle 5—Integrity and Confidentiality:** This states that organizations must establish appropriate security safeguards at technical and organizational levels to protect data from breaches, leaks, or unauthorized access.

- **Principle 6—Accountability:** This requires companies to not only follow these principles but also to demonstrate their compliance through proper documentation and processes.

- **Principle 7—Purpose Limitation:** This ensures that data is collected and used only for a clearly defined and legitimate purpose. Businesses can't repurpose the data for something else without proper justification or user consent.

Health Insurance Portability and Accountability Act (HIPAA)

In the United States, the Health Insurance Portability and Accountability Act (HIPAA) protects sensitive health information. It applies to healthcare providers, insurance companies, and any business that handles medical data. Data governance policies under HIPAA include:

- Data access policy, which limits who can access patient records. For example, a hospital cannot give a patient's medical records to anyone without their permission, unless the law allows it.

- Data encryption policy, which ensures that medical data is encrypted to prevent unauthorized access.

- Audit policy, which requires companies to log and monitor who accesses patient data.

- Data breach notification policy, which outlines how companies must inform patients if their health data is exposed.

California Consumer Privacy Act (CCPA)

The California Consumer Privacy Act (CCPA) is a state-level privacy law that gives California residents more control over personal data. While it shares similarities with GDPR, it is generally considered less strict. The CCPA applies to businesses that meet specific criteria, such as having annual revenues over $25 million, processing data for 50,000 or more consumers, or deriving 50 percent or more of revenue from selling consumer data. There are five key rights under CCPA:

- **Right to Know:** Consumers can request details about the personal data a business collects, including what is collected, why it is collected, and whether it is shared or sold.

- **Right to Delete:** Consumers can ask businesses to delete personal data, with some exceptions like legal or security reasons.

- **Right to Opt Out-of-Sale:** If a business sells consumer data, individuals have the right to opt out and businesses must provide a "Do Not Sell My Personal Information" link on their website.

- **Right to Nondiscrimination:** Businesses cannot discriminate against consumers who exercise their CCPA rights—for example, by charging higher prices or denying services.

- **Right to Correct Data:** Consumers can request corrections to inaccurate personal data.

SOC 2 (System and Organization Control 2)

System and Organization Control is not exactly a law, but it's a big deal if you're working in cloud services, especially software-as-a-service (SaaS) applications. It's a security checklist for companies that store customer data in the cloud. The checklist consists of five foundational principles:

- **Principle 1—Security:** This is the most fundamental part of SOC 2. It focuses on how well a company protects its systems from unauthorized access. It covers everything from setting up firewalls and encryption to enforcing strong passwords and multifactor authentication. The goal is to make sure that only authorized users can access sensitive data, preventing hackers or even internal employees from tampering with information.

- **Principle 2—Availability:** This principle checks whether the system is reliable and accessible when customers need it. It's not just about protecting data; it's also about making sure that the service is always up and running. It checks if companies have backup systems, disaster recovery plans, and performance monitoring tools to minimize downtime. For example, a cloud storage provider needs to prove that customers can access their files 24/7, even during unexpected outages.

- **Principle 3—Confidentiality:** This principle focuses on who can access sensitive information. Not all data should be visible to everyone in a company, especially personal or financial information. This principle makes sure companies have access controls that restrict sensitive data to only authorized individuals. It also looks at whether data is encrypted when it's being stored or transferred so that even if someone intercepts the information, they can't read it without the proper keys.

- **Principle 4—Processing Integrity:** This principle checks if data is processed correctly, on time, and without errors. This is especially important for systems that handle financial transactions or automated processes.

Imagine an online payment platform where every payment request needs to be processed accurately without altering the amount or duplicating transactions. Companies need to have controls in place to detect errors, delays, or unauthorized changes and fix them quickly.

■ **Principle 5—Privacy:** This principle focuses on how companies collect, store, and use personally identifiable information (PII). This includes things like customer names, emails, phone numbers, or any other data that can identify a person. Companies are expected to be transparent about what data they're collecting, why they need it, and how long they'll keep it. They should also ask for user consent before sharing data and only collect the information that's necessary for their services.

Each of these principles works together to help companies protect customer data, build trust, and comply with industry regulations. Even though SOC 2 isn't legally required, having the certification signals to customers that their data is in safe hands, which can be a big advantage in the cloud services industry.

Payment Card Industry Data Security Standard (PCI DSS)

If you're handling credit card data in any way, whether you're running an online store, a subscription service, or even just processing one-off payments, Payment Card Industry Data Security Standard (PCI DSS) is a mandatory security standard for you and any business that processes, stores, or transmits credit card information. The whole point of PCI DSS is to protect cardholder data from theft or misuse.

One of the biggest rules in PCI DSS is encryption. Credit card numbers should never be stored or transmitted in plain text; they need to be scrambled using encryption algorithms so that even if someone intercepts the data, they can't read it without the right decryption key. For example, if a customer enters their card number on a payment form, the system should encrypt that number before storing or sending it.

Another key rule is to never store card numbers in plain text, not even temporarily. If your system needs to store card data at all, it must be encrypted or masked. In many cases, companies are required to avoid storing card numbers altogether unless necessary.

Additionally, access to payment data should also be strictly limited. Only a small group of employees like those working in payment processing or fraud detection should have permission to view cardholder information. This is managed through role-based access controls (RBAC) that ensure employees only see the data they need to perform their jobs.

Regular security audits are another big part of PCI DSS. Companies are required to run vulnerability scans and system monitoring to check if there are any weaknesses in their systems. These audits help businesses spot security gaps before attackers can exploit them.

Data Classification Policy

Data exists in various forms and serves different purposes. Some data is openly available, whereas other data is highly sensitive and must be protected from unauthorized access. A data classification policy helps an organization categorize data based on its sensitivity and criticality, ensuring proper handling, security, and compliance with regulatory requirements. Organizations typically use a tiered classification system to define how data should be handled. As shown in Figure 10-2, the most common classification levels include:

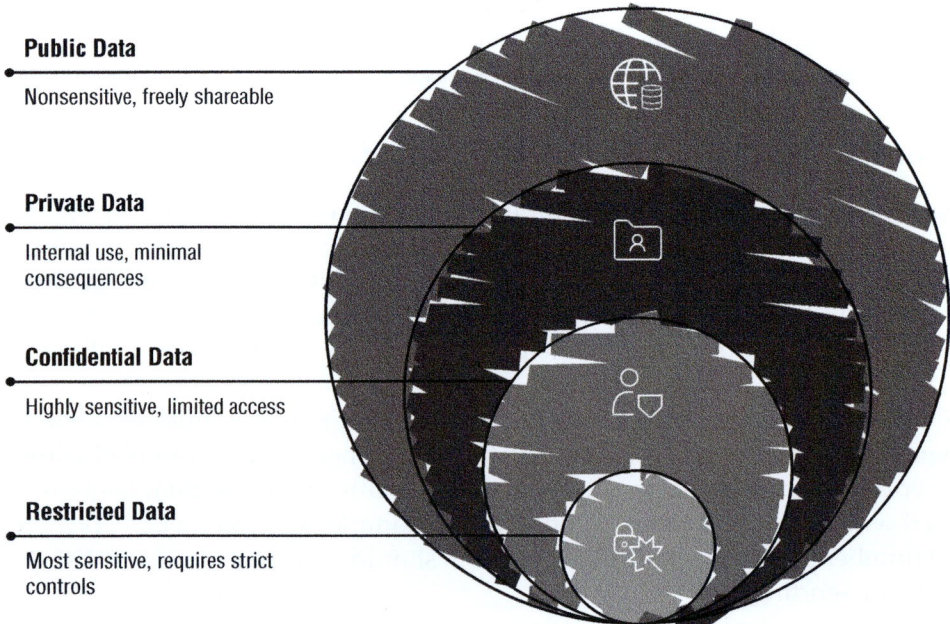

Public Data

Nonsensitive, freely shareable

Private Data

Internal use, minimal consequences

Confidential Data

Highly sensitive, limited access

Restricted Data

Most sensitive, requires strict controls

Figure 10-2: Data classification

- ▪ **Public Data:** This type of data is nonsensitive and can be freely shared with the public without causing harm to the organization, such as press releases, marketing materials, and publicly available financial reports.

- ▪ **Private Data:** This data is intended for internal use within an organization and not meant for public distribution. Unauthorized disclosure may have minimal consequences but is still undesirable. Examples include company policies, internal memos, and employee handbooks.

- **Confidential Data:** This data is highly sensitive data that is restricted to authorized personnel. If this data is exposed, it could result in financial loss, reputational damage, or legal consequences. Examples of this are customer data, financial records, business strategies, and employee personal details.

- **Restricted Data:** This type is the most sensitive form of data and is highly confidential. It requires strict access controls, encryption, and security measures. Examples are trade secrets, intellectual property, PII, medical records, and credit card information.

To successfully implement a data classification policy, as shown in Figure 10-3, organizations can follow these key steps:

Data Classification Policy Implementation

| Identify Data Assets | Define Classification Levels | Label Data | Apply Access Controls | Conduct Periodic Audits |

Figure 10-3: Data classification policy framework

Step 1: Identify data assets by conducting an inventory of all data within the organization and determining where data is stored.

Step 2: Define classification levels by establishing clear criteria for each classification level and ensuring consistency across departments and teams.

Step 3: Label data accordingly using metadata tags to indicate classification levels and automating this labeling where possible using data governance tools.

Step 4: Apply access controls based on classification levels—for example, public data may be accessible to everyone, whereas restricted data requires multifactor authentication.

Step 5: Finally, conduct periodic audits to ensure compliance with the classification policy and also update classifications as business needs and regulations evolve.

Data Retention and Disposal Policy

A data retention and disposal policy establishes clear guidelines on how long different types of data should be stored and the processes for securely disposing of data once it is no longer needed. This policy is important for compliance and operational efficiency, ensuring that data is retained for as long as necessary but not beyond its usefulness or legal requirements. It reduces the risks associated with holding unnecessary or outdated data and prevents excessive storage costs.

A data retention policy in an organization might look like this, and these periods are usually tailored based on industry standards and business needs.

DATA	RETENTION PERIOD	REASON FOR RETENTION
Customer records	5–7 years	Compliance with tax and consumer protection laws like GDPR, CCPA
Financial transactions	7+ years	Required by financial regulations like SOX, IRS
Employee records	3–6 years after departure	Compliance with labor laws
Emails	1–3 years	Internal business records
System logs	30–90 days	Security and troubleshooting
Backup data	30 days–1 year	Business continuity and disaster recovery

In my role as a data engineer, my team follows a policy that automatically deletes PII after 30 days to minimize data retention risks, because the longer PII is stored, the higher the risk of unauthorized access or data breaches. Once data reaches the end of its retention period, it can either be logically deleted by removing access to the data while retaining it in a secure archive; by overwriting it to prevent recovery; or by physically destroying it in cases where it exists in a storage media such as hard drives.

To effectively implement a data retention and disposal policy, organizations can:

- Set up automated retention schedules by using data management tools to apply retention rules consistently, so nothing slips through the cracks.

- Keep an eye on data storage and access by carrying regular audits, which help ensure that data is deleted on time and that everything stays in compliance.

- Review and update policies regularly, because regulations and the needs of the business change, so it's important to revisit your policies from time to time to keep them up to date.

Data Sharing Policy

The data sharing policy establishes guidelines on how data can be shared both internally, within the organization and externally (third parties, partners, vendors, or the public). The primary objective of a data sharing policy is to define who can share data, with whom, and under what conditions, and to facilitate controlled and responsible data exchange between entities. Internal sharing is the controlled exchange of data within the organization, while external sharing is sharing data with third parties, which requires additional security measures. A data sharing policy might look like this, defining which categories of data are shareable and under what conditions.

- Public data can be freely shared both internally and externally with no restrictions.

- Internal business data can be shared within the organization but requires management approval before being shared externally.

- Confidential data is restricted from internal sharing and strictly prohibited from external sharing, except under regulatory conditions such as NDAs or user consent.

- Financial records are restricted from internal sharing and highly prohibited from external sharing due to financial regulations like SOX (Sarbanes–Oxley Act).

We did not cover the data quality policy, which sets standards for accuracy, completeness, consistency, and timeliness, and the data security policy, which governs access control, encryption, authentication, and breach protection, as these topics were already explored in detail in previous chapters. In summary, policies provide some structure and guidance on how data should be handled. Without policies, different teams might make their own rules, leading to a lot of inconsistencies.

Processes

An effective data governance framework relies not just on policies but also on well-defined processes that ensure the policies are followed. These processes outline the workflows and methodologies for handling data throughout its life cycle, from creation and storage to usage and eventual deletion. Each process involves ongoing activities and decision-making steps to ensure data is properly governed. The key processes in data governance include:

- Metadata management
- Data lineage
- Incident management
- Master data management (MDM)

Metadata Management

Metadata is data that describes other data. It provides context about data, including where it comes from and how it is structured. When organizations manage metadata effectively, it's much easier to track the lineage of data and keep its quality in check. Imagine you own a fruit supply store, and you send fresh produce daily to retailers. Your grapes are first picked from the field and placed in baskets. A truck then transports those baskets to a warehouse, where they're sorted, checked for quality, and sent off to grocery stores. Now, let's say your retailers complain about spoiled grapes and you want to trace the journey of where those grapes might be coming from, like where it was grown, which truck carried it, or which warehouse it passed through. That's where metadata comes in: It acts like a digital record, helping you track the life cycle, from the field to the store.

Metadata management is the process of organizing, storing, and maintaining metadata to ensure that it is easily accessible, accurate, and usable. It involves:

- Collecting metadata from different sources like databases, reports, and data pipelines
- Storing and cataloging metadata in a central place like a metadata repository or data catalog
- Keeping metadata up to date so users always have the latest information
- Making metadata searchable so data engineers, analysts, and end users in general can easily find what they need

Types of Metadata

There are three main types of metadata: technical, business, and operational, all serving unique purposes.

- As shown in Figure 10-4, technical metadata is like the blueprint of data; it tells engineers how data is stored and structured. With technical metadata we can understand what columns exist in a table, what data types they have, and how different tables are related.
- Business metadata explains what the data means in a way nontechnical people can understand. For instance, suppose a marketing manager wants to analyze customer data to create a campaign. Business metadata helps them understand what a column like "active customers" might mean, and it ensures they use the right data. Business metadata might contain other information, like ownership information stating which department in an organization own a particular dataset.

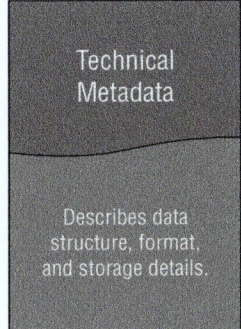

Technical Metadata

Describes data structure, format, and storage details.

Business Metadata

Provides context and meaning for business processes.

Operational Metadata

Tracks data usage, performance, and operational processes.

Figure 10-4: Types of metadata

■ Operational metadata tracks what happens to data over time and it's majorly for monitoring and debugging. If a data engineer notices an error in a financial report, they can make use of operational metadata to check when the data was last updated, where it came from, and what transformations were applied. Operation metadata also includes timestamps showing when data was last updated and data sources connected to that data.

Metadata is usually stored in specialized systems for storing, managing, and retrieving metadata called *catalogs*. Examples are Apache Atlas, used in big data ecosystems like Hadoop or Spark; AWS Glue Data Catalog, which stores metadata for AWS services like S3, Redshift, and Athena; Google Data Catalog, which stores metadata for Google Cloud services like BigQuery; and Microsoft Purview, a metadata repository for Azure data sources.

Benefits of Metadata Management

Metadata management makes data discovery faster, and it helps users quickly find the right datasets without manually searching through files or databases. A marketing analyst can search for "customer churn rate" and find the relevant dataset instantly.

Metadata management ensures that metadata is updated and consistent across systems, reducing errors. If a product price column changes from "integer" to "decimal," an effective metadata management process helps to inform engineers to update their queries.

Metadata management helps organizations track where data comes from and who has access, helping with regulatory compliance. A company can see who accessed sensitive customer data and when, ensuring security policies are followed.

Lastly, operation metadata helps trace how data moves through different systems, making it easier to debug errors. If a report shows incorrect revenue figures, data engineers can track the data lineage to find the issue.

Data Lineage

Data lineage refers to the visual representation of the journey that data takes throughout its life cycle within an organization. It's like a map that shows the flow of data from its origin through various transformations and processing until it reaches its final destination. When a data source changes, data lineage helps evaluate the impact on downstream reports and applications, and in case of errors, it also allows us to quickly trace the root cause and debug data pipeline issues.

A robust metadata management strategy can be combined with a data lineage process to create a unified repository for all data-related information, so we can think of metadata management and data lineage as two sides of the same coin. Data lineage helps keep things transparent, and this traceability makes troubleshooting easier because you can quickly pinpoint where things went wrong.

One of the biggest challenges with data lineage is just how complex modern data pipelines can get. If you're dealing with a simple pipeline with one input and minimal transformations, mapping its lineage is pretty straightforward, but when data moves through multiple systems, undergoes various transformations, and ends up in different places. Keeping track of all those movements isn't easy and it takes the right tools and careful planning.

Incident Management

Incident management is how organizations handle data security issues, whether it's a leak, a system failure, or any kind of security incident. It's a structured way of identifying the problem, figuring out how bad it is, responding to it, and making sure it doesn't cause too much damage. The whole point is to have processes in place to keep operations running smoothly while protecting data from being lost, exposed, or misused.

Key Components of an Incident Management Process

A strong incident management process minimizes disruption and ensures that the organization can respond quickly and effectively to incidents. Here are the key components involved:

- **Identification:** The first step is spotting issues early. Organizations use monitoring systems to watch for anything unusual like unauthorized access, system slowdowns, or security threats. Logs, alerts, and automated tools help catch problems before they get out of hand.

- **Classification:** Not every incident is the same, so companies categorize them based on severity, minor, major, or critical. They assess how the issue affects data security in terms of confidentiality and determine if they need to report it to regulators.

- **Incident Response:** Once an incident is confirmed, the response team jumps into action. Their priority is to stop the issue from spreading, and this could mean isolating systems, revoking access, or fixing vulnerabilities like applying patches.

- **Communication:** When a breach happens, communication is key. Internal teams need to be informed, and depending on the severity, external parties, like regulators, customers, or users may also need to be notified. The goal is to be transparent while protecting the organization's reputation.

- **Root Cause Analysis:** Once the dust settles, the next step is figuring out what went wrong. This involves forensic analysis to trace the root cause and then making changes, whether that's updating policies, fixing security gaps, or adding stronger protections to prevent it from happening again.

- **Documentation:** After everything is resolved, a postmortem review (a structured analysis that happens after an incident) helps assess how well the response was handled. At this stage, lessons learned get documented, security policies are updated where needed, and employees are trained to prevent similar incidents in the future. In summary, incident management is all about staying prepared, minimizing damage, and strengthening security for next time.

Best Practices for an Effective Incident Management Process

To stay ahead of security issues, organizations must be proactive when something goes wrong. Here are a few best practices that you can follow for effective incident response management:

- Regular audits and monitoring are important for maintaining a strong security posture. When systems are continuously scanned for vulnerabilities, organizations can identify weak points before attackers exploit them. This proactive approach ensures that security gaps are addressed promptly. Monitoring tools help spot suspicious activities early, allowing teams to take action before an incident escalates.

- Having incident response playbooks is like having a fire drill for cybersecurity. These playbooks outline step-by-step actions for handling different types of data breaches, ensuring that teams know exactly what to do in an emergency. A well-prepared response can significantly reduce downtime and limit the impact of an attack. Playbooks should cover various scenarios so that teams can respond quickly and effectively to any situation.

- Employee training is another critical layer of defense. Security isn't just the responsibility of the IT team, every employee plays a role in keeping data secure. Training programs should teach staff how to recognize common threats, especially phishing emails or suspicious links, and how to report them. When employees are well informed, they become the first line of defense against security breaches, helping to prevent incidents before they happen.

- Finally, simulated breach exercises put all these measures to the test. Just like emergency drills prepare people for real-life situations, cybersecurity simulations help organizations assess their response readiness. These exercises expose weaknesses in security protocols and provide an opportunity to improve them before an actual breach occurs.

Master Data Management

Let's understand what master data is first before diving into how we can manage it. Think of *master data* as the core, high-value information that's shared across an organization. It's the who, what, where of a business, things like customers, products, employees, suppliers, or locations. Unlike transactional data, like sales records that change frequently, master data is relatively stable and is used across different systems and departments. For a retail company, master data could be the customer details (name, address, loyalty number) or product catalog (product name, price) because they're referenced everywhere, on the website, in-store systems, and marketing databases.

Master data management is a key process in data governance because governance is all about ensuring data is accurate, consistent, and used correctly across the business. If your master data is messy, like duplicate customer records or inconsistent product names, your whole organization suffers from inefficiencies. While governance provides the rules and policies, master data management puts them into practice.

Let's look at some key master data management processes.

- **Agreeing Ownership of Attributes:** Think of this as deciding who owns what. In any business, different teams may use the same data but in different ways. For example, is the Product Price owned by the Finance team, the Sales team, or Marketing? Ownership means someone is responsible for maintaining and updating that attribute correctly. Without clear ownership, you might have multiple versions of the same data floating around.

- **Data Definition:** This step is about making sure everyone speaks the same language when it comes to data. If one team calls it Customer ID and another calls it Client Number, things can get messy. So, data definition involves standardizing terms, descriptions, and rules so that everyone knows what a data attribute means, what format it should be in, and how it should be used.

- **Defining Attributes:** This means setting clear rules and properties for each piece of important data. This ensures that everyone in the organization understands how a data attribute should be structured, stored, and used. Let's take the example of Product Name in a retail company. We need to define certain properties to make sure it's consistent and usable across different systems.

  Format: This defines the data type and length. Should it be text or can it contain numbers? How many characters should it allow? Should it allow special characters?

  Source: Where does this data come from? Does it come from the product catalog system? Is it entered manually by employees? Is it imported from a supplier's database?

  Valid Values: What are the acceptable inputs? Should abbreviations be allowed? Should brand names always be included? Can numbers be used in the name?

  Business Rules: Special conditions that must always be followed. Must each product name be unique? Should duplicate names be prevented?

- **Amending Attributes:** Over time, business needs change, and master data needs to evolve. Amending attributes means updating existing data fields, maybe a new regulation requires more details on customer records, or a product's price needs a new decimal format. The key here is making sure updates happen in a controlled way so they don't break systems or create inconsistencies.

- **Retiring Attributes:** At some point, some data attributes eventually become unnecessary. Maybe the company no longer tracks Fax Number for customers. Instead of deleting it recklessly, retiring an attribute means gradually phasing it out, ensuring it doesn't impact reports, databases, or integrations with other systems.

Without a solid master data management process, companies end up with duplicate data and outdated information. Good management ensures that everyone in the organization is working with one accurate version of the truth, which leads to fewer errors. Several master data management solutions help organizations manage master data efficiently, like Informatica MDM, SAP Master Data Governance, IBM InfoSphere MDM, Oracle MDM, and Talend MDM.

Roles in the Data Governance Framework

The data governance framework assigns specific roles to individuals or teams, as shown in Figure 10-5, each with clear responsibilities to ensure that policies are met and to create a system that protects data quality, privacy, and compliance. Let's break down the key roles and their responsibilities.

Data Owner

Decision-maker for a particular dataset

Data Steward

Acts as the caretaker of the data daily

Data Custodian

Technical expert who manages the storage and security

Chief Data Officer

Executive who oversees the entire data governance program

Figure 10-5: Data governance roles

Data Owner

The data owner is the decision-maker for a particular dataset. This person typically comes from the business side, such as a department head or senior manager, and is responsible for defining how the data should be used and creating policies. The data owner decides:

- What kind of data should be collected?
- Who is allowed to access the data?
- How long the data should be kept?
- What rules apply to the data?

The data owner makes the final decision if any questions or conflicts arise regarding the data. Their primary goal is to ensure that the data is aligned with business needs and regulatory requirements.

Data Steward

A *data steward* is a person from the business who has detailed knowledge of the data that is needed to support targeted business initiatives. They act as the day-to-day caretaker of the organization's data. While the data owner sets the rules, the data steward makes sure those rules are followed. They are responsible for:

- Evaluating data quality
- Cleaning up incorrect or duplicate data
- Adding business descriptions to data fields in a data catalog
- Working closely with data owners to ensure the data meets business requirements and working with IT to accelerate these processes

Data stewards help maintain consistent and reliable data across the organization, making it easier for others to trust and use the data. They are found in an organization and not made because there might be people already doing this unofficially in the organization without the role title.

Data Custodian

Data custodians are technical experts who manage the storage, security, and infrastructure of data. This role is usually performed by IT or engineering teams. Their main responsibilities include:

- Implementing access controls to restrict who can view or edit data
- Encrypting sensitive data to prevent unauthorized access
- Managing backups and recovery systems
- Ensuring the systems meet security standards

While data custodians don't make business decisions about the data, they play a critical role in protecting the data from breaches and loss.

Chief Data Officer (CDO)

The chief data officer (CDO) is the executive who oversees the entire data governance program. Not every company has a CDO, but in organizations that do, this person is responsible for:

- Defining the company's overall data strategy
- Aligning data governance efforts with business goals
- Advocating for data governance at the executive level
- Measuring the success of the data governance program

The CDO acts as the champion of data governance, making sure the entire organization understands the value of data as a business asset.

In summary, each role in the data governance framework contributes uniquely to the process. The framework works best when everyone understands their responsibilities and how they fit into the bigger picture. These roles are commonly found in organizations, especially those that handle large volumes of data or operate in regulated industries like finance, healthcare, or technology.

In many organizations, especially smaller ones, the same person might take on multiple roles. For example, a data steward might also act as a data custodian by not only cleaning the data but also managing its storage in databases. Although not every company uses the same job titles. Some companies might refer to data owners as data managers or data stewards as data quality analysts.

Larger companies with more advanced data governance programs are more likely to have a chief data officer and a formal data governance committee.

However, even without formal titles, the responsibilities still exist. Someone is always making decisions about data, cleaning and maintaining data, or securing the infrastructure. Understanding these roles helps organizations build more effective data governance programs, whether or not they have dedicated teams.

Data Management and Data Governance

We've discussed data governance extensively, but the definition of data management and data governance often overlap. Some sources tell you that data management allows you to manage your data, while data governance allows you to manage your data better. Let's understand the difference between them.

Data is not useful unless we can get value from it. The journey to making data valuable involves it getting cleaned, modeled, analyzed, and secured. When these processes are carried out daily, we can say that our data is being managed. Data management focuses on the operational aspects of handling data and maintaining its quality to support business *needs*. But how do we set clear rules on what clean data should look like, or how data should be secured and made accessible? This is where data governance comes in.

Data governance establishes the policies, standards, and accountability frameworks that define how data should be handled. It answers critical questions like what are the rules for accessing and modifying data, or what data quality metrics should we track?

In simpler terms, data management is about executing processes to handle data efficiently, whereas data governance sets the rules and guidelines that ensure data is managed properly.

Summary

- Data governance is the overall framework that ensures data within an organization is accurate, secure, consistent, and used responsibly. It involves setting policies, standards, and processes to manage data throughout its life cycle, from creation to deletion.

- Data governance acts like a blueprint for data security and data quality measures in an organization.

- A data governance framework consists of policies, processes, and roles and responsibilities, each of which plays an important role in ensuring an effective data governance strategy.

- Key regulatory policies include GDPR for global data privacy, HIPAA for healthcare data, CCPA for California consumer privacy, PCI DSS for payment security, and SOC 2 for cloud security compliance.

- The Service Organization Control, SOC 2, is a security checklist for companies that store customer data in the cloud.

- A data classification policy helps organizations categorize data into public, private, confidential, and restricted data categories based on its sensitivity.

- Metadata is data that describes other data, and there are three main types of metadata, namely technical metadata, business metadata, and operational metadata.

- Data lineage refers to the visual representation of the journey that data takes throughout its life cycle within an organization.

- Incident management is how organizations handle data security issues, whether it's a leak, a system failure, or any kind of security incident. The best practices for a good incident response are regular audits and monitoring, having incident response playbooks, and employee training.

- Master data is core, high-value data that's shared across an organization, and managing master data involves defining data, deciding ownership of attributes and making sure there is only one accurate version of the truth.

- Data governance roles include data owner, data steward, data custodian, and chief data officer, with each role contributing uniquely to the data governance goals of an organization.

- Data management and data governance definitions often overlap, but data management allows you to manage your data, while data governance allows you to manage your data better.

Big Data and Distributed Systems

In my experience, organizations across industries work with data of all sizes, ranging from gigabytes to petabytes and, in some cases, even more. Earlier chapters covered the basics of databases and data processing. Still, when data gets so large, it requires a completely different method of processing, one that is faster, more efficient, and built to scale.

Traditional databases and single-server architectures—that is, database systems that run entirely on a single machine—struggle to keep up with the scale and complexity of modern data because when large datasets are processed on a single machine, it leads to slow performance and a lot of scalability issues. Looking at big companies like Netflix, Google, and Amazon, which manage massive amounts of data without their systems crashing, raises an important question: What makes this possible? What technologies and strategies allow them to handle such enormous workloads seamlessly?

The answer lies in distributed computing and understanding the basic features of big data. With the right systems, businesses can process huge amounts of data more efficiently.

IN THIS CHAPTER, WE WILL EXPLORE:

- The fundamentals of big data
- The five V's of big data

- Key principles of distributed systems and their components
- An overview of big data processing and frameworks
- The design architectures of Apache Spark and Hadoop
- Various big data file types
- Choosing the right file types for big data projects

By the end of this chapter, you'll have a strong understanding of how big data is managed at scale and how distributed systems form the backbone of modern data engineering.

The Five V's of Big Data

We create data each time we scroll through a social media application, watch a YouTube video, buy something online, or even just walk around with our phone's location on. Now, imagine billions of people doing this every second and companies trying to collect, store, and manage this data. That's big data in simple terms.

Big data refers to extremely large and complex datasets that are so vast that traditional data tools like your average spreadsheet or small database can't handle them effectively. It's not just about the size; it's also about how quickly the data arrives, the different formats it comes in, and how unpredictable or messy it can be.

The five V's of big data are essential characteristics that define and help us understand the nature of big data. Originally, there were three V's—volume, velocity, and variety—but over time, more V's have been introduced as the field evolved, as shown in Figure 11-1. Let's break them down.

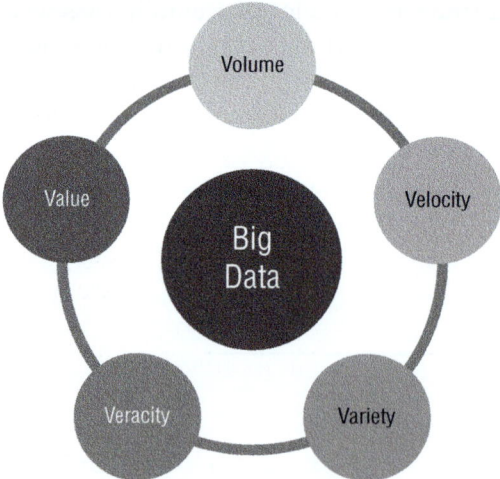

Figure 11-1: The five V's of big data

Volume

Volume refers to the amount of data being generated and stored, often on a massive scale. For instance, Meta (Facebook) alone processes terabytes of data daily, from user interactions like posts, comments, and likes, to video uploads, messaging, and more. To put that in perspective, one terabyte (TB) equals 1,000 gigabytes (GB), and one gigabyte can store about 250 songs or a few hours of video. Now, imagine what 1,000 gigabytes can hold, and Meta handles that kind of data volume several times over every single day. This scale isn't just about storage; it also presents challenges for data management, requiring powerful systems to collect, organize, and access such large quantities of information efficiently. What makes volume a uniquely big data concern is not only the sheer amount of data but also the need for scalable architectures and advanced algorithms that can process and analyze this data in a reasonable time frame, something traditional databases and tools simply aren't built to handle.

Velocity

Velocity is all about the speed at which data is generated, transmitted, and processed. In the past, data was collected in batches and analyzed at intervals, perhaps once a day or even once a week. But with big data, things move much faster. Many modern systems rely on data that is streaming in real time, meaning the data is continuously generated and needs to be analyzed immediately or within seconds of arrival. This is common in areas where quick insights are critical like financial trading, real-time fraud detection, and health monitoring systems. Velocity matters in small data too, but in big data, it's not just the speed, it's the scale and continuity of that speed that makes it defining, shifting organizations to a more proactive way of responding to events as they happen, rather than analyzing them later.

Variety

Big data differs from traditional data systems in terms of its diversity. Data no longer comes only in neat rows and columns like it used to in conventional databases. Instead, big data encompasses an entire spectrum of formats, and to manage it effectively, you need to understand the various forms it comes in. In the previous chapters, we discussed three major forms of data—structured, semi-structured, and unstructured. In the context of big data, these forms become even more significant, because the more data you have, the more crucial it is to organize and manage it properly, and that starts with understanding what kind of data you're dealing with.

Imagine a company that's analyzing customer feedback; they may have survey results in a structured format, email inquiries in a semi-structured format, and social media posts or product review videos in an unstructured format. Structured data can still be managed with traditional relational databases and SQL. But semi-structured and unstructured data require specialized tools like Hadoop, Spark, or machine learning models to extract insights. Most value in big data lies in semi-structured and unstructured forms, like customer reviews, video content, or clickstream data. Understanding the data type helps prioritize the right tools and processing strategies that can work across formats to extract value whether the data is numbers, words, images, or sounds.

Veracity

Veracity is all about the quality and reliability of the data you're working with. One of the challenges in big data is that the greater the volume and variety of data, the harder it becomes to ensure accuracy and consistency. The more data you collect, the higher the chance that some of it will be incomplete, inconsistent, or duplicated. Unlike small datasets that might come from a single source or system, big data often pulls from multiple sources. For example, social media data might include fake accounts or bots that are hard to interpret accurately. Veracity is critical because businesses rely on accurate data to make decisions; if the data is faulty, the entire decision-making process is compromised.

Value

It's not enough to simply collect large amounts of data quickly and from various sources; we need to do something useful with it. In big data systems, where information flows in from hundreds or even thousands of sources, often in real time, the challenge isn't lack of data but identifying what's meaningful. Value is about translating raw data into insights that result in decisions and actions that have a tangible impact on an organization or its customers. While smaller datasets can certainly offer valuable insights, the power of big data lies in uncovering patterns, trends, and connections that only emerge at scale. Take Spotify as an example; they use data on your listening habits to recommend new songs and playlists. This data-driven personalization enhances user experience, and that's only possible because of scalable infrastructure that can process millions of interactions per second.

Distributed Systems

Every time you watch a movie on Netflix, shop online, or search on Google, you're interacting with a distributed system hidden by a web page or application. They are everywhere. Distributed systems have always been popular in computer science, but in the context of data engineering, how did we start using them? Back in the day, businesses had one computer called a mainframe that did all the work, stored data, processed it, and ran programs. These were centralized systems, and they were massive, expensive, and not exactly flexible.

Over time, companies transitioned to client-server models, where a server handled requests from multiple clients. Think of it like a waiter serving different tables; the waiter represents the server, while the tables represent the clients. This approach worked well for a while, especially for websites, simple applications, and databases.

But then, data exploded when applications started generating way more data than one server could handle. What was the next step? Companies tried to make servers more powerful, with bigger hard drives, faster CPUs, and more RAM. But there was a limit; you can only make one machine so powerful before it becomes ridiculously expensive and still prone to crashing if overloaded.

Then this question came up: What if we used multiple servers and designed them to work together instead of beefing up one server, and this is how distributed systems came about. Popular companies like Google faced this problem early with their search engine where they couldn't store the entire Internet on one machine, so they built their own distributed systems to split the data across many machines. They also introduced what they called MapReduce, which later inspired Hadoop, an open source tool that lets the rest of us process big data across multiple machines. Fast-forward to today, and tools like Apache Spark and others have emerged, all designed with distributed systems at their core.

A distributed system is a collection of independent computers that appear to the user as a single system. These computers work together to achieve a common goal, coordinating actions and sharing resources, even though they might be physically located in different places.

Imagine trying to build a house by yourself. This would take a long time, and you'd probably be exhausted. Now imagine you have a team of skilled workers, each handling a different part of the construction like plumbing, wiring, roofing, and painting, all working together to finish the house faster and more efficiently. This is the basic idea behind distributed systems: breaking down a task into smaller parts, sharing the load across multiple machines, and working together to complete tasks that would be too slow or too big for one machine to handle.

Distributed systems are the backbone of modern data engineering. They're what makes it possible to handle and process huge amounts of data without everything slowing to a crawl or breaking down. As the amount of data in the world keeps exploding, knowing how distributed systems work isn't just a nice-to-have for data engineers; it's a must because these systems let you build data processing solutions that are scalable, so you can keep up with the demands of big data.

Distributed systems have unique characteristics that enable them to do their work efficiently, but before we explore them, let's figure out how they work.

When a task like processing a large dataset is being executed, that big task is divided into smaller tasks and these smaller tasks are distributed across computers called *nodes*. Each node is connected to a network, like the Internet or a local network, and they may be physically apart but are logically connected. Nodes communicate using protocols, rules for sending and receiving messages like HTTPS, and they agree on what tasks to do and who does what; this is called coordination. One node might be a leader (coordinator), or all nodes might be equal peers. All nodes work simultaneously (in parallel) to speed up the job, which is why distributed systems are scalable and fast.

While working, nodes often need to share data or results. They send messages back and forth. The system also handles issues like network delays and message loss. Nodes may also fail or crash, and distributed systems use techniques like replication, which is keeping copies of data and trying again if a node fails, in order to keep the system working. Once all nodes finish their tasks, the results are collected and combined. The system gives a final output to the user as if it were done by one computer.

The common features of distributed systems that make them super-efficient include:

- Scalability
- Fault tolerance
- Reliability
- Concurrency
- Resource management
- Consistency
- Availability
- Load balancing
- Latency

Scalability

Scalability is the ability of a system to continue to work correctly as the load increases. Load here can mean the number of requests per second received by a web server, the number of reads from versus writes to a cache, or the number of users on an application.

Imagine your company experiences a surge in data, maybe due to a Black Friday sale or a viral marketing campaign. As a data engineer, you notice that your current ETL pipeline is running slower due to the increased volume. To make sure the system can handle this spike in data, you may need to upgrade your data processing infrastructure by either increasing the number of nodes in your system to distribute the workload efficiently or implementing autoscaling in your cloud setup when demand increases. Scalability ensures that as data grows, the system can handle it without a drop in performance. There are two main ways we can scale our system: either horizontally or vertically, as shown in Figure 11-2.

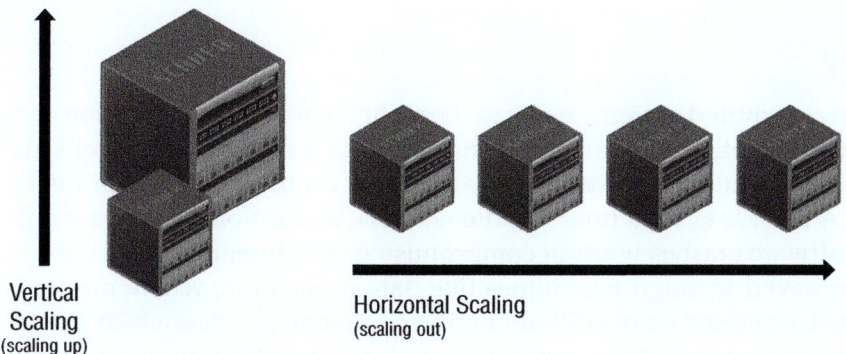

Vertical
Scaling
(scaling up)

Horizontal Scaling
(scaling out)

Figure 11-2: Vertical and horizontal scaling

- *Horizontal scalability*, also called scale-out, means you can add more machines to the system. For example, if your system is slow in processing data from 1 million users, you add 10 more servers to share the load, and you can keep adding more nodes as needed.

- *Vertical scalability*, also called scale-up, means you upgrade a single machine by adding more CPU or RAM. But the limitation here is that, eventually, there's a limit to how big machines can get, and they can be very expensive because you can't get infinite RAM.

Most companies use a mix of both methods; they use more powerful machines and add more machines to share the load. Also, every system is different, and although there's no one-size-fits-all, things like how users access the system and how fast it needs to respond according to your SLA requirements affect how you design your scaling strategy. In summary, scale-up when you can, scale-out when you need to, and always design based on your system's specific needs.

Fault Tolerance

Fault tolerance is the ability of a system to continue functioning even when some of its components fail. Distributed systems are built with redundancy, meaning that if one node fails, another can take over without disrupting the service. For instance, you might be running a batch job that processes customer transactions and a server crashes in the middle of execution. Without fault tolerance, this could mean losing hours of data processing. Here, distributed processing frameworks like Spark have checkpointing features to resume from the last successful state instead of restarting the entire job. Similarly, in distributed databases such as Apache Cassandra, data is stored across multiple nodes, ensuring that even if some nodes fail, the data remains accessible. Without fault tolerance, a single point of failure could bring down an entire system, leading to loss of data and service interruptions.

Reliability

Reliability in distributed systems refers to the ability of a system to function correctly and consistently over time, ensuring that data is not lost, operations are completed successfully, and users receive accurate results even in the presence of failures. A reliable system must handle network disruptions, hardware failures, and software crashes without compromising data integrity.

This is achieved through techniques like data replication, where multiple copies of data are stored across different nodes; automatic retries, which ensure that failed operations are retried until they succeed; and checkpointing, where the system periodically saves its state to recover from unexpected crashes. For instance, in financial transactions, banks use distributed databases with transaction logs to ensure that even if a failure occurs in the middle of a transaction, the system can roll back or retry the operation to maintain accuracy and consistency. Reliable distributed systems are designed to minimize downtime and prevent data loss, making them essential for applications where uninterrupted service and data correctness are critical.

While fault tolerance ensures that the system keeps running even when failures occur, reliability ensures that the system always produces correct results.

Concurrency

Concurrency allows multiple tasks or users to access and use the system at the same time, independently, without interfering with each other. In distributed systems, tasks are executed in parallel across different nodes. For instance, multiple users can query the database at once. Another prime example of concurrency is seen in online ticket booking systems like Airbnb or Booking.com. When multiple users try to book the same hotel room at the same time, the system must handle concurrent requests and ensure that the room is allocated to only one user while preventing double bookings or when a company has a shared database that allows multiple users to run ad hoc queries.

Resource Management

In a distributed system, there are limited resources like CPU (processing power), memory (RAM), storage (disk space), and network bandwidth (how fast data moves between machines). If these resources are not managed well, some machines might be overloaded while others sit idle, leading to slow and inefficient processing. To prevent this, resource managers allocate tasks to different machines based on their availability and workload. A good example is running queries on Apache Spark, only to notice that the cluster suddenly slows down. Upon investigation, you realize that some jobs are consuming too much memory. In such cases, resource management plays a crucial role in reallocating resources, adjusting memory limits, redistributing workloads, or scaling up the cluster to restore smooth performance.

Consistency

Consistency, in the context of distributed systems, ensures that all nodes in a distributed system have the same data at a given point in time. It prevents conflicts and ensures that users see the latest updates across all devices. A good example is Amazon's shopping cart. If a user adds an item to their cart using a mobile device, the same item should appear in the cart when they switch to a desktop browser. This requires strong consistency across Amazon's distributed database system. However, achieving strong consistency in large-scale distributed systems can be expensive. Some systems, like Twitter or Facebook, use an approach called eventual consistency, where updates propagate over time, ensuring that all nodes eventually converge to the same state.

Different consistency models exist:

- *Strong consistency*, where all nodes reflect updates immediately
- *Eventual consistency*, where nodes update asynchronously but will eventually sync
- *Causal consistency*, where operations that are causally related appear in order

Availability

Availability ensures that the system is accessible and operational at all times, even in the presence of failures. A practical example is Amazon Web Services (AWS), which offers a 99.99 percent uptime guarantee for its cloud services. This is achieved by deploying servers in multiple availability zones (data centers in different geographic locations). Even if one availability zone fails due to a hardware issue, another zone takes over, ensuring that services remain operational. Another example is WhatsApp or Facebook Messenger, which must be available 24/7 globally. If a server in one region goes down, users are automatically redirected to another server to maintain uninterrupted communication.

Load Balancing

A distributed system can distribute workloads across multiple nodes to prevent any single node from becoming overloaded, ensuring optimal performance.

A classic example is Google Search, which handles billions of search queries daily. Google uses *load balancers* to distribute incoming queries across thousands of servers worldwide, ensuring that no single server is overwhelmed. Similarly, in content delivery networks (CDNs) like Cloudflare, user requests are routed to the nearest or least-busy server to improve response times. Load balancing is important for handling large-scale distributed applications such as video streaming, online gaming, and high-traffic websites.

Latency

Latency is the time it takes for a request to get a response. Latency also affects performance, which is how quickly and efficiently tasks are completed. The goal in most distributed systems is to minimize latency and maximize throughput, that is, how many tasks are completed per time unit. When processing large datasets, queries are expected to be fast and responsive. Low latency is also essential for real-time analytics, dashboards, and recommendation systems, while higher latency can sometimes be acceptable for batch processing workflows.

Distributed Data Processing

Distributed data processing is a method of handling large volumes of data by breaking data into smaller chunks and processing them across multiple computers working together. Instead of relying on a single powerful machine, this approach distributes the workload across many machines, making data processing faster, more efficient, and scalable, especially for big data. Without distributed processing, big data engineering would struggle to handle the volume, velocity, and variety of modern data because that's the engine under the hood.

To achieve this, data engineers use frameworks designed to handle distributed workloads. Some of the most common ones are Apache Hadoop, Spark, Flink (for real-time streaming), and Apache Kafka.

Many other tools are available, each designed for specific use cases. Throughout this section, we'll explore some of these popular frameworks and how they help data engineers process massive datasets efficiently.

Apache Hadoop

As data started growing massively in the early 2000s, thanks to things like web apps, social media, and just about everything going online, tech giants like Google ran into a serious problem: How could they store and process mountains of data that simply wouldn't fit on one machine? Their answer? Spread the load.

In 2003 and 2004, Google shared two game-changing ideas with the world: (1) the Google File System (GFS), a way to stash huge amounts of data across many computers; and (2) MapReduce, a method for breaking data tasks into smaller pieces and processing them at the same time on different machines. These ideas laid the foundation for what we now call *distributed data processing*.

Inspired by Google's approach, Doug Cutting and Mike Cafarella built an open source version and called it Hadoop. It went on to become one of the first big tools that helped engineers process data at scale.

Hadoop is an open source framework that enables distributed storage and processing of large datasets using clusters of commodity hardware—affordable, regular computers. Traditional systems store and process data on a single machine. But what if your data is so big it can't fit or process efficiently on one machine? Hadoop breaks big data into small pieces, stores them across multiple computers, and processes them in parallel, making the entire process faster and scalable.

Hadoop has the same features a distributed system would typically have; it adds more machines to handle more data, making it scalable. If one machine fails, others take over, which makes it fault-tolerant and efficient. It also processes data where it is stored, minimizing data movement. The Hadoop engine is powered by three main components: the Hadoop Distributed File System (HDFS); MapReduce, the processing engine; and Hadoop YARN, the resource manager.

Hadoop Distributed File System (HDFS)

Hadoop Distributed File System (HDFS) is the primary storage system used by Hadoop for managing big data. It is designed to store vast amounts of data across many machines in a distributed manner. HDFS works by breaking down large files into smaller fixed-size blocks, typically 128 MB or 256 MB, and distributing them across multiple machines in a cluster.

As seen in Figure 11-3, the local file system represents a single machine with a 10 TB storage capacity. In a local file system, all data is stored on one machine, making it a single point of failure (if the machine crashes, all data is lost). In a distributed file system, like HDFS, data is distributed across multiple machines. The figure shows four machines, each with 10 TB of storage, effectively scaling storage to 40 TB. These nodes are connected and work together to store and process data.

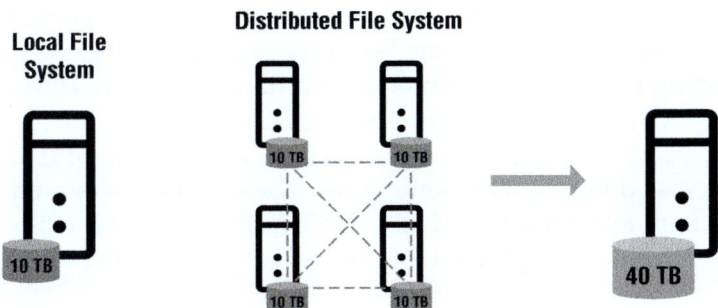

Figure 11-3: A local file system and a distributed file system

The HDFS Architecture

The HDFS architecture, shown in Figure 11-4, is how data is stored, replicated, and accessed within a Hadoop cluster. Let's break it down step by step.

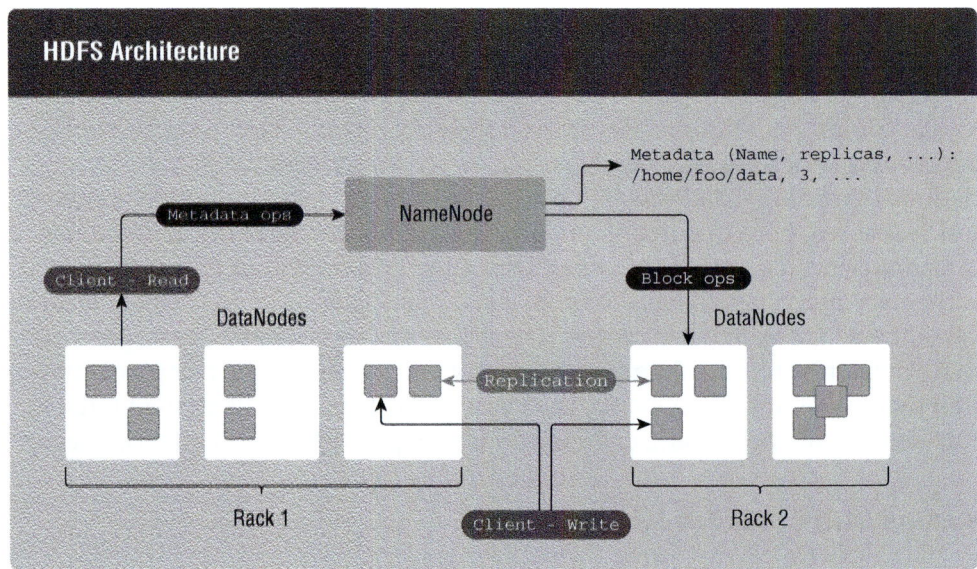

Figure 11-4: Hadoop's distributed file system architecture

The *NameNode* acts as the master node of HDFS. It maintains metadata such as filenames, directories, permissions, and replication details. It does not store actual data; instead, it keeps track of which DataNodes store which data blocks.

DataNodes are also known as the storage workers. These are the machines responsible for storing actual data blocks. DataNodes store, replicate, and retrieve data as requested by clients. In Figure 11-4, DataNodes are grouped into Rack 1 and Rack 2, representing physical separation in a data center to ensure redundancy and fault tolerance.

The *HDFS client* (a user) interacts with the HDFS system to read or write data. A client can request to write a file, and the system stores it in blocks across multiple DataNodes, or the client can request to read a file, and data is fetched from the relevant DataNodes. In this case, the NameNode provides the client with metadata, including locations of the block the data is stored on. If the NameNode fails, a secondary or standby NameNode takes over.

As illustrated in Figure 11-4, replication occurs in HDFS by storing multiple copies of each block across different racks and nodes. These blocks are stored redundantly to ensure fault tolerance. By default, HDFS follows a default replication factor of 3, and each block is replicated three times across different nodes.

This means that if one node fails, the data can still be retrieved from another node holding a replica. The replication process is shown in Figure 11-4, where blocks are duplicated across racks for reliability.

Physically, HDFS spans across a network of machines, often using commodity hardware, affordable, off-the-shelf computers that are not specially designed for high-performance computing. Logically, it appears as a single, unified file system to users and applications. Data is written and read through APIs or command-line tools, and the entire system can scale horizontally. From a visualization standpoint, HDFS is typically monitored through web interfaces that show data node status, storage usage, and file system health.

Companies use HDFS for tasks like log processing, recommendation systems, fraud detection, and data archiving. It's especially useful in environments where traditional storage systems can't handle the size, speed, or complexity of the data.

MapReduce

MapReduce is the processing component of Hadoop, designed to generate and process large datasets in parallel across a distributed cluster of computers. The core idea is to divide a task into smaller subtasks, process them independently, and then combine the results. The MapReduce process has two major phases: Map and Reduce, often preceded by data input and followed by output. Figure 11-5 shows how the MapReduce process works:

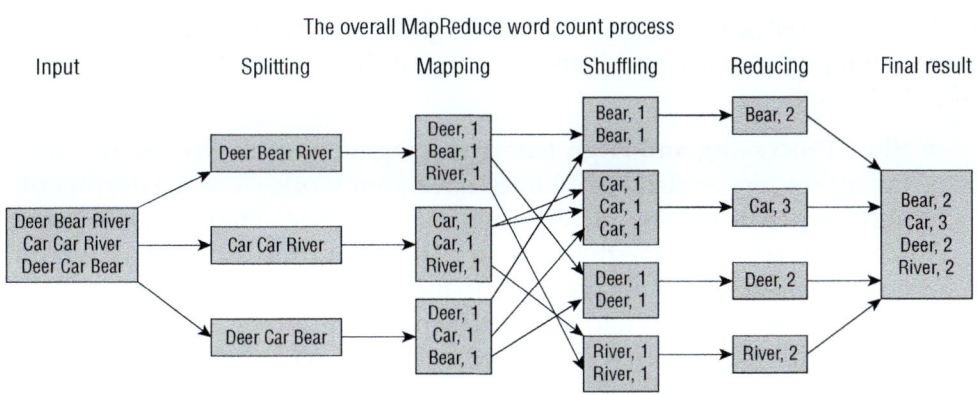

Figure 11-5: The MapReduce process

- **Input splitting:** Large data files in HDFS are divided into fixed-size blocks, typically 128 MB as discussed earlier, and each block is processed independently. If we had a 1 GB file, Hadoop would split that into about 8 blocks. Each block can then be processed independently and in parallel.
- **Map Phase:** Each block of data is fed into a Map function, which processes the input and emits key-value pairs in this format: word, countOfWord.

- **Shuffle and Sort:** The system automatically groups all values by key, shuffling them across nodes to prepare for the reduce phase. This ensures that all values associated with the same key are sent to the same reducer.

- **Reduce Phase:** Each reduce function takes the grouped key and associated list of values and processes them to output a result.

- **Output:** The final results are written back into HDFS or another storage system.

The entire process is parallelized and fault-tolerant. If any task fails, it can be restarted on another node without affecting the overall job. However, MapReduce is less popular today than Apache Spark, which is faster and more versatile. It's still foundational in many legacy systems and big data workflows, especially where batch processing of large datasets is required.

Yet Another Resource Negotiator—YARN

Hadoop YARN is a resource management and job scheduling system for Hadoop. It is responsible for allocating system resources like CPU and memory and also managing tasks across a cluster of machines. If a task fails, it's YARN's job to reschedule it on another node.

Limitations of Hadoop MapReduce

Hadoop MapReduce was great for handling large amounts of data, but it has some major performance problems that made it slow and inefficient. Let's discuss the limitations.

- **Slow Processing and High Latency:** Imagine you are writing an essay, but after every sentence, you must save your work, close the document, and reopen it before writing the next sentence. That's exactly how MapReduce worked. After each step in a data processing job, it would save results to disk before moving to the next step. Then, when it needed those results again, it had to read them back from the disk. This write-read-write-read process happened over and over, making everything very slow.

- **Not Ideal for Real-Time or Repeated Workloads:** MapReduce was not good for tasks that needed fast results or repeated calculations. Let's say you are learning a dance routine. If you had to read the instructions from a book before every move, you'd never finish. You'd rather remember the steps in your head and practice quickly. But MapReduce doesn't "remember" anything; each time it runs a step, it has to load everything from the disk again. This made it bad for real-time analytics and also for machine learning, where calculations needed to be repeated over and over again.

■ **Waste of Resources:** When a MapReduce job is finished, it releases the computer power it was using. If another job needed to run, it had to request computer power again from scratch. This caused gaps and delays between jobs, making things inefficient.

To address these limitations, Apache Spark was introduced.

Apache Spark

Apache Spark is an open source, distributed computing system designed for big data processing. It was born out of a need for faster data processing than what was possible with Hadoop MapReduce. In 2010, Spark was open sourced, and by 2014, it became a top-level Apache project. Its rise was fast and attracted a lot of attention because it could process data up to 100 times faster than Hadoop MapReduce, thanks to its in-memory computing capabilities. At its core, Spark is a distributed data processing engine that enables you to write applications in Java, Scala, Python, R, and SQL, which can run on a single machine or across clusters.

The foundational data structure in Spark is called a *resilient distributed dataset (RDD)*, as shown in Figure 11-6. Imagine you have a huge list of names that you want to process. If you use just one computer, it might take a long time. But if you split the list into smaller parts and give each part to a different computer, they can all work at the same time. This is what an RDD does: It splits a large dataset across multiple machines so that Spark can process it faster.

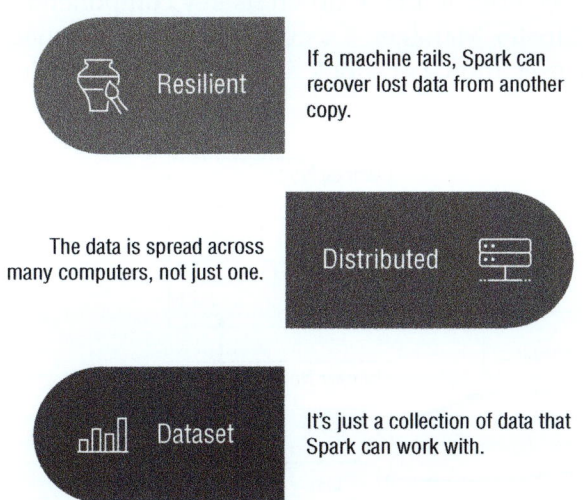

Figure 11-6: Apache Spark RDD description

When Spark loads data into an RDD from a file or database, the RDD divides the data into small chunks and spreads them across multiple computers. Spark then processes each chunk in parallel (all at once), making it very fast. Spark can also cache (store) RDDs in memory, so it doesn't have to reload data from disk each time, unlike Hadoop. Later on, Spark introduced easier and more user-friendly tools for working with data called DataFrames and Datasets. DataFrames are conceptually similar to tables in Excel, with rows and columns, making them intuitive for many users. Datasets provide a similar tabular structure but offer more control and type safety for programmers working in strongly typed languages like Scala. These tools help you better organize and understand data, especially when it has structures. However, in the architecture section that follows, we continue to refer to RDDs (resilient distributed datasets) because they form the fundamental low-level data structure underpinning Spark. Understanding RDDs is important for grasping how Spark achieves fault tolerance at its core, while also appreciating how DataFrames and Datasets have provided a more user-friendly and efficient way to work with data.

Another interesting thing about Spark is that it uses something called lazy evaluation. This means that when you tell Spark to do something with data, like to filter data or sort it, Spark doesn't do it immediately. Instead, it waits until you ask for the final result, like counting the data, aggregating or saving it, and then it quickly figures out the best way to do everything. This helps Spark save time and work more efficiently.

Apache Spark Architecture

The core of Spark's architecture is based on the driver–worker model. To understand how Spark executes tasks, we need to break down its key components, which are the Driver Program, Cluster Manager, Executors, and the internal mechanisms that coordinate task execution. Let's look at these components in detail in Figure 11-7.

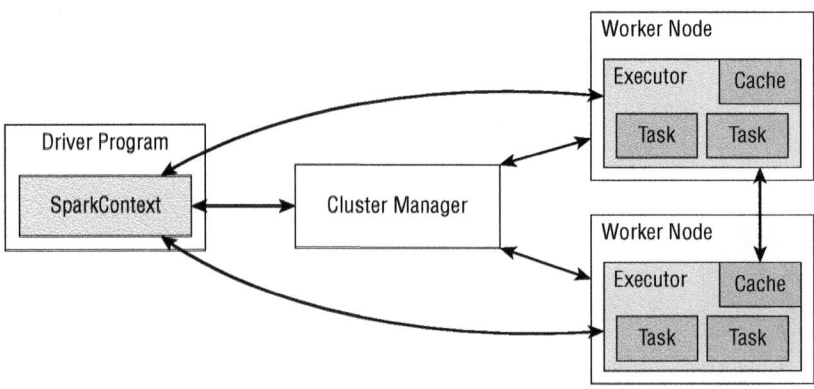

Figure 11-7: Apache Spark architecture

Driver Program

Every Spark application begins with a Driver Program, which serves as the central controller of execution. It runs the user's main function, defines the logic of data processing, and coordinates with other components to ensure smooth execution. The Driver Program initializes the SparkContext, which acts as the entry point for interacting with Spark. The SparkContext requests resources from the cluster and establishes communication between the Driver and the rest of the system.

A Spark job refers to the entire sequence of computations that is triggered when an action is called on a dataset. When a Spark job is submitted, the Driver analyzes the transformations applied to the data and constructs a directed acyclic graph (DAG), which is a logical representation of an execution plan. One of the main responsibilities of the Driver is managing the DAG of computations. This DAG determines the sequence of operations (such as functions applied to the data) and helps optimize how Spark executes tasks across the cluster.

Figure 11-8 is a DAG in Apache Spark that shows how Spark breaks your code into stages and connects them with dependencies. Let's understand what's happening in Stages 0–3.

Stage 0 begins the job by reading data using `newAPIHadoopFile`, which loads input from a Hadoop-compatible file system. Immediately after, a map transformation is applied to process each record individually. A map is commonly used for parsing the raw input into a structured format. The output of this stage is passed on to the next stages.

In Stage 1, a different dataset is loaded into an RDD named `newLogRDD`. This data undergoes two successive filter operations. These filters likely remove irrelevant or malformed records. The final filtered RDD from this stage is sent to Stage 2 for joining with other datasets.

Stage 2 is the most complex and central stage in the DAG. It has multiple branches converging. One branch receives input from both Stage 0 and Stage 1, and performs a cogroup, which most likely joins the two datasets on a common key. After the cogroup, a `mapValues` transformation reshapes the grouped values, and `flatMap` likely flattens the nested structure into a simpler form.

Simultaneously, another path in this stage reads additional data via `newAPIHadoopFile`, applies a filter, transforms it using map, and then combines it using union with the earlier transformed dataset. This union merges the two datasets into one cohesive RDD for further processing.

In the final stage, Stage 3, a `reduceByKey` operation aggregates the records, often used for summing up metrics or counting events per key. This is followed by a coalesce, which reduces the number of partitions, in order to optimize the performance when writing the final output.

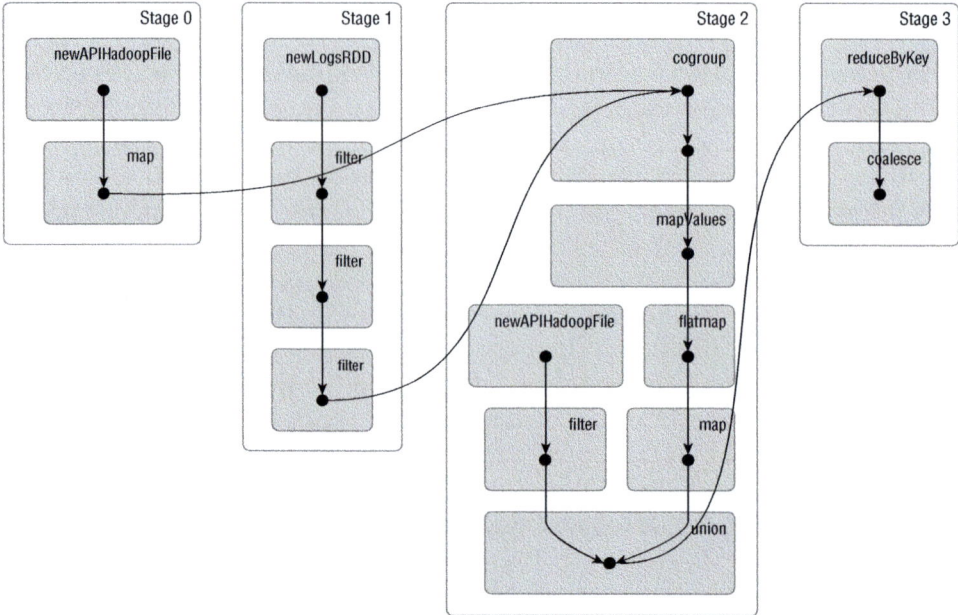

Figure 11-8: A DAG representing a simple Spark job

Cluster Manager

The Cluster Manager is the component responsible for managing and distributing resources across the cluster. It acts as a bridge between the Driver Program and the physical infrastructure, ensuring that resources such as CPU and memory are allocated efficiently.

When the Driver requests resources, the Cluster Manager assigns them by provisioning worker nodes within the cluster. Depending on the deployment mode, Spark can work with different types of cluster managers, like YARN, which is used in Hadoop ecosystems, Kubernetes for containerized workloads, or Spark's built-in Standalone Mode. Regardless of the specific cluster manager, its main role is to provide the necessary computing power for the Spark job to execute.

Executors

Once the Cluster Manager assigns resources, Spark launches executors on the worker nodes. Executors are distributed processes that perform the actual computations defined in the user's code. Each Spark application gets its own set of Executors, which are dedicated solely to that application and remain active for its duration.

Executors perform two primary functions, which are executing assigned tasks and storing intermediate data in memory or on disk. Tasks are the smallest units of execution in Spark and correspond to operations like mapping, filtering, or reducing data. The Driver schedules these tasks across available Executors based on the DAG, ensuring parallel execution to maximize efficiency. Since Executors also cache data, they enable Spark's in-memory computing capabilities, reducing the need to repeatedly read from disk and improving performance.

DAG Scheduler and Task Execution

Spark's execution process follows a structured pipeline. When a user writes transformations such as `.map()`, `.filter()`, or `.groupBy()`, Spark does not execute them immediately. Instead, it constructs a logical execution plan in the form of a DAG, as seen in Figure 11-8. This DAG captures all dependencies between transformations and helps Spark determine the most efficient way to execute the job. The DAG Scheduler is responsible for breaking down the execution plan into stages, where each stage contains tasks that can run in parallel. These stages are then passed to the Task Scheduler, which assigns individual tasks to Executors based on resource availability.

Understanding Spark's execution model is key to writing efficient and reliable Spark applications. The Driver Program orchestrates the workflow, the Cluster Manager allocates resources, Executors perform distributed computations, and the DAG Scheduler ensures optimized execution.

Apache Spark is a versatile distributed engine that supports a wide range of data engineering tasks, from batch processing to real-time analytics to even training and deploying ML models at scale. For any data engineer, learning Spark is non-negotiable. It opens the door to building scalable and efficient data pipelines that process massive datasets. In Table 11-1, you can see the comparison between Apache Spark and Hadoop across a couple of features.

Table 11-1: Comparing Apache Spark and Hadoop MapReduce

FEATURE	APACHE SPARK	HADOOP MAPREDUCE
Processing speed	Much faster, because it processes data in memory	Slower, because it writes intermediate data to the disk after every step
Data processing	Uses DAG to optimize and execute tasks efficiently	Uses a step-by-step process, meaning each task must finish before the next one starts
Storage	Stores data in memory, only writing to disk when necessary	Writes data to the disk after each step, which causes a higher read/write overhead
Language	Provides high-level APIs in Python, Scala, Java, and R, making it versatile	Requires writing low-level Java code

Continues

Table 11-1 (*continued*)

FEATURE	APACHE SPARK	HADOOP MAPREDUCE
Fault tolerance	Uses RDDs to automatically recover lost data	Uses HDFS replication (stores multiple copies of data across nodes)
Resource management	Uses YARN or Spark's resource manager	Uses YARN for resource allocation
Use case	Can handle batch, real-time, machine learning, and graph processing in one system	Mainly designed for batch processing
Machine learning support	Has a built-in ML library for AI/ML tasks	Has no built-in ML library
Adoption	Widely used in modern data engineering projects	An older technology, but is still used in legacy systems

Big Data File Types

When working with big data, you'll come across a variety of file types and formats, each suited for different storage, processing, and analysis needs. Big Data file types are data serialization formats designed to store and exchange data efficiently at scale, especially within big data ecosystems where data needs to move efficiently between components. *Data serialization* here is the process of converting data into a specific format that can be easily stored, transmitted, and reconstructed later.

These file types act as specialized containers for data, each designed for a specific purpose. Some focus on speed, others on compression, schema evolution, or query performance. The choice of file type directly affects storage efficiency, processing speed, and scalability. Let's explore some common file types:

- Avro
- Parquet
- ORC

Avro

Avro is a binary, row-based serialization format developed within the Apache Hadoop ecosystem. It stores both the data and its schema together in the same file, enabling schema evolution, which is the ability to change data structure over time without breaking systems.

As mentioned earlier, with Avro, data is serialized in a compact binary form. A separate schema that is usually defined in JSON format to describe the structure of the data, like its fields and data types. When reading the file, tools use this schema to deserialize the data correctly. Avro is ideal for write-heavy systems because it's a row-based format. When writing data, it writes rows sequentially, which is fast and efficient.

Strengths:

- Avro is efficient and compact due to its binary format.
- It has excellent support for schema evolution, allowing you to add or remove fields safely.
- It's good for write-heavy applications and row-wise operations.
- It can be used across different systems seamlessly, making it cross-platform.
- It's an excellent choice for real-time streaming projects.

Weaknesses:

- It's not human-readable, and it requires a tool to interpret.
- It's less efficient for column-based analytics.
- It requires schema management and understanding for proper use.

Parquet

Parquet is a columnar, binary file format designed for efficient data storage and analytical querying and is widely used in data lakes and analytics platforms. In analytics, you often query only a few columns out of many and Parquet stores data column by column instead of row by row. With this style of storage, Parquet reads only the columns you need, not the entire dataset, saving time and resources.

Parquet also applies compression and encoding techniques per column, which boosts efficiency. For example, if we have 100 rows with the same `country` value, `=United States, count=100"`. This reduces the file size and speeds up reading because less data needs to be loaded into memory.

Parquet files also store the schema inside the file itself. This makes it self-describing, so tools can automatically understand the data without needing external schema definitions. In contrast, Avro separates the schema from the data and the schema is maintained separately. Parquet files are ideal for analytics queries where users often need to read a few specific columns from large datasets.

Strengths:

- Parquet is highly compressed, saving storage costs.
- It is fast for queries involving specific columns, as only relevant data is read.
- It supports filtering data before reading it.
- It is compatible with many cloud storage solutions.

Weaknesses:

- It has slower writes due to the overhead of organizing data by columns.
- It is not suitable for small, frequent updates.
- It is not human-readable and not ideal for simple key-value lookups.

Optimized Row Columnar (ORC)

ORC is a high-performance columnar data storage format that stores data in an optimal way for column-based operations like filtering and aggregation. ORC is like a super-efficient way of storing big tables of data, especially when you have lots of rows and columns, like in a huge Excel sheet. Instead of storing all the data row by row, ORC organizes the data into sections called stripes.

As shown in Figure 11-9, each stripe contains many rows, but it stores the data in columns rather than rows. So, instead of having a whole row of data

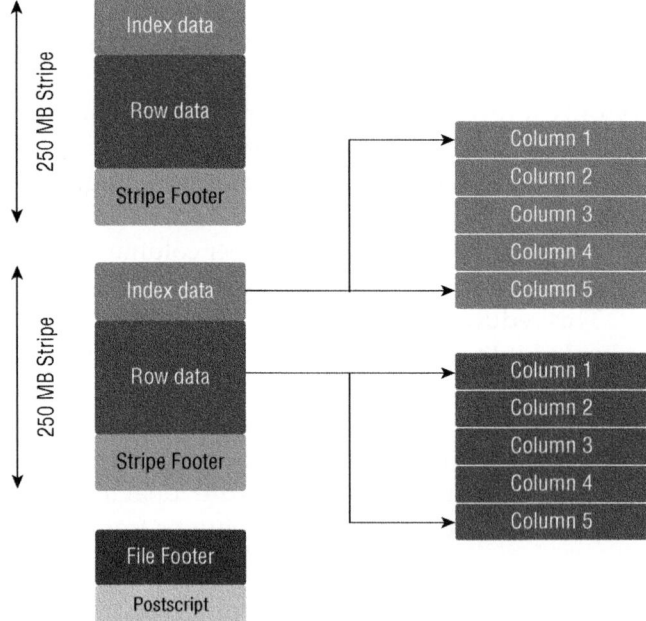

Figure 11-9: ORC file format

saved together, each column in a row is stored separately, making it easier and faster to access just the specific columns you need. This is helpful when you're working with big amounts of data and you want to perform operations like filtering or adding up numbers quickly, because the system doesn't have to load all the data, just the parts you're interested in.

ORC saves important metadata about the data, such as column names, types, and structures at the end of the file. This metadata helps tools quickly understand the content without reading the whole file.

Strengths:

- ORC has smaller file sizes than Parquet in many cases.
- It is optimized for fast reads and writes in Hive.
- It has built-in indexes and metadata for faster query execution.
- It also supports schema evolution.

Weaknesses:

- ORC has less cross-platform support outside the Hadoop ecosystem.
- Like Parquet, it is not ideal for write-heavy or streaming scenarios.
- ORC is not human-readable, and it requires processing tools to access and interpret its contents.

Choosing the File Type

Choosing the right file format is important when working in big data environments because efficiency, speed, and storage matter. While different file formats are designed for different use cases, using the right one can save money, speed up your system, and make your work easier. These are a few questions that would guide your decision.

1. **How Will You Use the Data?**
   Start by asking, "What am I going to do with this data?" If your goal is to run analytics or reports, formats like Parquet or ORC are perfect because they are fast and optimized for reading large amounts of data. If you are sharing data between systems or working with web APIs, then Avro is better because they are easier to use for sending and receiving data. For real-time streaming, like with Kafka, Avro is often the best option.

2. **Do You Need to Save Storage Space?**
   Some file formats compress data automatically, which helps save disk space and reduces storage costs, which is an important consideration for big data environments. If space-saving is important, choose Parquet, ORC, or Avro, as they support compression and they're efficient for storing and processing large datasets.

3. **Do You Want Faster Read Performance?**
   If you need to read or analyze data quickly, especially large datasets, you should choose a columnar format like Parquet or ORC. These formats allow your system to read only the columns it needs, which makes queries much faster.

4. **Do You Need to Include Schema in the File?**
   A schema is like a blueprint that describes the structure of your data, like what each field means and what type it is. Avro, Parquet, and ORC embed the schema inside the file, which helps tools read the data correctly and ensures consistency.

5. **Will Your Data Structure Change Over Time?**
   If your data's schema may evolve, for example, by adding new fields or changing data types, Avro is a smart choice. It is built to handle schema evolution, meaning it can manage changes over time without breaking. Parquet and ORC also support this, but Avro handles it best, especially in streaming systems.

6. **What Tools and Technologies Are You Using?**

   Your choice might depend on the tools or platforms you're using. For example, AWS technologies work best with Parquet. Hadoop often prefer ORC or Parquet, and Apache Kafka uses Avro widely.

Summary

- Big data refers to extremely large and complex datasets that traditional data processing tools cannot handle efficiently.

- Big data is characterized by five main properties, often called the five V's of big data: Value, Velocity, Veracity, Variety, and Volume.

- Volume refers to the amount of data being generated and stored, often on a massive scale.

- Velocity is the speed at which data is generated, transmitted, and processed.

- Big data varies in terms of how diverse it can be. It doesn't just come in only neat rows and columns.

- Veracity is all about the quality and reliability of the data you're working with.

- Value is about translating raw data into insights that result in decisions and actions that have a tangible impact on an organization or its customers.

- A distributed system is a collection of independent computers (or nodes) that work together as a single system to achieve a common goal.

- Key components of distributed systems are scalability, fault tolerance, reliability, availability, consistency, and resource management.

- Fault tolerance is the ability of a system to continue functioning even when some of its components fail.

- Reliability in distributed systems refers to the ability of a system to function correctly and consistently over time.

- Concurrency allows multiple tasks or users to access and use the system at the same time, independently, without interfering with each other.

- Resource management ensures tasks are allocated to different machines based on availability and workload.

- Consistency, in the context of distributed systems, ensures that all nodes in a distributed system have the same data at a given point in time.

- Availability ensures that the system is accessible and operational at all times, even in the presence of failures.

- Load balancers ensure that workloads are distributed across multiple nodes to prevent any single node from becoming overloaded.

- Latency is the time it takes for a request to get a response.

- There are two main types of scaling: horizontal and vertical. Horizontal scaling involves adding more machines to a system, whereas vertical scaling involves upgrading a single machine.

- In distributed systems, three consistency models exist: strong, eventual, and casual consistency. This design is due to how expensive achieving consistency can be.

- Distributed data processing is a method of handling large volumes of data by breaking data into smaller chunks and processing them across multiple computers working together.

- Some common frameworks help us achieve distributed data processing are Apache Hadoop, Spark, and Kafka.

- Hadoop is an open source framework that enables distributed storage and processing of large datasets using clusters of commodity hardware—affordable, regular computers.

- Apache Hadoop is powered by three main components: the Hadoop Distributed File System (HDFS); the processing engine, MapReduce; and the resource manager, Hadoop YARN.

- Hadoop Distributed File System (HDFS) is the primary storage system used by Hadoop for managing big data.

- MapReduce is the processing component of Hadoop, designed to generate and process large datasets in parallel across a distributed cluster of computers.

- Hadoop YARN is a resource management and job scheduling system for Hadoop.

- Due to the limitations of MapReduce, Apache Spark was introduced as a faster alternative due to its in-memory capabilities.

- Apache Spark is an open source, distributed computing system designed for big data processing.

- In Spark, a cluster manager is the component responsible for managing and distributing resources across the cluster and an executor is a distributed process that performs the actual computations defined in the user's code.

- There are three major big data file types: Parquet, Avro, and ORC. These file types act as specialized containers for data, each designed for a specific purpose. Some focus on speed; others on compression, schema evolution, or query performance.

- Avro is a binary, row-based serialization format developed within the Apache Hadoop ecosystem.

- Parquet is a columnar, binary file format designed for efficient data storage and analytical querying.

- ORC is a high-performance columnar data storage format that stores data in an optimal way for column-based operations like filtering and aggregation.

- The most important considerations for choosing a file type are understanding how the data would be used, the storage or performance concerns, and most importantly, the likelihood that the structure of your data will change over time.

Data Engineering on the Cloud

In the early days of computing, computers were very large and expensive. Organizations that could afford them had mainframes housed in dedicated rooms where the temperature was controlled, and users interacted with them through terminals. With this setup, every single byte of processing or storage was managed internally. As personal computers and servers became more affordable, many companies transitioned to building their on-premises (in-house) infrastructure. This meant buying physical servers, installing them in racks, and having a dedicated IT team to manage everything from hardware maintenance to software updates.

However, this setup had several limitations. First, it required heavy capital investment because companies had to predict their future computing needs, which, to be honest, often changed. If they underestimated, they couldn't handle sudden spikes in traffic. If they overestimated, they wasted money on hardware that won't be used. Second, maintaining on-premise systems was complex. IT teams had to worry about cooling, power supply, backups, disaster recovery, hardware failures, and security, all while trying to support the business's evolving data needs.

Later on, a game-changing idea began to emerge along with questions like, "What if companies could access computing power over the Internet?," without having to buy and maintain the hardware themselves. This idea wasn't entirely new, because something similar was happening during the time-sharing mainframe era, where multiple users could access a single mainframe computer at the same time, each from their terminal. These systems switched between users very quickly, so quickly that it felt like everyone had their dedicated machine, even though they were all sharing one big computer. But cloud computing did not become a reality until Amazon launched Amazon Web Services (AWS) in 2006. AWS became the first major player to successfully commercialize cloud computing at scale. With their services, developers could now store data and run machines virtually on demand, paying only for what they used.

This was revolutionary because it lowered the barrier to entry for startups and allowed large companies to become more agile. Soon after, Microsoft Azure and Google Cloud Platform (GCP) followed suit, along with IBM Cloud, Oracle Cloud, and others. Over the next decade, cloud providers kept adding services, not just machines that can be used virtually, but also databases, analytics tools, and developer-friendly services. This laid a good foundation for modern data engineering practices. The cloud wasn't just about hosting servers anymore; it became a powerful ecosystem that changed how we collect, process, store, and analyze data.

In this chapter, we will be exploring the following:

- Understanding the concept of the cloud
- Comparing cloud and on-premises setups for data storage and processing
- Exploring cloud service models
- Choosing between IaaS, Saas, and PaaS for different data engineering tasks
- Understanding object, block, and file storage for storing large-scale data
- Leveraging cloud-based compute services for data transformation
- Setting up virtual private clouds, subnets, and gateways for secure data movement
- Technical trade-offs between serverless, managed, and self-managed data infrastructure
- Best practices for optimizing cost for storage on the cloud

Cloud Computing

The *cloud* refers to a network of remote servers on the Internet that store, manage, and process data, rather than using a local computer or personal device. It is often referred to as "someone else's computer" because when you use the cloud, you're essentially renting storage, compute power, and other services on physical machines owned by cloud providers, and these machines are housed in massive data centers around the world. So essentially, you're using someone else's computer, just a very sophisticated one. *Cloud computing* refers to the on-demand delivery of IT resources and services over the Internet. Instead of owning and maintaining physical data centers and servers, companies can rent these resources and gain access to them any time and from anywhere.

In an organization, we generally consider two main development architectures: on-premise and cloud-based solutions. Both approaches serve the same goal, efficiently managing and processing data, but they differ significantly in how they handle infrastructure.

On-Premises

An *on-premises* setup is where data infrastructure is managed on physical hardware that resides within your organization's premises. This means you own the servers, storage devices, processing frameworks, and networking equipment, and you're in complete control of every aspect of your data engineering systems—data pipelines, ETL jobs, and storage.

The key advantage of on-premises solutions is control. Because the hardware and software are under your organization's roof, you can customize the architecture to your specific needs. There's also a sense of security because all the data stays within your internal network, reducing the exposure to external threats.

However, this all comes at a cost. The upfront capital expenses for buying physical hardware, setting up data centers, and ensuring that they are properly maintained can be expensive. You also need a dedicated team of engineers and systems administrators to manage the infrastructure, monitor performance, and handle scaling as your data needs grow.

Cloud

A *cloud-based* setup, on the other hand, involves using cloud service providers to host and manage your data infrastructure. These services provide preconfigured data storage, compute power, and other tools that you can use on demand.

One of the most significant advantages of cloud-based solutions is scalability. You can easily scale up or down based on demand without worrying about buying additional hardware. This flexibility is useful for businesses with fluctuating data needs. The cloud also provides a pay-as-you-go model, meaning you pay only for what you use, which can be a cost-effective solution for growing companies.

Another major benefit is the ease of setup. Cloud providers offer fully managed services for databases, storage, and data processing, which means you don't need to worry about setting up servers, configuring networks, or managing hardware.

From a security perspective, cloud providers invest heavily in securing their data centers and offer advanced security features like encryption, identity management, and compliance with various regulatory standards, and these usually exceed what many organizations can afford to implement themselves. However, this also means you're somewhat reliant on the provider for ensuring security and compliance, which can be a concern for businesses with very sensitive data.

Making the Right Choice

In summary, both on-premises and cloud-based data engineering have their strengths and weaknesses. On-premises may be the right choice for businesses that prioritize control, security, and compliance and have the resources to manage the infrastructure. Cloud-based solutions are ideal for organizations looking for scalability, flexibility, and reduced maintenance overhead, especially if they're growing or uncertain about their future needs. Many companies today adopt a hybrid approach, using both on-premises and cloud infrastructure to take advantage of the best of both worlds, depending on the type of data and the specific requirements of each project.

Core Cloud Concepts

Cloud computing is built on a set of core elements, and understanding these elements is key to knowing how everything fits together and helps you navigate the rest of this chapter better. Your data engineering workflows depend on how well you can leverage cloud infrastructure, and that starts with mastering the core concepts. In this section, we'll break down the following concepts:

- Storage
- Compute
- Networking

Storage

Cloud storage is one of the foundational elements of modern data engineering. It allows us to store and manage massive amounts of data without the need for on-premises hardware like traditional hard drives or servers. The beauty of cloud storage lies in its scalability, which is important because we work with large datasets that are constantly growing.

When we talk about cloud storage, we're usually referring to services provided by cloud providers. These platforms provide various storage solutions designed to support different use cases and performance needs. There are different ways to organize and store data depending on your needs. The three primary types of cloud storage are object, block, and file storage, as shown in Figure 12-1. Each type offers unique advantages and is better suited for different scenarios.

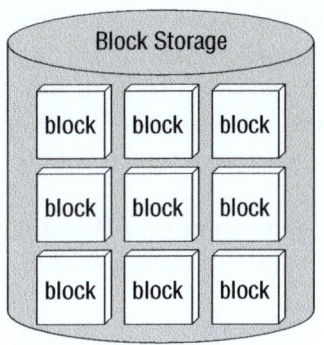 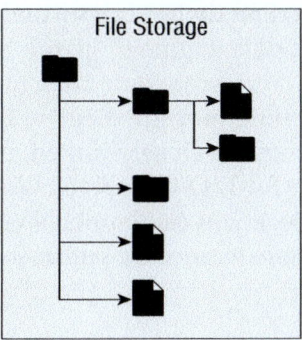 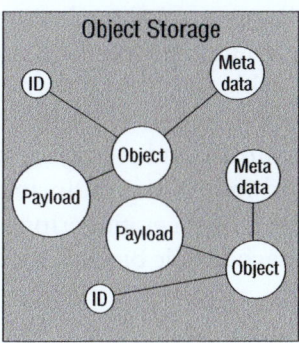

Figure 12-1: Cloud storage models

Object Storage

Object storage is one of the most popular forms of storage in the cloud. It is designed to store large amounts of unstructured data such as files, images, or videos. Unlike traditional filesystems that use folders and files, object storage manages data as objects, where each object consists of the data itself, metadata, and a unique identifier called an object ID, as shown in Figure 12-1, and this data is usually accessed by an API.

How does this work? Instead of saying "go to folder X and open file Y," you say, "give me object 12345 from bucket Z." This type of storage is ideal for highly scalable storage because it has a flat structure, and there's no folder-tree system to manage, which makes it suitable for long-term archiving, big data analytics, and storing files that don't need to be accessed quickly or regularly.

A great example is when raw IoT data or clickstream logs are stored in Amazon S3, Google Cloud Storage, or Azure Blob Storage, to be later processed by tools like Spark or Databricks.

Block Storage

Block storage is similar to the hard drives you might have in a local server. As you can see in Figure 12-1, it stores data in chunks, or blocks, and each block has its own address. This makes block storage more like a traditional filesystem; when a file is uploaded, it is split into blocks, and each block is stored individually and given a unique ID/address. When the file is read or written, the system finds the relevant blocks, assembles them, and serves the file with the operating system or database managing the logic and structure.

Block storage is typically used when you need fast access to data. For example, if you're running a database, block storage is often the preferred choice because it allows for quick reads and writes. It's also useful when you need to set up custom filesystems that are not supported by object storage. Block storage allows you to attach storage directly to your virtual machines (VMs), enabling low-latency access to data. In data engineering, this is important because certain workloads, like performing large-scale data transformations, require fast, consistent access to disk. Attaching storage directly to the VM ensures that the compute and storage resources are closely linked, minimizing network delays and improving performance for I/O-intensive tasks.

In a data engineering project, you can launch a virtual machine on AWS and attach Elastic Block Store to store temporary intermediate files during a Spark job.

File Storage

File storage, also known as file-level storage, is one of the most familiar types of storage. If you think about how you store files on your computer, that's essentially how file storage works in the cloud. It's based on the traditional filesystem structure, where data is stored in files and folders. In a cloud environment, file storage allows you to organize and manage data just like you would in a directory on your personal computer but with the added benefits of scalability and reliability.

In file storage, the system hierarchically manages the data, meaning that data is organized within folders (directories), and each file has a specific name and path. File storage is typically used when you need to share files or access them in a structured, organized way, especially when multiple machines or users need to access the same files simultaneously. Using Azure Files or Amazon EFS (Elastic File System) to store shared ETL scripts or job logs for a team of data engineers working on Airflow DAGs is an example of how file storage is used.

Key Factors for Choosing a Cloud Storage Solution

When working with cloud infrastructure, choosing the right type of storage is important. Let's compare the various types of storage under these key factors:

- Scalability
- Performance
- Cost
- Use case

Scalability

Object storage is known mostly for its scalability. Since it's built to handle large volumes of unstructured data, as your data needs expand, it scales horizontally by distributing data across multiple nodes and regions. This makes object storage ideal for workloads that experience significant data growth over time, such as media libraries, log storage, and backup systems.

Block storage also scales well but has a different approach. Block storage tends to scale vertically, meaning you have to increase the size of individual storage units or attach more blocks to the system. While it's still highly scalable, it can require more management and planning.

File storage can scale, but it's not as straightforward as object or block storage. File storage is often limited by the underlying filesystem, which may have restrictions on the number of files or the amount of data that can be handled efficiently. It is best suited for applications that require filesystem semantics and don't need to scale to the extreme levels that object storage can achieve.

Performance

In data engineering, performance is critical when choosing the right storage type for a given workload. Object storage, like Amazon S3 or Azure Blob Storage, is highly scalable and cost-effective, making it ideal for storing large volumes of raw or processed data. However, it doesn't provide the fastest access speeds because each object must be retrieved via a unique identifier, which can introduce latency. This is acceptable for batch processing but not ideal for real-time analytics or low-latency tasks.

Block storage, on the other hand, offers the best performance. Since it stores data in fixed-size blocks and allows direct read/write access, it's ideal for I/O-intensive data engineering tasks, such as running relational databases or high-speed data transformation jobs using Spark on virtual machines.

File storage falls in between. It supports structured, hierarchical file access and is useful when multiple data engineering jobs or users need shared access to scripts, datasets, or logs. While it performs better than object storage in these scenarios, it may not scale or respond quickly enough for large-scale, high-throughput processing pipelines.

Cost

Cost is one of the biggest advantages of object storage. Due to its distributed nature and simple architecture, object storage is very cost-effective. Cloud providers offer pricing models that allow you to store data at different price points based on how frequently you need to access it. Infrequently accessed data can be stored at a much lower cost.

Block storage is generally more expensive than object storage because it's optimized for high performance. Pricing for block storage depends on factors like the type of volume and storage capacity. While it provides excellent performance, the cost can become significant.

File storage falls between object and block storage in terms of cost. It's more expensive than object storage because it includes the overhead of maintaining a filesystem structure, but it's generally more affordable than block storage.

Use Case

Object storage is the go-to solution for massive amounts of unstructured data. It's a perfect choice for cloud backups, media and entertainment content, log storage, and data lake environments. If you're dealing with a situation where data is accessed infrequently but needs to be durable and stored for the long term, object storage is your best bet. It is optimized for scalability and cost-efficiency when storing this kind of data.

Block storage is best suited for performance-intensive applications. It's commonly used for databases, virtual machines, and high-performance applications that need low-latency data access. It's also the ideal choice for environments where the data needs to be frequently written to or updated. In data engineering workflows, especially when maintaining source systems or staging transactional data, databases like PostgreSQL or MySQL require fast, consistent input/output operations per second. Block storage offers low-latency access and high throughput, which are critical for frequent reads and writes.

File storage is optimal when you need a traditional filesystem structure with directories and files. It's commonly used for applications that require access to shared files, such as content management systems, home directories, or network drives. Many businesses use file storage for collaboration tools where multiple users need to access and update files in a familiar structure. When data engineers work in teams, they often share transformation scripts, configuration files, or documentation. These require a traditional folder structure and simultaneous access from multiple machines or users. File storage provides this shared filesystem environment.

Compute

Compute services on the cloud provide the processing power needed to run applications, perform calculations, and handle workloads. In data engineering, compute services on the cloud provide the processing power required to ingest, transform, and analyze large volumes of data. These services can be used to run ELT jobs on distributed data processing frameworks like Apache Spark, execute SQL queries in cloud warehouses, and orchestrate complex workflows across multiple stages of the data pipeline. We will be discussing virtual machines and containers.

Virtual Machines

Virtual machines are cloud-hosted computers that you can spin up on demand. They give you full control, you choose the operating system, install your tools, and configure your environment. It's like having your server but without the physical hardware. Virtual machines are ideal for workloads that require customization. A common use case for virtual machines is setting up a custom ETL environment using tools like Apache Airflow, Python libraries, or Spark clusters that require specific configurations. For example, if you're processing large CSV files with custom logic using Pandas and need to schedule jobs with Airflow, a virtual machine allows you to install all dependencies, tune performance settings, and manage the pipeline exactly how you want.

Virtual machines give you a lot of flexibility and control when you're testing new tools, working with complex dependencies, or need to manage resource allocation. The trade-off, of course, is that you're responsible for managing the OS, applying patches, and handling scale manually. A best practice is to use VMs when you need customization or isolation.

Containers

Imagine you're working on a data pipeline that processes marketing analytics data, and different teams are responsible for different parts of the pipeline. One team writes the ingestion scripts in Python, and another handles transformations using Java. Although this division of labor works in theory, things get messy fast when all these jobs are deployed into the same environment.

You start to run into version conflicts; some people use Python 3.9, others use 3.10. Java libraries might clash. Dependency issues show up, and soon, someone drops the dreaded line, "But it works on my machine." This slows down development and makes debugging painful, especially in fast-moving projects.

To solve this, we use containers. A container is a lightweight, portable unit that packages your code, its dependencies, and its runtime environment into a single executable unit. Each stage of the pipeline is containerized. What this means is that every team packages their code, dependencies, and environment. These containers are like sealed boxes: they include everything needed to run the job and behave the same way whether they're running on a developer's laptop or in a cloud production environment.

Networking

In traditional infrastructure, networks consist of routers, switches, and physical cables that connect machines. In the cloud, we use virtual networks, software-defined systems that mimic those physical networks. A network is a collection of connected devices like servers, databases, or containers that can communicate with each other. It allows different services you create to talk to each other securely and efficiently. If a network isn't set up correctly, your pipeline might fail to move data, connect to databases, or even start at all.

As a data engineer, learning networking fundamentals is essential because modern data systems are highly distributed and cloud-based. Here are a few ways a good networking knowledge can be helpful:

- In data movement, you would work with data that flows between multiple sources, processing tools, and storage. So understanding network latency and protocols helps you build efficient pipelines.

- Networking knowledge is key to securing your data. You'll need to configure VPCs, subnets, and access rules to control how services talk to each other, especially in the cloud.

- When your pipeline fails or slows down, networking is often the bottleneck. Knowing how to check connectivity or port blocks can save hours of debugging.

- Tools like Airflow, Spark clusters, and Kafka often run across multiple nodes in the cloud. You'll need to understand how these services discover and communicate with each other over internal IPs.

Let's explore key networking concepts through the lens of data movement to help you understand how it fits into your day-to-day operations:

- Virtual private cloud (VPC)
- Subnets
- IP addresses
- Gateways

Virtual Private Cloud (VPC)

A virtual private cloud (VPC) is your isolated network space within a cloud provider. It functions like a private data center that you fully control, allowing you to define which services are allowed to communicate and how traffic flows. For instance, you might deploy your ETL jobs, storage systems, and databases all inside the same VPC to keep traffic private and secure. This isolation is useful when building data pipelines, as it ensures that components like your ingestion layer, transformation jobs, and output targets can interact with a high security. You can configure your pipeline to access an internal dataset without ever exposing it to the public Internet, keeping compliance and data governance in check. As shown in Figure 12-2, VPC ensures that your services don't interact with the public Internet unless explicitly allowed, which is important for protecting sensitive data.

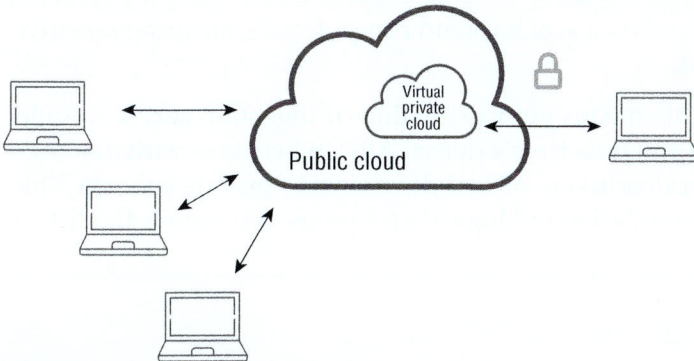

Figure 12-2: A virtual private cloud

Subnets

Inside a virtual private cloud, which acts like your personal data center in the cloud, you don't just throw all your resources into one big space. Instead, you divide that space into smaller segments called subnets, as shown in Figure 12-3. You can think of a subnet as a room within a house. A subnet (short for subnetwork) allows you to group related resources together. For example, you might have, one subnet that holds your compute resources and another subnet that holds your databases. For data engineers, this segmentation is crucial because it helps control which parts of your data pipeline are exposed to the Internet and which remain protected.

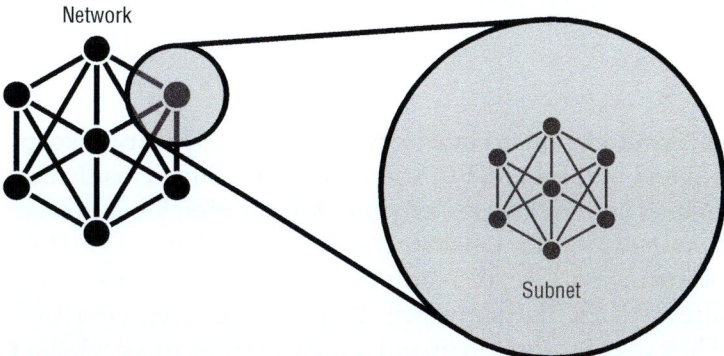

Figure 12-3: A subnet

There are two types of subnets:

- *Public* subnets can access the Internet and are commonly used for resources that need to fetch updates or interact with APIs.

- *Private* subnets are restricted to internal communication and are ideal for databases, data warehouses, or backend compute jobs, ensuring sensitive data stays isolated.

For data engineers, this means your extraction or ingestion services could run in public subnets to pull data from external APIs, whereas sensitive storage and transformation workloads stay locked down inside private subnets. This setup creates security boundaries and logical groupings that reduce the risk of accidental exposure.

IP Addresses

Each resource in a VPC, whether it's a virtual machine, a container, or a database, has an IP address. These addresses serve as the unique identifier that allows one service to communicate with another. There are two types of IP addresses: private IPs, which are used for communication inside the VPC, and public IPs, which are used to communicate with the Internet. In your day-to-day, you will often need to configure your jobs to talk to databases or APIs using their IP addresses. Knowing whether to use a private or public IP is important for ensuring access and maintaining security. Using the correct IP type is important. Your ETL jobs and data processing clusters should typically use private IPs to connect securely within the VPC, avoiding unnecessary exposure to the Internet. Conversely, when your pipeline needs to pull data from an external source, you'll configure public IPs to allow outbound Internet access without exposing your internal resources. A practical way to observe this is when provisioning cloud resources, you'll often need to reference or configure IP addresses to establish network connectivity between multiple services.

Gateways

In a cloud environment, your virtual private cloud is like a walled city. It keeps your infrastructure isolated and secure. But sometimes, the things inside that city, like your data pipeline, your databases, or your orchestration tools, need to communicate with the outside world, whether it's fetching code from GitHub, sending logs to a monitoring service, or reading data from S3. That's where gateways come in. Gateways act like controlled doorways between your VPC and other networks. They decide who can go out, who can come in, or whether communication stays internal or reaches the broader Internet. In a typical data engineering workflow, your pipelines don't just sit still. They talk to APIs, download packages, access external data, and interact with cloud storage and databases. If the right gateway isn't configured, your job will fail, not because of your logic, but because your code couldn't even reach what it needed. Learning how to configure gateways correctly is critical because your pipelines often depend on external services for data ingestion, dependency management, or monitoring. Without proper gateway setup, your ETL jobs might fail not due to logic errors, but because they cannot reach these essential external resources.

Cloud Service Models

Having covered the core cloud concepts, let's now explore cloud service models. These models define the various ways cloud computing services are delivered to users. They describe the layers of responsibility between the cloud service provider and the customer. In these models, the cloud provider offers a variety of resources, from infrastructure to fully managed applications, and the customer chooses the level of control and responsibility they want. These models are designed to help businesses and individuals access computing resources in a flexible and cost-effective way without needing to manage physical hardware or complex IT infrastructure. In data engineering, cloud service models shape how much of the data infrastructure you're responsible for building and managing yourself, versus what the cloud provider handles for you. At the core, it's about deciding where you want to spend your time, maintaining systems or building data solutions.

The three primary cloud service models are:

- Infrastructure as a service (IaaS)
- Platform as a service (PaaS)
- Software as a service (SaaS)

Infrastructure as a Service

As seen in Figure 12-4, the *Infrastructure as a Service (IaaS)* model provides the foundational building blocks of cloud computing. It offers virtualized hardware resources, like servers, storage, and networking, on a pay-as-you-go basis. In this service model, users are responsible for managing everything from the operating system upward, which means they install, configure, and maintain the operating system applications, runtime, and data. Here, you're deeply involved in setting up environments for data storage, processing, and scheduling. Imagine you're building a pipeline to process millions of product transaction records daily. In an IaaS model, you provision virtual machines (software-based emulations of physical computers), configure the operating system, install processing frameworks, and manage your own job scheduler.

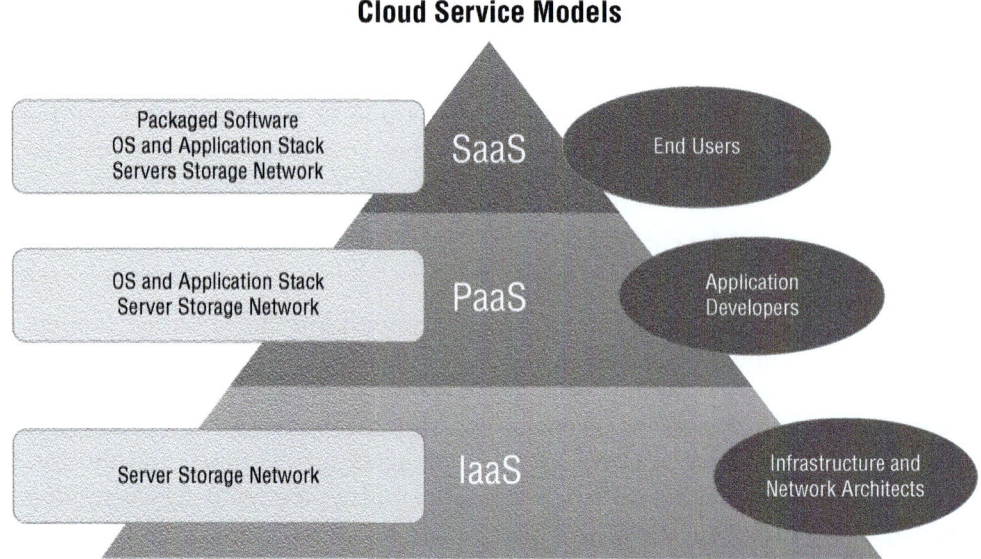

Cloud Service Models

Figure 12-4: Cloud service models

The main advantage of IaaS is its high flexibility and control. Since you have full access to the infrastructure, you can customize the environment to fit specific requirements. For example, say you're working on a batch data pipeline that processes CSV files from multiple clients. You set up virtual machines, choose the exact version of Python you want, install libraries like Pandas or PySpark, and write custom scripts. However, the downside is that you are also responsible for maintaining and updating everything, which requires technical expertise, but this model is a good fit when you need a tailored solution and have a capable technical team.

Platform as a Service

The *platform as a service (PaaS)* model sits one level above IaaS, as shown in Figure 12-4. With the PaaS model, the cloud provider manages the infrastructure, operating system, and runtime, leaving users to focus solely on developing and deploying their applications. It abstracts away the infrastructure and gives us a platform to develop, run, and manage our applications. This is a dream for engineers who don't want to worry about server configurations or scaling issues and want to get apps to market fast without dealing with infrastructure management. In platform-based models, you focus more on designing and running data workflows. The underlying systems, like compute, scaling, and scheduling, are already handled. In the scenario we mentioned in IaaS, you define the logic of your ETL pipeline using a built-in framework, and the platform handles the scheduling, scaling, and underlying compute. You spend less time managing servers and more time refining data transformations and ensuring quality.

A popular example of PaaS for data engineering is Google Cloud Composer (a managed Apache Airflow service), Azure Data Factory, or AWS Glue Studio, which allow engineers to build and schedule data workflows without managing the underlying infrastructure. The biggest benefit of PaaS is increased productivity. You can deploy data processing jobs using tools like Apache Airflow or build data APIs using FastAPI, without worrying about servers or underlying infrastructure, which makes it best suited for startups or teams focused on rapid development. On the flip side, PaaS can sometimes limit your control over configurations or the environment, which might be a challenge for legacy applications. If your pipelines rely on very specific configurations or custom dependencies, PaaS might limit your control over the runtime environment.

Software as a Service

Software as a service (SaaS) is the most accessible and widely used model. With Saas, the cloud provider delivers fully functional software over the Internet, which users access through a web browser or app. Think of it as buying a subscription to an app that solves a specific business problem. We're talking about ready-made, fully managed software applications. All the underlying infrastructure, operating systems, and software updates are handled by the provider. With SaaS models, the priority shifts almost entirely to the data itself, defining what to extract, how to transform it, and where to deliver it. The infrastructure is abstracted away. Your job becomes more about ensuring correctness, speed, and efficiency in delivering insights. You simply configure a data workflow through a web interface, set your source, define some basic transformations, and specify where the output should go. You don't worry about how jobs are executed behind the scenes. SaaS tools like Snowflake, BigQuery, or Fivetran simplify many tasks by abstracting infrastructure, offering built-in scalability, and enabling fast querying or integration with minimal setup.

The key strength of SaaS is its simplicity and convenience. These platforms are ideal when you need to move quickly, ingest data from multiple sources, or collaborate with nontechnical teams. It's also cost-effective because most SaaS tools follow a subscription-based model. While Saas offers a great out of the box, it offers the least flexibility; you can't customize the application beyond the options the provider gives you, because the software is designed to do a specific thing. Moreover, since your data is stored on the provider's servers, it raises privacy concerns, especially in industries with strict data regulations like healthcare or finance. You may have limited visibility into how and where your data is stored, which makes it harder to enforce encryption standards and access control. SaaS is perfect for everyday users and businesses looking for ready-to-use solutions that don't require technical intervention.

Choosing Between IaaS, PaaS, and SaaS

Choosing the right cloud service model isn't a one-size-fits-all situation. In Figure 12-5, we can see what you manage and what the service provider manages under the different models. The choice depends on what the business is trying to accomplish, the level of control needed, how experienced the team is, and the business's long-term goals.

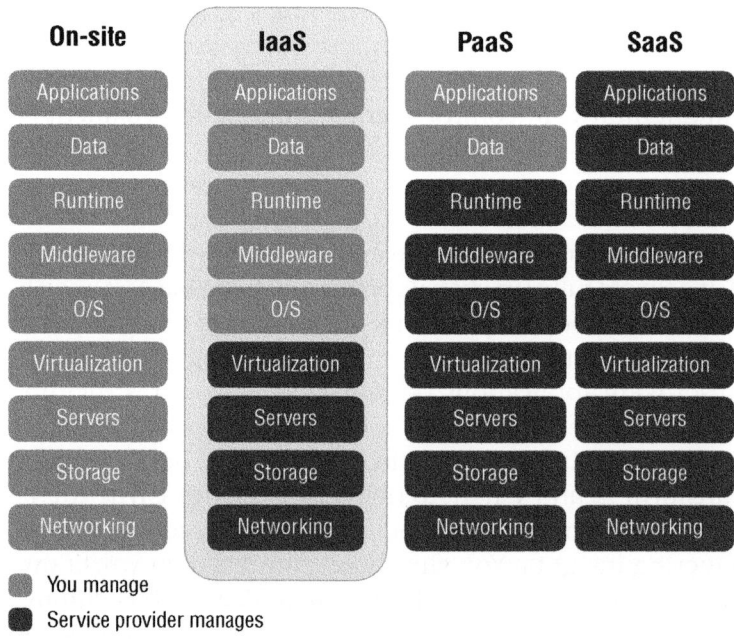

Figure 12-5: Comparing IaaS, SaaS, and PaaS

Let's look at some of the factors you must consider when you decide which model is appropriate for your situation.

Your Organization's Needs

The first step is to analyze your organization's needs, especially around data volume, velocity, processing complexity, and security requirements. In data engineering, the decision between IaaS, PaaS, and SaaS goes beyond just technical expertise or control; it's about how much of the data infrastructure you need to manage directly. If your team has technical skills in handling large-scale data processing like building custom Spark clusters or managing Kafka infrastructure, IaaS provides the control needed to fine-tune performance, manage networking for secure data pipelines, and scale storage and compute independently. It's best suited for organizations building bespoke data platforms from scratch.

If your priority is speeding up data pipeline development and reducing maintenance overhead, PaaS solutions like Google Cloud Composer or Azure Data Factory enable engineers to focus on data workflows rather than provisioning infrastructure. This model supports mid-sized teams or projects where data orchestration, ingestion, and transformation are key, but the team prefers a managed environment.

For teams looking to move fast with minimal setup, SaaS tools like Snowflake, BigQuery, or Fivetran handle most of the heavy lifting like data storage, scaling, patching, and even parts of data transformation, making them ideal for small teams or nontechnical users integrating data into dashboards and business intelligence (BI) tools. However, they may fall short if your organization needs deep customization, granular security control, or advanced lineage tracking.

In terms of flexibility, IaaS offers full control, ideal for custom ETL jobs, advanced monitoring, and optimizing performance at scale. PaaS offers balance, with flexibility over logic and workflows but limitations in infrastructure tuning. SaaS is the most rigid, optimized for ease of use but less suited to organizations needing fine-grained control over data architecture, transformation logic, or privacy compliance.

Cost Efficiency

Cost is a significant factor when choosing a cloud service model. IaaS may seem cost-effective at first, but keep in mind that managing infrastructure comes with its costs, both in terms of time and money. You'll need to invest in a skilled team to manage everything, and if you're not careful, scaling can get expensive. For data engineering teams, this means budgeting not just for storage and compute but also for monitoring tools, cluster tuning, and data transfer between zones or services, especially when working with large datasets.

PaaS simplifies many aspects of management, which can lower overhead costs. With managed services for orchestration, transformation, and pipeline scheduling, you can reduce engineering effort, but you'll pay for convenience, especially when running frequent or complex data workflows. But depending on how much you use the platform, costs can rise as your needs grow. SaaS usually comes with predictable pricing models in the form of subscriptions, and it's often the most affordable option upfront, especially for smaller businesses. For example, using a SaaS data warehouse like Snowflake or BigQuery can help eliminate infrastructure concerns, but pay-per-query or storage usage models mean that poorly optimized queries or unnecessary data scans can drive up costs quickly. However, depending on how many licenses you need, the costs can add up.

Security

IaaS offers more control over security, but you'll be responsible for managing the security of your virtual machines, storage, and applications. This means you must secure your data processing environments, databases, and storage layers yourself, ensuring data encryption, access controls, and compliance are properly configured. If your security needs are complex and you have the right expertise, IaaS gives you flexibility. PaaS simplifies security, but you'll still need to handle security at the application level. This is often the case with managed data platforms and ETL services, where the cloud provider secures the underlying infrastructure, but data engineers need to secure data pipelines, manage user permissions, and enforce data governance policies. The platform provider secures the infrastructure, but your application's security is still your responsibility. SaaS takes care of security and compliance for you, which is great if you're dealing with sensitive data, but you have to ensure your provider meets your specific compliance requirements. This is important for data engineers who rely on SaaS analytics or reporting tools handling sensitive datasets. You must validate that the provider's compliance certifications align with your organization's data privacy requirements.

Scalability

At some point, your organization would need to increase or decrease its IT resources based on demand. IaaS and PaaS are built to scale quickly. This means being able to scale data processing clusters, storage capacity, and ETL workflows to handle growing volumes of data or spikes in query load. But scaling infrastructure with IaaS can require more manual intervention and careful planning to avoid bottlenecks. Data engineers using IaaS might need to provision additional servers, optimize distributed computing resources, or reconfigure data storage solutions to maintain pipeline performance. PaaS handles a lot of the scaling automatically, so it's a great choice if you need quick and seamless scaling without worrying too much about the infrastructure behind it, allowing data engineers to focus more on building data transformations and analytics rather than managing compute resources. SaaS is typically easy to scale for user numbers or features, but it's not as customizable when it comes to optimizing performance for your specific needs. This means SaaS tools may be suitable for scaling dashboards or reporting usage quickly, but data engineers may find them limiting if they need fine-tuned control over data processing performance or complex pipeline customization.

Time to Deploy

The faster you can deploy a solution, the sooner you can start benefiting from it. Time to deploy refers to how long it takes to set up, configure, and implement a cloud solution before it's ready for use. IaaS will take more time to set up and configure. This means setting up servers and installing and configuring data processing frameworks, databases, and security settings, all of which can extend deployment timelines for data pipelines or analytics environments. You need to prepare the environment and configure everything, which can slow down deployment. PaaS is quicker to set up, especially if you just need a platform to develop your applications. This allows data engineering teams to rapidly deploy managed data warehouses, ETL tools, or streaming platforms with minimal configuration. Much of the environment is already preconfigured for you. SaaS is the fastest. Since everything's ready to go, you can implement the solution right away and start using it. This is especially useful for data engineers who want to quickly spin up analytics dashboards without worrying about infrastructure setup.

Integration with Existing Systems

Many organizations already have legacy systems in place, and making sure your cloud solution works smoothly with these systems helps everything run without any issues. If you have existing legacy systems or specific requirements, IaaS may be the best choice. IaaS allows you to customize and configure your infrastructure to connect legacy databases, on-premises data warehouses, or custom data sources, enabling seamless data ingestion and processing across hybrid environments. You can integrate your infrastructure as needed and ensure it fits with your current systems. PaaS might require more effort for integration, especially if the platform doesn't support some of your legacy systems. This can mean data engineers must find work-arounds to connect managed data services with older systems, which can add complexity to pipeline development. SaaS is easiest to integrate if it fits into your workflow. But if it doesn't, integration could be challenging. Data engineers relying on SaaS analytics or ETL tools benefit from quick setup when SaaS aligns with existing workflows, but they may struggle if the SaaS lacks connectors or APIs for legacy data sources, limiting data accessibility or requiring additional integration layers.

Long-Term Strategy

Lastly, organizations need flexibility to grow and innovate. Picking a cloud solution that doesn't align with your long-term goals prevents you from scaling, customizing, or adapting as your business changes. A long-term strategy defines how well a cloud solution can adapt and grow with your organization's evolving needs over time. If you plan to build custom applications, scale infrastructure, or pivot your tech stack, IaaS and PaaS are better suited. For data engineering teams, this means choosing platforms that can handle growing data volumes, evolving pipeline complexity, and new analytics requirements without forcing costly migrations or redesigns. SaaS is perfect for short-term or specific business needs but may require switching to a more customizable solution if your requirements grow. Data engineers might initially use SaaS BI or data integration tools for quick wins but may later need to migrate to PaaS or IaaS solutions for greater control over data workflows, performance tuning, and compliance.

A Hybrid Approach

Ultimately, it's all about what works best for your team, your current needs, and where you want to be in the future. It's not always an either-or choice; you could use a combination of all three, depending on what different parts of your organization require. In many real-world scenarios, organizations use a mix of all three models because each model provides different levels of abstraction and control. Data engineering often leverages a hybrid approach, using IaaS for custom data infrastructure, PaaS for managed data platforms, and SaaS for analytics and visualization, to balance agility, control, and speed across their data ecosystem.

Cloud Management Models

While cloud service models define what kind of service the provider delivers, cloud management models define the level of operational responsibility shared between the user and the cloud provider. This relationship varies across the three main service models, IaaS, PaaS, and SaaS, with increasing levels of management responsibility handled by the provider as you move from IaaS to SaaS. In other words, the chosen service model directly influences the management model, determining how much control the user retains versus how much operational burden the cloud provider assumes. As organizations adopt cloud services, one of the key decisions they face is how much control they want over their infrastructure versus how much responsibility they're willing to offload to the cloud provider. These models, which offer flexibility based on business needs, technical skillsets, and scalability goals, are as follows:

- Serverless
- Managed
- Self-managed

Serverless

Serverless represents an architecture where cloud providers manage all the infrastructure, like servers, so you don't have to worry about any of it. The concept is simple: You write functions or small pieces of code that are executed in response to specific events, and the cloud automatically handles the rest.

Let's say you're building a system where data is continuously flowing, and maybe users are uploading files or new records and they are being added to a database. In such cases, a serverless model works like a charm. For data engineers, this means you can build event-driven data pipelines that automatically process incoming data without managing or provisioning servers, which simplifies scaling and reduces operational overhead. Every time a file is uploaded, it triggers a serverless function to process that file, maybe converting it into a different format or extracting some data from it. The beauty of this is that you don't need to have a server running 24/7, waiting for someone to upload a file. You just let the serverless function fire up automatically when that event happens, and it processes the task quickly; this makes it event-driven.

Another good scenario is when you have small, stateless tasks, meaning the task doesn't need to remember anything between executions. For example, suppose you have a function that checks whether new records in a database meet certain criteria, and, if they do, sends an email notification. This task is fast and doesn't require any complex database state to be stored. Serverless is perfect for that; you just write the logic, and the platform takes care of everything else. In data engineering, this enables lightweight transformations, validations, or alerts within pipelines, allowing you to build scalable and cost-efficient workflows that respond immediately to data changes or anomalies.

Challenges with Serverless

The serverless model does have some challenges:

Cold Start Latency   One of the big downsides of serverless is the cold start problem. If a function hasn't been triggered for a while, it can take a few seconds to warm up when it's called again, adding an unnecessary delay. For data engineering workloads that require near-real-time processing or low-latency responses, cold starts can introduce unwanted delays in event-driven data pipelines, and this may also impact the freshness of data insights.

Limited Execution Time   Serverless functions often have time limits on how long they can run. If you need to process a huge file or run a long-running task, serverless might not be the best fit because your function could time out before finishing. Large-scale ETL jobs or complex batch data transformations often exceed typical serverless time limits, so data engineers may need to rely on other compute options like containerized jobs or managed clusters for those workloads.

Complex Debugging   Since you don't have direct access to the underlying infrastructure, debugging can be tricky. If something goes wrong, you might have to rely on logs and error messages from the cloud provider, and sometimes, that's not enough to get to the root cause. It can be harder to troubleshoot compared to self-managed setups where you have full control. This lack of control can complicate diagnosing data pipeline failures or performance bottlenecks, making observability tools, detailed logging, and monitoring even more critical in serverless data architectures.

Managed

A managed service is when the cloud provider takes care of most of the heavy lifting for data processing, including infrastructure management, scaling, and sometimes even optimization, and you have access to a range of high-level tools and features for managing your data pipeline. For example, cloud providers give you services where you don't need to manage the underlying database hardware or the infrastructure; it's managed for you, but you get full access to the system's features. This is common in managed data warehouses like BigQuery or Snowflake where data engineers can run complex queries and transform data without worrying about tuning servers or storage. Another example is opting for a fully managed ETL service and not having to worry about server configurations or Apache Airflow upgrades. Most managed services come with built-in redundancy. This means they're designed to stay up and running even if something goes wrong, whether it's hardware failure or network issues. There are automatic failover mechanisms that make sure your system is always available, which is super important for data pipelines that need to run without interruptions.

Challenges with Managed Services

The managed model has some challenges:

Less Flexibility   Managed services are great for standard use cases, but they can be a bit restrictive. If your workload requires custom configurations or very specific needs, you might feel limited by the provider's available options. This means certain complex or highly customized data transformations, pipeline orchestration, or performance tuning might not be possible with managed services, requiring workarounds or hybrid solutions that combine managed and self-managed components.

Vendor Lock-In   Another thing to consider is vendor lock-in. Once you're deep into a managed service's ecosystem, migrating away from it can be challenging. For example, if you're using one cloud platform, moving your data to another platform could require significant effort, both in terms of data migration and learning the new platform's quirks. Data engineering teams face risks here, especially with proprietary data formats, APIs, or orchestration tools that tie your pipelines to one cloud provider, making future transitions expensive and time-consuming. This is why designing systems with interoperability in mind is important.

Self-Managed

Self-managed services allows you to take full control over your infrastructure. By using IaaS, you can rent virtual machines from the cloud provider and build out your clusters. While cloud platforms can simplify provisioning, you're still responsible for handling everything else, from OS patches to scaling and troubleshooting. Examples of self-managed services include running Apache Hadoop or Apache Spark on virtual machines. For data engineers, self-managed infrastructure offers the flexibility to customize every aspect of the data processing environment, from tuning cluster configurations to installing specific versions of tools and libraries, which is essential when dealing with complex, performance-sensitive data workloads or legacy systems.

Let's say you have very specific requirements for how you process data; maybe your algorithm requires a custom setup that isn't available in managed services, or you're working on a pipeline where you need precise control over the specific software versions and tools installed on your system. In this case, self-managed infrastructure is ideal because you can install, configure, and manage everything in a way that perfectly suits your needs. This level of control enables advanced data engineering tasks such as deploying custom ML pipelines to be possible.

Challenges with Self-Managed Models

Challenges with self-managed models include the following:

High Maintenance   With self-managed solutions, you're responsible for maintenance. This includes tasks like applying updates and patches, and troubleshooting issues when something goes wrong. It can take up a lot of your team's time. This means that data engineers would spend considerable effort on infrastructure upkeep instead of focusing on building and optimizing data pipelines.

Scalability Issues   Scaling your infrastructure is your responsibility. Unlike managed services that automatically scale to meet demand, with self-managed systems, you need to plan for scaling, which means setting up the right architecture upfront. If you don't design it well, scaling to handle a large volume of data can become a nightmare, especially if you're working with unpredictable growth. This adds complexity to data engineering workflows, especially for big data projects, where unexpected spikes in data volume require rapid scaling to maintain performance and avoid pipeline failures.

Putting It All Together

In summary, an organization can use a combination of serverless, managed, and self-managed models within the same data processing architecture. It helps them leverage a hybrid approach to take advantage of the strengths of each model in different parts of their data pipeline.

Cost Optimization

One of the most important yet often overlooked skill is understanding how to design cost-efficient systems in the cloud. When you're running pipelines, storing massive datasets, or processing workloads at scale, the cost can add up quickly. And trust me, in most organizations, once your data team starts spending, finance will come knocking. That's why you need to go beyond building systems that work—you need to build systems that scale responsibly.

Cost optimization means thinking strategically about how you run workloads, when you run them, what resources you use, and how data is stored. Every design decision you make, from choosing a VM type to setting a data retention policy, has a dollar impact. This section discusses various strategies you can use to optimize cost on the cloud.

Understanding Cloud Pricing Models

To manage costs, you have to understand how you're being charged. Most cloud platforms follow similar pricing principles; you're billed based on compute time, storage used, data transfer, and API calls. For compute, you're typically charged per second or minute based on the type of instance and resources (CPU, memory, GPU) you allocate. For storage, the cost depends on volume, tier (hot/cold/archive), and access frequency. There are three main pricing models you'll run into when working with cloud computing, and each one has its advantages depending on the type of workload you're running:

On-Demand Instances   This is the most flexible option. You spin up resources whenever you need them, pay per second or per hour, and shut them down when you're done. There is no long-term commitment or upfront costs. We usually use on-demand for things like testing, development, or one-off jobs. The downside is, it gets expensive fast if you're running long, consistent workloads this way. You can use on-demand instances for experimental pipelines, quick data validation jobs, or testing new transformations.

Reserved Instances   After running experiments, you can predict the amount of compute you need long term. Especially for a core service that runs 24/7, it's smarter to go with reserved instances. Here, you commit to using a particular instance type for one or three years, and in return, the cloud provider gives you a big discount. Production data pipelines or ETL jobs that process data regularly are candidates for reserved instances because they help to control ongoing costs.

Spot Instances   Cloud providers often have leftover compute capacity that nobody's using. They'll sell it to you at a cheaper rate, but the catch is, they can take it back at any time. They're great for workloads that can handle interruptions, like large-scale data processing or Spark jobs. If a job gets killed midway, it must be able to checkpoint, retry, or pick up from where it left off. We typically use this model for noncritical batch jobs that can run when resources are available, so you can design batch processing jobs to leverage spot instances for cost savings while ensuring fault tolerance.

The best practice is to match your workload type with the right pricing model or mix them. Use on-demand for development, reserved instances for production pipelines, and spot instances for batch or parallel jobs that can handle interruptions.

Rightsizing Resources

The key is to not overdo it. If a job only needs two vCPUs, giving it eight doesn't make it faster; it just burns more money. I've seen teams spin up huge machines just to be safe and then wonder why the bill tripled. Instead, use monitoring tools to see how much CPU and memory your jobs are actually using. Then right-size your compute so it matches the need, no more, no less. You can instrument your pipelines and clusters to track resource utilization and adjust configurations accordingly.

Smart Job Scheduling

Not everything needs to run immediately. For non-urgent or batch jobs, schedule them during off-peak hours like overnight or during weekends, when spot instance pricing is cheaper. If you're working with serverless, design your pipeline to be event-driven so that it only runs when there's data to process.

Storage Optimization

Data isn't just expensive to process; it's also expensive to store, especially at scale. Cloud providers offer storage tiers to help balance cost and performance depending on how often data is accessed.

Hot storage is optimized for frequent access. Active datasets, like real-time logs, current analytics data, or streaming inputs, are stored here for rapid read/write operations, whereas cold storage is much cheaper but slower to retrieve. It is ideal for backups, archived event data, or historical records that are not needed often. The key to managing storage cost is life cycle policies. Most storage systems let you define rules that automatically move data between tiers based on age or usage. For example, logs older than 30 days could move from hot to cold storage. After 90 days, they might be deleted or moved to an archive.

The best way to do this is to audit your storage buckets regularly. Asking questions like, "Do we still need this in hot storage? When was it last accessed? Is it part of a regulatory requirement?" Automation here can save thousands of dollars annually.

Shutting Down Idle Resources

One of the easiest ways to save on cloud costs is by shutting down resources when they're not in use. For example, if you're running dev or test environments, there's no reason they should be running overnight or on weekends. You can automate this or write your own scripts to stop or terminate unused instances. Also, don't forget to clean up temporary environments after demos or testing; those forgotten resources can quietly run up a big bill. The goal is to treat cloud infrastructure like a utility; turn it off when you're not using it. This also applies directly to data engineering clusters, interactive query engines, and test data environments.

Use Serverless Where Possible

Another cost-efficient strategy is to leverage serverless computing for lightweight tasks or workloads that don't require full-time infrastructure. Some dedicated tools let you run code without provisioning or managing servers, and you only pay for the actual execution time. It's perfect for things like event-driven functions, scheduled jobs, or lightweight APIs. Plus, it scales automatically, so you don't pay for idle time or over-provision for peak loads. Data engineers can use serverless architectures for small transformation functions or alerting mechanisms.

Monitoring and Alerting

As you start working with cloud infrastructure, one of the most important habits to build is monitoring proactively. A good starting point is setting budgets and alerts to give you early warnings before things get out of hand. Make it a routine to track daily usage patterns so you can quickly identify anomalies, like a sudden spike in compute or storage that might indicate an error or misconfiguration. Don't just rely on intuition; use visibility tools to get a clear, detailed picture of where your money is going.

Summary

- The cloud refers to a network of remote servers on the Internet that store, manage, and process data. Cloud computing refers to the on-demand delivery of IT resources and services over the Internet.

- An on-premises setup is where data infrastructure is managed on physical hardware that resides within your organization's premises. A cloud-based setup involves using cloud service providers to host and manage your data infrastructure.

- Cloud service models refer to the different ways cloud computing services are delivered to users. They are infrastructure as a service (IaaS), platform as a service (PaaS), and software as a service (SaaS).

- IaaS provides virtualized infrastructure like servers and storage, PaaS offers a platform to develop and deploy data pipelines, and SaaS delivers ready-to-use data solutions over the Internet.

- There are multiple criteria for choosing which model to use, such as your organization's needs, cost, scalability, time to deploy, interaction with existing systems, and long-term strategy.

- The cloud offers three ways to manage cloud services: self-managed, where you manage everything; managed, where the provider handles infrastructure; and serverless, where you focus only on code while the provider manages scaling and infrastructure automatically.

- Cloud computing is built on three major blocks; storage, compute, and networking. Storage handles data persistence, compute powers processing and workloads, and networking connects resources and enables data transfer across systems.

■ There are three primary types of cloud storage. Block storage splits data into fixed-size blocks for fast access, file storage organizes data in a hierarchy like traditional folders, and object storage stores data as objects with metadata, ideal for unstructured data and scalability.

■ A compute service is a part of cloud computing that provides the processing power needed to run applications, perform calculations, and handle workloads. In data engineering, compute services power batch processing jobs, real-time data flows, and analytics workloads.

■ Virtual machines are cloud-hosted computers that you can spin up on demand. They're useful when you need full control over the environment, like for custom Spark jobs or running database clusters.

■ A container is a lightweight, portable unit that packages your code, its dependencies, and its runtime environment into a single executable unit. They're ideal for deploying reproducible, modular data services and pipelines.

■ In cloud networking, VPCs provide isolated network environments, subnets segment the VPC into smaller networks, IP addresses identify devices, and gateways enable communication between different networks or the Internet.

■ Data engineers must often configure IP addresses and VPC's to secure pipelines and ensure systems can access each other efficiently and securely.

■ Best practices for optimizing cost on the cloud is understanding cloud pricing models, rightsizing resources, using serverless where possible, shutting down idle resources, and effectively monitoring and managing resources.

13

Building a Career in Data Engineering

Congratulations! You're almost done with the book, and now you're ready to embark on the most exciting part of your journey, which is launching your career as a data engineer. With all the technical skills you've learned, the path to landing your first job can be overwhelming. This chapter is designed to help you transition from learning to doing. It will guide you through the process of positioning yourself for success in data engineering interviews and understanding what companies are looking for.

BY THE END OF THIS CHAPTER, YOU'LL BE EQUIPPED WITH THE FOLLOWING KNOWLEDGE:

- The different types of data engineering roles available, and which one aligns best with your skills and interests
- How to ace a data engineering interview, from technical assessments to behavioral questions
- A typical data engineering job description and how to identify patterns
- Data engineering project recommendations to improve your portfolio

- Tips for optimizing your résumé to stand out and increase your chances of landing interviews
- How to think like a data engineer and tackle problems from a problem-solving perspective

With this, you'll be ready to step into the job market with confidence and make your first big leap toward becoming a successful data engineer.

Types of Data Engineering Roles

If you've ever searched for data engineering jobs online, you've probably seen different job titles that all sound similar but seem to ask for very different skill sets. One role might emphasize the knowledge of cloud infrastructure. Another might want you to be fluent in SQL and build dashboards or machine learning (ML) pipelines.

In practice, data engineering has evolved into multiple specialized subfields, each shaped by the kind of data a company works with, its stage of growth, and its technical priorities. So while two job descriptions might both say Data Engineer, what they actually need can range from building infrastructure and pipelines to preparing data for ML or supporting AI-powered apps. We'll break down the three major flavors of data engineering roles you're likely to encounter and walk you through what each role focuses on, what their daily work looks like, the kinds of tools they use, and where they tend to sit in the data ecosystem.

Types of Data Engineers

Among the different specialties of data engineers, I'll group them into three categories, as seen in Figure 13-1:

- Platform data engineer
- Analytics data engineer
- AI/ML data engineer

Platform Data Engineer

This role is all about building the foundation. It's more focused on making sure the data systems are scalable, reliable, and performant. If you enjoy DevOps or cloud architecture, you'll probably feel right at home here. You'll be designing data platforms, setting up distributed systems like Hadoop or Spark clusters, configuring cloud services, and managing orchestration tools. In this role, you'll seldom work with SQL or dashboards. Instead, your focus will be on making sure everything behind the scenes operates smoothly, securely, and at scale.

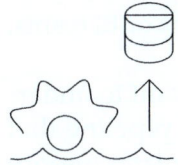

Platform Data Engineers

Build and maintain core data infrastructure. Ensure data systems are scalable, reliable, and efficient.

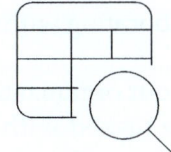

Analytics Data Engineers

Transform raw data into clean, usable datasets. Support dashboards, reports, and business insights.

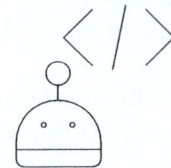

AI/ML Data Engineers

Prepare and optimize data pipelines. Specifically for training and deploying machine learning models.

Figure 13-1: Data engineering roles

As a platform or infrastructure data engineer, you will:

■ Design, build, and maintain data infrastructure and platforms

■ Develop frameworks and automation for the ingestion, processing, and storage of large-scale datasets

■ Implement data governance, security, and monitoring of best practices across pipelines and storage layers

■ Continuously optimize platform performance, scalability, and cost-efficiency

Key skills include the following:

■ Strong experience with distributed data systems

■ Infrastructure as code (IaC) tools

■ Deep understanding of cloud platforms and their data services

■ Expertise in building scalable storage and compute systems

■ Knowledge of observability tools for monitoring and alerting

Analytics Data Engineer

This is probably the most well-known type of data engineer, and what most people imagine when they hear the term. The focus here is on building data pipelines, cleaning raw data, transforming it into structured formats, and making it ready for analysts or dashboards. If you're someone who loves SQL and enjoys digging into messy data and collaborating with data analysts or BI teams, this is your zone.

For instance, the marketing team in your organization might want to understand user churn. In this role, you'll be tasked with building a pipeline that extracts user logs from a database, transforms that data, and calculates metrics like session duration or last active time. This role is all about making data useful and accessible to decision-makers. It also requires the most collaboration with downstream teams.

As an analytics data engineer, you will:

- Build and maintain ETL/ELT pipelines to support reporting, dashboards, and business analytics
- Develop complex SQL queries and transformations to organize and prepare data for analysis
- Integrate data from multiple internal and external sources into centralized systems
- Ensure data quality, deduplication, and consistency across analytical datasets
- Collaborate closely with analysts, business intelligence teams, and stakeholders to understand reporting needs and deliver accurate, trusted data

Key skills include the following:

- Strong SQL expertise for building analytical datasets
- Experience with ETL tools and frameworks
- Familiarity with data modeling and data warehousing concepts
- Knowledge of orchestration tools for managing ETL workflows

AI/ML Data Engineers

An AI/ML data engineer combines data engineering principles with AI expertise to build, manage, and maintain robust data pipelines specifically for AI and ML models. This infrastructure powers large language models, chatbots, recommendation engines, and generative AI tools. While a traditional data engineer might focus on analytics or reports, an AI data engineer focuses on feeding clean, structured, and relevant data into AI models and ensuring those models run smoothly in production.

As an AI/ML data engineer, you will:

- Build and maintain infrastructure that can store and process the petabytes of data needed to power models
- Design, build, and maintain ETL/ELT pipelines for AI-driven data workflows
- Integrate data from multiple structured and unstructured sources, including APIS and third-party platforms
- Ensure data quality, deduplication, and consistency across datasets powering AI systems

Key skills include the following:

- Strong proficiency in SQL for data extraction, transformation, and analysis
- Experience with data processing tools like Spark
- Experience in filtering and processing datasets for training multimodal data
- Expertise in API integration and building custom connectors to ingest diverse datasets

An Organization's Structure

While we've explored these data engineering roles separately, the reality in most organizations is that the lines between them are not always so clear-cut. Depending on the company size, industry, and maturity of the data function, you might see these roles exist as distinct positions on separate teams, or they might be merged into a single, hybrid role with overlapping responsibilities. For instance:

- In a startup, one data engineer might handle everything from building a data warehouse, designing pipelines, enabling analytics, and even deploying machine learning models into production.
- In a large tech company, there might be separate teams specializing deeply in their lane.
- In consulting or product-facing roles, engineers are expected to adapt quickly and move across domains depending on the needs of the project or client.

These titles may differ, but the core skill set is rooted in the same foundations. As the field evolves, companies are always seeking engineers who can move across these domains, understand the end-to-end data journey.

Landing Your First Data Engineering Role

We've discussed different types of data engineering roles and how to identify them. Now, it's time to get practical about landing your first job. In this section, you'll learn what a typical data engineering job description looks like, the anatomy of a data engineering interview, and additionally, how to position yourself effectively on your résumé.

A Typical Data Engineering Job Description

The following sidebar shows a sample job description. Learning how to analyze a job description, not just at face value, but with a critical eye, is an important skill. You'll start identifying patterns like which skills are truly essential, which ones are nice-to-have, and which responsibilities you should be prepared to talk about. This allows you to prepare smarter and avoid wasting time on areas that don't matter as much for the roles you're targeting. Also, recognizing these expectations early will help you better prepare for the realities of the role and stand out during interviews.

A SAMPLE JOB DESCRIPTION

Job Overview

We are seeking a talented and motivated data engineer to join our dynamic team. As a data engineer, you will be responsible for designing, building, and maintaining scalable and efficient data pipelines that enable data-driven decision-making across the organization. You will work closely with data scientists, analysts, and other stakeholders to ensure seamless data integration, transformation, and availability.

Key Responsibilities

- Design, develop, and maintain ETL (Extract, Transform, Load) pipelines to support data integration from various sources into data warehouses or data lakes.

- Collaborate with cross-functional teams (data scientists, analysts, product teams) to gather data requirements and ensure data is available, accurate, and reliable.

- Build and optimize data pipelines for batch and real-time processing using frameworks such as Apache Spark, Apache Kafka, or AWS Lambda.

- Implement and maintain data warehouses and data lakes using technologies like Amazon Redshift, Google BigQuery, or Snowflake.

Skills and Qualifications

- Strong proficiency in SQL and experience with relational databases (MySQL, PostgreSQL, etc.)

- Proficiency in programming languages such as Python, Java, or Scala for data engineering tasks

- Experience working with cloud platforms (AWS, Google Cloud Platform, Microsoft Azure) and services like AWS S3, Redshift, BigQuery, or Databricks

- Solid understanding of data warehousing concepts, dimensional modeling, and star/snowflake schemas

- Knowledge of data security and governance best practices

- Excellent communication skills and the ability to work in a collaborative team environment

Why Join Us

- Work in a fast-paced, innovative environment where your ideas and contributions will have a significant impact

- Collaborate with talented and motivated colleagues across different departments

- Opportunity to work on cutting-edge technologies and data engineering challenges

- Competitive salary and benefits package

It's easy to get overwhelmed by the long list of tools and technologies companies mention; one company might ask for Airflow, another for Azure Data Factory, and another for AWS Glue. But here's an important thing to remember: Tools are just tools. They are flavors of the same fundamental concepts. What truly matters are the foundations behind those tools.

For example, whether a company uses Apache Airflow or Azure Data Factory, the underlying principle is the same: You're just orchestrating and scheduling data workflows. If you understand the concept of orchestration and how data pipelines work, learning a new tool is just a matter of picking up the different interface or syntax. Companies know that technology stacks change all the time, so they prioritize candidates who can adapt, not just candidates who know a particular tool today.

Reading job descriptions gives you clarity on the core technical skills you need to master. For most data engineering roles, a strong foundation in SQL, Python, cloud platforms, and building ETL pipelines is non-negotiable. When you know what's consistently expected, you can focus your learning and projects around these high-impact skills, instead of trying to learn everything at once.

Another benefit of studying job descriptions is that it helps you map your current learning to real-world applications. It becomes easier to see how the concepts and tools you've studied show up in actual job tasks. This connection not only boosts your confidence but also helps you explain your skills more effectively during interviews.

How to Build a Winning Résumé

Your résumé is the very first impression you make on a company, sometimes even before they see your portfolio. You could have all the right skills, but if your résumé doesn't present them clearly and confidently, you might not even get a chance to show what you can do. A poorly crafted résumé can close doors before you even get in the room. In this section, we'll talk about how to position yourself on paper so that your résumé actually works for you and not against you. A good résumé should have the following sections.

Experience Section

In this section, you list your work experience with your most recent job first. For each role, focus on accomplishments rather than just listing tasks. Always quantify your impact when possible, and also focus on high-impact roles and not just "any" role. The following sidebar shows a sample experience section.

SAMPLE EXPERIENCE SECTION OF A DATA ENGINEERING RÉSUMÉ

XYZ Company | Data Engineer | June 2025

- Designed and implemented ETL pipelines, reducing data processing time by 40%
- Built and maintained a real-time data pipeline using Apache Kafka and Spark, improving data flow efficiency by 25%
- Optimized SQL queries for data extraction, leading to a 20% decrease in query runtime

Skills Section

This section highlights your technical skills. It helps recruiters quickly identify your proficiency, and so, it's always best to categorize them. The following sidebar shows a sample skills section.

SAMPLE SKILLS SECTION OF A DATA ENGINEERING RÉSUMÉ

XYZ Company | Data Engineer | June 2025

- **Programming languages:** Python, Scala, and SQL
- **Data warehousing:** Amazon Redshift, Google BigQuery, Snowflake
- **ETL tools:** Apache Airflow

- **Big data:** Apache Spark, Hadoop, Kafka
- **Databases:** MySQL, PostgreSQL, MongoDB
- **Cloud platforms:** AWS/Azure

Projects Section

For beginners or people with little or no work experience, including a projects section can demonstrate your skills. When learning a new skill, one of the best ways to solidify your knowledge is by building real projects. It's not enough to just learn concepts in theory; you need to show that you can apply them to solve real-world problems. Let's go through a list of practical project ideas that will help you put your knowledge into action. By working through these projects, you'll gain hands-on experience and create concrete examples you can showcase during interviews. To build these projects, you'll need access to real-world datasets. Thankfully, several platforms offer free, high-quality datasets across a range of domains, like Kaggle, HuggingFace, Google Datasets, and DataGov.

SAMPLE PROJECTS

Data pipeline for web scraping: Build a data pipeline that scrapes data from websites and stores it in a database or data warehouse. This project will help you practice web scraping, data extraction, and storage in databases like MySQL or PostgreSQL.

ETL pipeline with data transformation: Design an ETL pipeline that extracts data from a source, transforms it, and loads it into a target system like a data warehouse or a cloud storage solution.

Data warehouse with star schema: Build a simple data warehouse with a star schema for an e-commerce or retail business. You can create tables for facts and dimensions and practice SQL queries for reporting and analysis.

Real-time data streaming with Apache Kafka: Set up a real-time data streaming pipeline using Apache Kafka. You can simulate real-time sensor data or log data and stream it into a system like Apache Spark for processing.

Log data analytics pipeline: Build a pipeline that collects log data from an application or server; processes it for analysis, like counting error rates; and visualize it in a dashboard.

Cloud-based data lake project: Create a simple data lake using a cloud storage service. Ingest raw data files into different folders (raw, processed, curated) and practice organizing and tagging. You'll get hands-on experience with the idea of a data lake architecture.

Batch data processing with Apache Spark: Set up a batch data processing workflow using Apache Spark. You can work with a large public dataset and write Spark jobs to clean, transform, and summarize the data. This helps you get comfortable using distributed computing to handle big datasets.

Event-driven architecture with cloud functions: Create a simple event-driven pipeline where a cloud function triggers when a new file is uploaded to a bucket, processes the file, and stores the result in a database. This project teaches you about serverless processing and reactive systems.

Be sure to add these projects to your résumé with a clear description of the projects, tools used, and a link to view either the architecture or the working solution.

Education and Certifications

List your academic background, including your degree(s) and any relevant certifications. Obtaining industry-recognized certifications also helps you improve your credibility.

> **TIP**   Many companies use applicant tracking systems (ATSs) to screen résumés. Ensure your résumé includes relevant keywords from the job description. Also, avoid using excessive jargon or nonstandard abbreviations that ATSs may not recognize.

Preparing for a Data Engineering Interview

The structure of data engineering interviews differs by the company, but the expectations are usually the same. As shown in Figure 13-2, most data engineering interviews are broken into a few common stages: a technical screen, a coding or SQL assessment, a system design interview, and a behavioral interview. Some companies may combine these steps, whereas others may spread them across multiple rounds. Let's look at the popular rounds.

The Résumé Review or Recruiter Screen

This is the warm-up interview, which is usually not technical. A recruiter wants to know if you're worth moving forward based on two things: Do you meet the baseline qualifications in terms of tech stack, years of experience, or background? The recruiter also checks if you can communicate well and articulate your journey clearly. The best way to prepare for recruiter screens is to review your résumé, research the company and role you're applying to, and prepare questions to ask the recruiter about the interview process, role, or company.

Interview Types

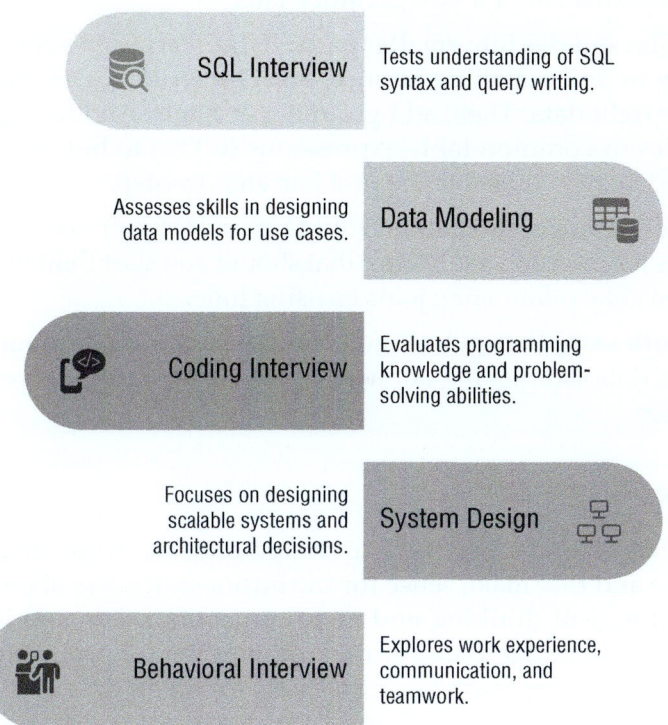

SQL Interview — Tests understanding of SQL syntax and query writing.

Assesses skills in designing data models for use cases. — **Data Modeling**

Coding Interview — Evaluates programming knowledge and problem-solving abilities.

Focuses on designing scalable systems and architectural decisions. — **System Design**

Behavioral Interview — Explores work experience, communication, and teamwork.

Figure 13-2: Common stages of a data engineering interview

SQL *Interview*

The first technical screen for data engineering roles is often a SQL interview, and for good reason. SQL is the language of data, and companies want to know if you can work with real-world datasets, write efficient queries, and think logically. Doing well in a first-stage SQL interview is not just about writing a query that works; it's about showing clear thinking, good habits, and understanding of best practices. In a SQL interview, you would meet with an engineer on the team who would assess your ability to write SQL code to solve business problems. In some cases, you might be given a dataset that contains 2–4 separate tables. Here are some tips for approaching the questions:

▪ **Understand the problem clearly before writing code:** Read the question carefully and reread it to be sure you understand what's being asked. Also, pay attention to details like whether they want a specific aggregation or a filter condition. If you're allowed to ask clarifying questions, especially in live interviews, don't be afraid to ask. It shows thoughtfulness, not weakness.

- **Plan your approach out loud:** Try to talk through your plan before you start typing. This gives the interviewer insight into your thought process and can even earn partial credit if you get stuck later.

- **Break down complex queries into smaller parts:** If the query seems complicated, don't try to do everything at once. Start by writing a simple query to select the right data. Then, add grouping or filters. Another tip is using subqueries or common table expressions (CTEs) to help you organize your work better and solve the problem step-by-step.

- **Aim for correctness before optimization:** Your first goal is to get a correct query that answers the question. Only after that should you start thinking about optimizations like minimizing joins or using indexes.

- **Test your logic with sample inputs:** Before submitting, think through small, hypothetical data samples in your head and walk your interviewer through the solution.

Data Modeling Interview

Data modeling interviews test whether you can design data structures that are efficient and scalable and that make sense for the business. It's less about coding and more about logical thinking and communication. The goal is to create models that can aid better decision-making that would profit the business. Here's a step-by-step approach you can follow to solve a data modeling problem:

- **Clarify the requirements first:** Always start by asking clarifying questions, "Who will use this data?," "How often will the data be updated?," "What types of queries will be run against it?" Understanding access patterns and business goals is important because a model that's perfect for reporting might be wrong for real-time querying.

- **Identify key entities and relationships:** Break the problem down into entities and relationships and show how they connect. The best way to do this is to think in terms of nouns and actions—for example, Customers place Orders for Products.

- **Apply normalization thoughtfully:** Start by designing a normalized model, with entities in different tables instead of repeating information, but also mention when denormalization might be helpful and the trade-offs.

You can get good at data modeling interviews with practice by designing models for everyday systems, like a ride-sharing app, a music-streaming service, or an e-commerce platform. Doing these repeatedly helps you get more confident.

The Coding Interview

In this stage, you will be writing code with a programming language to solve various business problems. Here, companies are trying to understand if you can think logically and write clean and efficient code with a coding language of your choice.

- **Get comfortable with data structures:** Practice parsing and manipulation on strings and arrays, and get familiar with hash maps and dictionaries for counting and grouping. You might encounter questions like finding duplicates in a list, grouping log entries by IP address, or parsing a CSV to find the most frequent user.

- **Write clean code:** Interviewers don't just care if your code works; they care about how easy it is to read and understand. Practice writing clear function names, using proper indentation and making your code modular.

The System Design Interview

In this stage, depending on the company and the expectations for the role you're applying for, you might be asked to design an end-to-end data pipeline or architecture. This might happen live in the interview, or it could be a take-home challenge. Interviewers typically want to understand several key things:

- **Your understanding of the problem statement and discovery process:** Interviewers want to see if you ask the right clarifying questions before jumping into the design. It's important to fully understand data volume, update frequency, latency needs, and business goals.

- **The tools you would use and why:** Rather than just naming tools, you should explain why you chose a particular tool and how the tool works behind the scenes. You should also discuss trade-offs like cost, performance, and ease of maintenance.

- **How you handle failures:** Good system design includes planning for inevitable failures. You should also discuss strategies to keep the pipeline reliable.

- **How do you ensure data quality and freshness?** Talk about implementing validation checks, schema enforcement, and monitoring to make sure bad or stale data doesn't silently break your pipeline.

- **How you would scale the pipeline:** Interviewers want to know how your design would handle an increase in data volume, user base, or query load. This is where strategies like autoscaling, partitioning, and sharding are used.

- **Bonus points:** If you proactively mention how you would handle monitoring, automation, and security, it shows you think like a real-world engineer who is ready to build production-ready systems.

The Behavioral Interview

A lot of engineers focus on building technical skills but forget that soft skills also matter. Behavioral interviews are used to assess how you work with others, how you solve problems, and how you handle challenges, not just your technical skills. Companies want to know if you'll be a good teammate and collaborator.

In a behavioral interview, you might be asked these kinds of questions:

- A challenging project you've worked on
- A time you made a mistake and how you fixed it
- A time you led a project or initiative
- A time you went above and beyond your regular responsibilities
- An instance when you took the initiative to fix or improve something
- A time you worked with a difficult teammate or cross-functional team
- A situation where you had to quickly learn something new
- A time you had to handle a large workload under pressure
- How you prioritize tasks or handle conflicting priorities
- A situation where you missed a deadline—what did you learn?
- A project where you improved a system or process

To answer these questions, focus on using the STAR (Situation, Action, Task, and Result) method. STAR keeps you organized and focused, and it makes it easy for interviewers to follow your story and assess your impact. Let's explain each section:

- **Situation:** Briefly explain the context, where you were working, and what the project or challenge was.
- **Task:** Explain your responsibility or what you were trying to achieve. What was the problem you had to solve or the goal you needed to meet?
- **Action:** Describe the specific steps you took to address the task. Focus on what you did, even if it was a team project, and avoid using the word "we."
- **Result:** Share the outcome with your interviewer. What happened because of your action? Try to use numbers or impact if you can.

This is a sample reply:

> **At my internship at XYZ Company, we were facing frequent ETL pipeline failures during high-traffic hours. My task was to investigate the failures and implement a solution to improve pipeline reliability.**

> I analyzed log files to identify bottlenecks, optimized SQL queries, and implemented retry mechanisms for failed jobs. After the changes, pipeline failure rates dropped by 85%, and we were able to handle 2× more traffic during peak hours.

Thinking Like a Data Engineer

Becoming an exceptional data engineer is not just about learning tools and writing code—it's about developing a mindset. Data engineers are problem-solvers at heart. They think about how systems fit together and how to design solutions that scale as data grows. Let's talk about how you can develop a mindset that will set you apart not just in interviews, but throughout your career.

Think in Systems

Always remember that you're not just writing a piece of code—you're building part of a system. A lot of people, early in their careers, focus on making a script work for today's problem, and that's fine at first. But as you grow, you have to start thinking bigger. Ask yourself, if I step away tomorrow, can someone else pick this up? If the data doubles in volume, will it still work? Systems thinking means designing pipelines that are modular, resilient, and easy to monitor.

Learn to Prioritize Data Quality

In an organization, the data you move and transform will directly influence major business decisions. If your pipeline lets bad data slip through, you're not just creating technical debt; you're eroding trust. That's why it's important to treat data validation by setting up schema checks, null checks, and so forth. These shouldn't be an afterthought; they should be core parts of your pipeline, because it's easier to build in data quality checks from the beginning than to fix trust once it's broken.

Design for Failure

No matter how perfect your design is, something will eventually fail, and that's normal. APIs will time out, databases will go down, and some weird corner case will pop-up, but good engineers plan for that reality from day one. What happens if your data source is unavailable? What if the schema changes unexpectedly? With robust systems, always expect things to go wrong. That means using retries, backoffs, checkpointing, and alerting. It's not about eliminating failure; it's about recovering from it quickly and gracefully.

Balance Business Context with Technical Choices

It's easy to get excited about the newest tools, but you need to make choices based on business needs, and you must be able to balance technical excellence with a strong grasp of business needs. Does the marketing team need real-time insights, or is batch good enough? Should we use a managed warehouse or set up open source tooling ourselves? The best engineers understand how to map technical architecture to business value. The tools and technologies you choose must serve the organization's goals, not just be the latest or most complex solution. When designing a solution, always consider both the technical feasibility and the business context, as that will guide your decisions.

Optimize for Clarity, Then Speed

It's tempting to dive straight into optimizing your pipeline for speed and performance, but clarity should always come first. Your queries, pipelines, and workflows should be understandable by the next person on your team. Once your logic is clean and correct, then you can profile and optimize. Premature optimization leads to brittle systems, but clear pipelines are easier to debug, test, and scale.

Think Beyond the Tool

You need to develop a mindset of understanding the tools you're using and why these tools exist by learning the underlying design patterns. Tools change, but patterns stay. Thinking like a data engineer means going beyond syntax and into strategy. A lot of new data engineers get caught up in learning the latest tools and frameworks. While tools are important, the mindset of a data engineer is less about being tool-agnostic and more about understanding the data infrastructure.

Master Automation

Data engineering is a repetitive job, and automation is key to efficiency. Once you've built a pipeline or workflow, you should be thinking about how to automate it, monitor it, and scale it. Automation isn't just about scheduling jobs; it's about creating systems that run smoothly, without needing constant human oversight. The more you automate and orchestrate, the more reliable and scalable your data pipelines will be.

Finally, always stay curious. Data engineering is a constantly evolving discipline, and the best engineers are the ones who never stop asking questions or seeking better ways to solve problems.

Summary

- Platform data engineers are more involved in building the foundation and making sure the data systems are scalable, reliable, and performant.

- Analytics data engineers focus more on building data pipelines, cleaning raw data, transforming it into structured formats, and making it ready for analysts or dashboards.

- An AI data engineer combines data engineering principles with AI expertise to build, manage, and maintain robust data pipelines specifically for AI and machine learning models.

- To land a data engineering role, you need to learn how to study job descriptions, build a winning résumé, and prepare well for interviews.

- Adding your experience, skills, projects, and relevant certifications to your résumé makes you stand out as a candidate.

- A typical data engineering interview consists of SQL, data modeling, coding, system design, and behavioral interviews.

- The SQL interview evaluates your ability to interpret data requirements and write effective SQL queries to meet those needs.

- Data modeling interviews test whether you can design data structures that are efficient and scalable and that make sense for the business.

- The coding interview involves writing code in a programming language to solve various business problems.

- System design interviews assess how well you can architect scalable, reliable systems from the ground up.

- Behavioral interviews are used to assess how you work with others, how you solve problems, and how you handle challenges, not just your technical skills.

- To answer behavioral questions, focus on using the STAR method. STAR stands for Situation, Action, Task, and Result.

- Becoming an exceptional data engineer is not just about learning tools and writing code—it's about developing a mindset. You need to think in systems, prioritize data quality, design for failure, master automation, and most importantly, balance business context with technical choices.

Sample Interview Questions

In this chapter, we'll walk through sample interview questions that cover some of the most important areas in data engineering interviews. Think of this appendix as a set of flashcards, something you can quickly flip through when preparing for interviews to refresh your memory and sharpen your thinking. Use it to test yourself, spot any weak areas, and build the confidence you need to walk into your interviews.

SQL

What is the difference between INNER JOIN, LEFT JOIN, RIGHT JOIN, and FULL OUTER JOIN?

INNER JOIN returns rows when there's a match in both tables. LEFT JOIN returns all rows from the left table and matches rows from the right. RIGHT JOIN does the opposite. FULL OUTER JOIN returns all rows from both tables, matching where possible and filling in NULLS where there's no match.

What are indexes, and how do they improve performance?

Indexes are special lookup tables that the database uses to speed up data retrieval. They allow queries to find rows faster, especially in large datasets, but can slow down inserts and updates due to maintenance overhead.

What is the difference between WHERE and HAVING clauses?

WHERE filters rows before grouping, whereas HAVING filters groups after aggregation. Use WHERE for raw data filtering and HAVING when dealing with GROUP BY queries.

What does GROUP BY do?

GROUP BY aggregates rows that have the same values in specified columns, allowing you to perform aggregate functions like SUM, COUNT, or AVG on each group.

Explain the difference between UNION and UNION ALL.

UNION combines two result sets and removes duplicates, whereas UNION ALL includes all rows, including duplicates. UNION ALL is generally faster since it skips the duplicate check.

What is a window function? Give an example.

Window functions perform calculations across rows related to the current row, without collapsing them. Unlike aggregate functions (like SUM, AVG, COUNT), which collapse rows into a single result, window functions retain the original rows and add new information alongside them. For instance, this query assigns a unique rank to each employee within their department based on descending salary order.

```
SELECT
  id,
  name,
  department,
  salary,
  ROW_NUMBER() OVER (PARTITION BY department ORDER BY salary DESC) AS
rank_in_dept
FROM employees;
```

ID	NAME	DEPARTMENT	SALARY	RANK_IN_DEPT
2	Bob	HR	75,000	1
5	Eve	HR	70,000	2
1	Alice	HR	60,000	3
4	David	IT	95,000	1
6	Frank	IT	80,000	2

Explain ACID properties in the context of SQL databases.

ACID stands for Atomicity, Consistency, Isolation, and Durability. They make sure operations are completed fully, without corruption, even during failures.

What is the difference between DELETE, TRUNCATE, and DROP?

DELETE removes specific rows and can be rolled back. TRUNCATE removes all rows faster and resets identity, but cannot be rolled back easily. DROP removes the entire table structure and data.

What's the purpose of COALESCE() in SQL?

COALESCE() returns the first non-null value in a list. It's useful for handling NULLS gracefully, especially when selecting fallback values.

How do you handle NULLS in SQL joins?

Use IS NULL or IS NOT NULL in filters. In joins, outer joins are useful when you expect NULLS on one side and still want to retain unmatched rows.

What is a CTE, and how is it different from a subquery?

A CTE (common table expression) is a temporary result set defined with WITH. Unlike subqueries, CTEs are more readable and reusable, and can be self-referenced (useful for recursion).

What's the difference between scalar and aggregate functions?

Scalar functions return a single value per row (e.g., UPPER(), LEN()), while aggregate functions summarize data over many rows (e.g., SUM(), AVG(), COUNT()).

How do you optimize a slow SQL query?

You check for missing indexes, avoid selecting all rows, reduce subqueries, use CTEs for clarity, and analyze query plans to determine performance.

What is a surrogate key, and how is it different from a natural key?

A surrogate key is a system-generated unique identifier (like an auto-increment ID), whereas a natural key is derived from real-world data (like email or SSN). Surrogate keys are preferred for flexibility and stability.

What is a CASE statement, and when would you use it?

The CASE statement is SQL's version of if-else logic. It allows you to apply conditional logic in queries, and it's also useful for categorizing data or customizing output based on certain rules.

What's the difference between EXISTS and IN?

IN checks if a value exists in a static list or subquery result set. EXISTS checks for the presence of rows in a correlated subquery and often performs better for large datasets, especially when checking for existence rather than matching values.

Explain how RANK(), DENSE_RANK(), and ROW_NUMBER() differ.

All three are window functions for ranking rows. ROW_NUMBER() gives unique sequential numbers. RANK() skips numbers for ties. DENSE_RANK() assigns the same number to ties but doesn't skip ranks.

What is a transaction in SQL?

A transaction is a sequence of operations performed as a single unit of work. It ensures data integrity through BEGIN, COMMIT, and ROLLBACK, and adheres to ACID properties for consistency.

What is a self-join, and when is it useful?

A self-join is when a table is joined to itself. It's useful for hierarchical relationships, like finding manager–employee pairs or comparing rows within the same table (e.g., finding people in the same department).

What is a data type mismatch, and how do you avoid it?

A data type mismatch occurs when columns being compared or operated on have incompatible types. You avoid it by ensuring consistent data types or using CAST() and CONVERT() functions to align them.

Data Modeling

What are the types of data models?

There are three types: conceptual, which outlines high-level business entities; logical, which defines structure and relationships; and physical, which implements the model in a particular database.

What is an entity?

An entity is a real-world object or concept represented in a data model. For example, a Customer or an Order is an entity in a sales database.

What is an attribute?

Attributes are properties that describe an entity. For example, a Customer entity may have attributes like Name, Email, and PhoneNumber.

What is normalization? Why is it important?

Normalization is the process of organizing data to reduce redundancy and improve integrity. It involves breaking a database into smaller, related tables. It helps ensure consistency, reduces update anomalies, and makes queries more efficient.

What is a primary key and a foreign key?

A primary key uniquely identifies each row in a table. A foreign key is a field that links one table to the primary key of another, enabling relational integrity between tables.

What is denormalization?

Denormalization is the process of combining tables to reduce joins and improve query performance, often at the cost of some redundancy.

What are the different types of relationships in data modeling?

The common types are one-to-one, one-to-many, and many-to-many relationships between entities.

What is referential integrity?

Referential integrity ensures that foreign keys accurately and consistently reference primary keys in related tables.

What is a star schema?

A star schema has a central fact table connected to dimension tables. It's simple and optimized for read-heavy analytical queries.

What is a snowflake schema?

A snowflake schema is a normalized form of a star schema where dimension tables are further split into subdimensions.

What are fact and dimension tables?

Fact tables store measurable data, whereas dimension tables store descriptive attributes.

When would you choose a star schema over a snowflake schema?

Choose a star schema when simplicity and performance are more important than storage efficiency; it requires fewer joins.

What is a slowly changing dimension (SCD)?

SCD tracks changes in dimension data over time. Type 1 overwrites data, Type 2 keeps history, and Type 3 stores a limited change history using a flag.

What is a surrogate key?

A surrogate key is a system-generated key used as a primary key instead of a natural key to simplify joins and indexing.

What are the advantages of using surrogate keys?

They reduce data size and simplify updates since they remain static even if natural keys change.

What is dimensional modeling?

Dimensional modeling is a design technique for data warehouses focused on ease of querying, usually involving facts and dimensions.

How do you decide between normalized and denormalized models?

Normalized models are used for transaction databases, and denormalized models are used for analytics systems to optimize performance based on use case.

What is a data mart?

A data mart is a subset of a data warehouse designed for a specific department or use case, typically modeled using a star schema.

What is cardinality in data modeling?

Cardinality defines the numerical relationship between entities. It affects how tables are joined.

What is a composite key?

A composite key is a primary key made of two or more columns used together to uniquely identify a row.

Data Pipelines

What are the key components of an ETL pipeline?

The three main components are extract (pulling data from various sources), transform (cleaning and converting data) and load (writing data into a storage or analytics system).

What is the difference between ETL and ELT?

In ETL, transformation happens before loading into the destination. In ELT, raw data is loaded first, and transformation happens within the destination system, typically used in modern cloud-based systems.

How do you handle data quality in ETL pipelines?

By applying validations during transformation, like null checks and type checks, using logging for failed records, and alerting systems for anomalies.

How do you manage schema changes in ETL?

By using schema versioning to track and manage changes to a database or data structure over time

What are DAGs?

DAGs (directed acyclic graphs) represent the workflow of tasks, where each node is a task and edges represent dependencies.

How do you monitor ETL jobs?

Through logging, alerting systems, dashboards, or tools

How do you ensure idempotency in ETL jobs?

By designing ETL steps so that rerunning them does not produce duplicates. This can be done by using UPSERTS, deduplication logic, or versioning. For example, if a pipeline loads yesterday's sales data into a warehouse, an idempotent process ensures that even if the load runs twice by mistake, the sales numbers don't double and they stay correct.

What is the difference between batch and streaming ETL?

Batch ETL processes data in chunks at intervals, whereas streaming ETL processes data in near real time as it arrives.

What is a watermark in streaming pipelines?

A watermark tracks the progress of event time in streaming data and helps handle late-arriving data appropriately.

How would you load large volumes of data efficiently?

By using partitioning, parallel processing, and compression techniques to reduce I/O and improve speed.

How do you handle duplicate records in ETL?

By using deduplication logic during transformation, based on primary keys, timestamps, or unique constraints.

What's the difference between full load and incremental load?

Full load replaces the entire dataset each time, whereas incremental load only updates the changes (new or modified data).

How do you implement incremental loading?

By using techniques like change data capture (CDC), timestamps, or version columns.

What is CDC (change data capture)?

CDC is a method of capturing only the data that has changed in the source since the last load, reducing ETL time and load.

What is data lineage, and why is it important?

Data lineage traces the flow of data from source to destination, helping in debugging, impact analysis, and auditing.

How do you handle failed ETL jobs?

By implementing retry logic, capturing failure logs, and setting up alerts for monitoring.

What is data partitioning, and why is it useful?

Partitioning splits data into segments (like by date or region) to improve query performance and parallelism during processing.

How do you ensure pipeline scalability?

By using distributed processing frameworks like Spark and designing modular pipelines

What is backfilling in ETL pipelines?

Backfilling refers to reprocessing or loading historical data into the system, typically after a bug fix or schema update.

Apache Spark

How is Spark different from Hadoop MapReduce?

Spark processes data in memory, making it faster than MapReduce, which writes data to disk between each stage. Spark is also easier to develop and supports iterative algorithms better.

What is an RDD?

An RDD (resilient distributed dataset) is the fundamental data structure in Spark representing an immutable, distributed collection of objects that can be processed in parallel.

What is the difference between RDD, DataFrame, and dataset?

RDD is low-level and offers full control, a DataFrame is a distributed collection of data organized into named columns, and a dataset combines RDD and DataFrame features, adding type safety.

What is lazy evaluation in Spark?

Spark doesn't execute transformations immediately. It waits until an action (like collect or count) is called, allowing for optimized execution planning.

What are transformations and actions in Spark?

Transformations (like map, filter) define a new RDD/DataFrame, whereas actions (like collect, count) trigger the execution of the transformations.

What is a SparkSession?

A SparkSession is the unified entry point to Spark functionality.

How does Spark achieve fault tolerance?

Through lineage and RDDS. If a partition is lost, Spark recomputes it using the transformation history from the original data.

What are partitions in Spark?

Partitions are chunks of data distributed across the cluster for parallel processing. More partitions usually mean better parallelism.

What is a wide transformation in Spark?

Wide transformations (like `groupByKey`, `join`) require shuffling data across the cluster and are more expensive than narrow transformations.

What is a shuffle operation in Spark?

Shuffling is the process of redistributing data across partitions, often caused by wide transformations, but the process is expensive.

How do you optimize Spark jobs?

By using techniques like caching, avoiding shuffles, choosing appropriate joins, broadcasting small tables, and tuning parallelism.

What is Spark SQL?

Spark SQL lets you execute SQL queries on structured data using DataFrames or datasets.

What are accumulators in Spark?

Accumulators are variables used for aggregating information (e.g., counters or sums) across tasks and are only readable by the driver.

How does caching work in Spark?

You can use `cache()` or `persist()` to store intermediate results in memory to avoid recomputation and improve performance for iterative tasks.

What is Spark Streaming?

Spark Streaming is a component of Spark that enables processing of real-time data streams using micro-batches.

What is coalesce vs. repartition in Spark?

Coalesce reduces partitions without shuffle, whereas repartition increases or redistributes partitions with shuffle.

System Design

How would you design a batch processing system?

When designing a batch processing system where data arrives in bulk (daily or hourly), I would use a scheduler such as Apache Airflow to trigger processing jobs at set intervals. These jobs would read input data from sources like files or databases, perform necessary transformations such as aggregation and cleaning, leverage Apache Spark for distributed processing, and then store the output in a data warehouse or data lake.

How do you handle failures in a data pipeline?

To handle failures in data pipelines, I would implement retries. I'd also use checkpoints or save intermediate states, especially for streaming pipelines, so that processes can resume from the last known good point. As monitoring and alerting are important, I'll integrate notifications via email to inform teams of failures. Additionally, orchestration tools like Airflow help manage dependencies and failure handling systematically.

What is data partitioning, and why is it important?

Data partitioning involves splitting large datasets into smaller, more manageable parts based on keys like date or region. This is important because it significantly speeds up query performance by limiting data scans to relevant partitions.

How would you design a simple data warehouse for an e-commerce company?

A data warehouse design for an e-commerce company would include fact tables such as Orders, Transactions, and Website Visits, paired with dimension tables like Customers, Products, Time, and Location. I would use a star schema for simplicity and maintainability. Data would be loaded daily from operational databases via batch processes, and analytics would be performed through SQL queries to generate reports and dashboards for business insights.

How would you design a data pipeline for real-time fraud detection?

For real-time fraud detection, I would ingest transactional events using a messaging system like Kafka. Processing would be done with stream processors such as Apache Flink or Spark Structured Streaming to apply fraud detection rules and anomaly checks. Real-time feature stores can enrich events with historical user behavior. The flagged transactions are then sent to alert topics, and all data is archived for audits. Key considerations here would include minimizing latency, ensuring data quality through schema validation, and implementing fault tolerance with checkpoints and monitoring.

How would you scale a warehouse for analytics across departments?

I would scale a data warehouse for analytics across departments by organizing data into data marts using star or snowflake schemas. For scalability, cloud warehouses offer elastic scaling, allowing separate compute clusters per department to prevent query interference. Data governance would be enforced with role-based access control.

How would you handle production ETL failures?

I would handle this by enforcing schema validations and designing my pipelines to be modular. For detection, orchestration tools like Airflow manage retries and send alerts on failures. When failures occur, I would triage by reviewing logs to identify the failing step, then roll back or patch as needed. Backfill jobs would also be used to recover missed data windows safely.

How would you design a data pipeline to ingest and process streaming data?

I'd use Kafka as the ingestion layer. For real-time processing, tools like Apache Flink or Spark Structured Streaming would apply necessary transformations, such as parsing, filtering, and enrichment. Raw data would be stored in data lakes, and processed data would be loaded into a data warehouse for analysis. Finally, results would be exposed via dashboards or APIs.

How would you design a data pipeline to handle schema evolution?

To handle schema evolution, I'd store data in schema-on-read formats like Parquet or Avro and use a schema registry to track versions.

Data Engineering Glossary

ACID — Set of properties (Atomicity, Consistency, Isolation, Durability) ensuring reliable database transactions.

Ad Hoc Query — A one-time query created for a specific analysis purpose, not regularly scheduled.

Aggregate Function — A function that performs a calculation on a set of values (e.g., SUM, AVG).

Algorithm — A step-by-step method for solving a problem or performing a task.

Alias — Alternative name for a database table or column, often used for simplicity.

Anomaly Detection — Identifying unusual patterns in data that do not conform to expected behavior.

ANSI SQL — A standardized version of SQL agreed upon by the American National Standards Institute.

API — Application programming interface; allows software components to communicate.

Append-Only — A data storage model where new data is only added, not modified.

Array — A data structure that holds a collection of elements, typically of the same type.

Artificial Intelligence — The simulation of human intelligence processes by machines.

Asset — A valuable piece of data, system, or infrastructure in an organization.

Authentication — Verifying the identity of a user or system.

Authorization — Granting access permissions to users or systems.

Autoscaling — Automatically adjusting resources based on system load.

Availability — Measure of a system's operational performance and uptime.

Backup — A copy of data stored separately to prevent data loss.

Batch Processing — Processing data in large blocks at scheduled times.

Big Data — Extremely large datasets that require specialized tools to manage and analyze.

Blob Storage — Object storage service for unstructured data like images and videos.

BLOB — Binary Large Object; stores large binary data like images or files.

Bottleneck — A point of congestion that limits system performance.

Bucket — A logical storage container in cloud object storage.

Build Pipeline — Automated process that builds, tests, and prepares code for deployment.

Business Intelligence — The technologies and strategies used for data analysis to inform business decisions.

CDC — Change data capture; identifies and captures changes made to data.

Cache — Temporary storage that helps speedup data retrieval.

Cartesian Join — Join that matches each row of one table with all rows of another table.

Catalog — Central repository that manages metadata about data assets.

Checkpointing — Saving the current state of a system to allow recovery after failure.

CI/CD — Continuous integration/continuous deployment; automating software development practices.

CLI — Command-line interface; text-based way to interact with software.

Cloud Computing — Delivery of computing services over the Internet.

Cluster — A group of servers or computers working together.

Cold Data — Infrequently accessed data that is stored in low-cost storage solutions, which are cheaper than primary or frequently accessed (hot) storage options.

Columnar Database — A database that stores data by columns rather than rows.

Compliance — Adhering to laws, regulations, and standards.

Compression — Reducing the size of data to save storage or transmission time.

Concurrency — Ability of a system to handle multiple operations at once.

Confidentiality — Ensuring information is accessible only to those authorized.

Consistency — Guarantee that a system will reach a correct state after a transaction.

Container — A lightweight, stand-alone package that contains software and its dependencies.

Contextual Data — Data that provides context about other data.

Continuous Data — Data that can take any value within a range.

Control Flow — The order in which operations or tasks are executed.

Correlation — Statistical relationship between two variables.

Cron Job — A scheduled task run at specified intervals on Unix systems.

CRUD — Create, Read, Update, Delete; basic operations for managing data.

Data Aggregation — Process of gathering and summarizing data.

Data Anonymization — Protecting privacy by removing identifiable information.

Data API — An interface to allow applications to access and manipulate data.

Data Catalog — Tool that organizes, manages, and searches metadata about datasets.

Data Cleansing — Process of detecting and correcting corrupted or inaccurate data.

Data Engineer — Professional who designs and builds systems for collecting, storing, and analyzing data.

Data Governance — Policies and processes that ensure data integrity, security, and usage.

Data Integration — Combining data from different sources into a single view.

Data Lake — Storage repository that holds raw data in its native format.

Data Lineage — Tracking the movement and transformation of data through systems.

Data Mart — Subset of a data warehouse focused on a specific business line.

Data Mesh — Decentralized approach to managing data architecture.

Data Migration — Moving data from one system to another.

Data Modeling — Designing data structures for storage and retrieval.

Data Pipeline — A series of processes that ingest, process, and store data.

Data Profiling — Analyzing data to summarize its structure, content, and quality.

Data Quality — Measure of the condition of data based on factors like accuracy and completeness.

Data Replication — Copying data from one location to another.

Data Retention — Policies for how long data is kept before being deleted.

Data Scientist — Professional who analyzes and interprets complex data.

Data Security — Protecting data from unauthorized access or corruption.

Data Sharding — Splitting a database into smaller pieces for scalability.

Data Silo — Isolated data storage not easily shared across systems.

Data Steward — Person responsible for ensuring data quality and governance.

Data Stream — Continuous flow of data generated in real time.

Data Synchronization — Keeping multiple data sources updated consistently.

Data Warehouse — Centralized repository for structured data used for reporting and analysis.

Database — Organized collection of data that can be accessed electronically.

Database Normalization — Organizing data to minimize redundancy.

Dataset — Collection of related data typically presented in a table.

Deadlock — A situation where two processes are waiting on each other indefinitely.

Deduplication — Removing duplicate copies of repeating data.

Default Value — A preset value assigned if no specific value is provided.

Delta Lake — Storage layer that brings ACID transactions to data lakes.

Denormalization — Adding redundancy to speed up read operations.

Deployment — Releasing a system or feature into a production environment.

Distributed System — A system where components are located on different networked computers.

DNS — Domain Name System; translates domain names into IP addresses.

Document Store — A NoSQL database designed to store and retrieve documents.

Downsampling — Reducing the resolution or frequency of data collection.

Drift — Changes in data, schema, or system behavior over time.

Dynamic Partitioning — Automatically creating table partitions based on incoming data.

Egress — Data leaving a system or network.

Elasticity — System's ability to dynamically scale resources up or down.

ELT — Extract, Load, Transform; loading data before transforming it.

ETL — Extract, Transform, Load; classic method for data integration.

Entity — An object or concept about which data is stored.

Entity Relationship Model — Diagram showing relationships between data entities.

Environment — The setup where software runs (e.g., dev, test, production).

Epoch Time — Number of seconds since January 1, 1970 (UTC).

Event-Driven Architecture — System design based on events triggering actions.

Exploratory Data Analysis (EDA) — Analyzing datasets to summarize their main characteristics.

Export — Sending data from one system to another format or location.

Failover — Automatic switching to a backup system in case of failure.

Federated Query — Query that retrieves data from multiple sources in one operation.

Field — Single piece of data in a record or table.

File System — System that manages how data is stored and retrieved on storage devices.

Filter — Operation to remove unwanted data based on conditions.

Flink — Open source stream-processing framework.

Foreign Key — A key used to link two tables together.

Full Outer Join — Combines all records from two tables, matching where possible.

Function — A reusable block of code that performs a specific task.

Garbage Collection — Automatic memory management process.

Git — A version control system for tracking changes in code.

GitHub — Hosting service for Git repositories.

Granularity — Level of detail represented by data.

Graph Database — A database that uses graph structures for semantic queries.

Hash Partitioning — Distributing data based on a hash function.

Health Check — Monitoring system that checks if components are working properly.

High Availability — System design that minimizes downtime.

Hive — Data warehouse infrastructure built on top of Hadoop.

Horizontal Scaling — Adding more machines to handle increased load.

Hot Data — Frequently accessed data stored in high-performance storage, usually stored in RAM.

IAM — Identity and Access Management; controls user access.

IDEMPOTENT — Operation that can be applied multiple times without changing the result.

Imputation — Filling in missing data values with substituted values.

Index — Data structure that improves the speed of data retrieval.

Ingestion — Process of collecting and importing data for use.

Infrastructure as Code (IaC) — Managing infrastructure using configuration files.

Instance — Single virtual machine running on a cloud platform.

Integration Test — Test to check whether combined parts of an application are working together.

Interactive Query — User-driven queries typically used for ad hoc analysis.

Interoperability — Ability of systems to work together.

IoT — Internet of Things; network of interconnected devices.

IP Address — Numerical label assigned to each device on a network.

Job — A scheduled unit of work in data processing.

Join — Combining rows from two or more tables based on a related column.

JSON — JavaScript Object Notation; lightweight data-interchange format.

Kafka — Distributed streaming platform.

Key — A field that uniquely identifies a record in a table.

Key-Value Store — Simple database using keys and associated values.

Kubernetes — System for automating deployment and management of containerized apps.

Latency — Delay between a request and its corresponding response.

Layered Architecture — Organizing a system into layers for better separation of concerns.

Load Balancer — Distributes network or application traffic across multiple servers.

Logging — Recording system events for monitoring or debugging.

Lookup Table — Table used to map, translate, or enrich datasets.

Machine Learning — Field of AI that uses data to train algorithms to make decisions.

MapReduce — Programming model for processing large datasets.

Materialized View — Precomputed table derived from a query.

Metadata — Data that describes other data.

Migration — Moving data or applications to a new environment.

Monitoring — Observing system performance in real time.

Namespace — Logical grouping of names to avoid conflicts.

Normalization — Organizing data to minimize duplication.

Notebook — Interactive document combining code, visualizations, and text.

NoSQL — Nonrelational database system for large, distributed data.

Null Value — A field with no assigned value.

Object Storage — Storage architecture that manages data as objects.

OLAP — Online analytical processing; systems optimized for query and analysis.

OLTP — Online transaction processing; systems optimized for transactional tasks.

On-Premises — Computing infrastructure hosted in-house rather than in the cloud.

Orchestration — Coordinating automated tasks and data flows.

Outlier — Anomalous data point significantly different from others.

Paginated Query — Query that retrieves results in chunks rather than all at once.

Parquet — Columnar storage file format.

Partition — Dividing a database or table into parts for performance.

Payload — Actual data transmitted over a network.

Performance Tuning — Optimizing systems for better efficiency.

Pipeline Orchestration — Managing the sequence and dependency of data processing tasks.

Platform as a Service (PaaS) — Cloud service that provides a platform for app development.

Primary Key — Unique identifier for table records.

Privacy by Design — Embedding privacy features in systems and processes from the start.

Polling — Regularly checking for updates or changes in data.

Polyglot Persistence — Using different types of databases for different needs.

PostgreSQL — Popular open source relational database known for extensibility.

Primary Key — Unique identifier for each record in a database table.

Privacy — The right to control access to personal information.

Process — An instance of a running program.

Profiling — Measuring code or system performance.

Projection — Selecting specific columns in a database query.

Provisioning — Preparing and equipping a system to provide services.

Pub/Sub — Publish-Subscribe messaging pattern for event-driven systems.

Query — A request for data or information from a database.

Query Optimization — Techniques to improve the speed and efficiency of database queries.

Queue — Data structure or service that stores messages or tasks to be processed.

RDBMS — Relational database management system; database based on relational model.

Real-Time Processing — Immediate processing of data as it is ingested.

Record — A complete set of fields representing a single item in a table.

Recovery — Process of restoring a system after a failure.

Redundancy — Duplication of critical components for fault tolerance.

Referential Integrity — Ensuring relationships between tables remain consistent.

Replication Lag — Delay between the primary and replica databases syncing.

Resharding — Redistributing data shards across servers.

Resilience — System's ability to handle failures and continue operating.

Resource Allocation — Assigning system resources to tasks.

REST API — Representational State Transfer; architecture for building web services.

Retention Policy — Rules about how long data is kept.

Reverse ETL — Moving data from a warehouse back into operational systems.

Rollback — Reverting database changes after a failed transaction.

Root Cause Analysis — Identifying the underlying cause of a problem.

Row-Level Security — Restricting access to rows in a database table.

Row-Oriented Database — Database that stores data by rows.

Runtime — The period during which a program is running.

Sampling — Analyzing a subset of data to infer characteristics about the full dataset.

Sandbox — Isolated environment for testing and development.

Scalability — Ability to handle growing amounts of work or expand.

Schema — Structure that defines the organization of data in a database.

Schema Evolution — Adapting a database schema as requirements change.

Schema Registry — Store and manage schemas for data serialization.

Scope Creep — Gradual expansion of project goals beyond original objectives.

SDK — Software development kit; tools for building applications.

Secure Socket Layer (SSL) — Protocol for encrypting Internet communications.

Security Audit — Examination of a system's security measures.

Self-Healing System — System capable of identifying and fixing problems autonomously.

Semi-Structured Data — Data that doesn't fit neatly into tables (e.g., JSON, XML).

Serialization — Converting an object into a format for storage or transmission.

Serverless — Cloud model where cloud providers manage the server infrastructure.

Sessionization — Grouping user activities into sessions for analysis.

Sharding — Splitting a database horizontally to spread load.

SLA (Service Level Agreement) — Contract defining service expectations between provider and client.

Slowly Changing Dimension (SCD) — Data warehouse technique to manage data that changes slowly over time.

Snapshot — A read-only copy of data at a specific point in time.

Snowflake Schema — Data warehouse schema with normalized tables.

Soft Delete — Marking data as deleted without actually removing it.

Spark — Open source distributed data processing engine.

Spatial Data — Data that represents the location, size, and shape of objects.

SQL Injection — A security attack that exploits vulnerabilities in SQL queries.

SQL — Structured Query Language; standard language for relational database management.

SSH (Secure Shell) — Protocol for secure network communication.

Stateful Application — Application that keeps track of client session information.

Stateless Application — Application that treats each request independently.

Streaming Data — Data continuously generated by sources.

Structured Data — Organized data that fits neatly into a table.

Subquery — Query nested inside another query.

Surrogate Key — Artificial key used instead of a natural key in a database.

Synthetic Data — Artificially generated data used for testing or training.

Table Scan — Reading every row in a table to find results.

Tagging — Adding metadata labels to data or resources.

Task — A unit of work in a workflow.

Tenant — A group of users sharing access to common infrastructure in a multi-tenant architecture.

Throughput — Amount of work a system can perform over a given time.

Time Series Data — Data points indexed in time order.

Tokenization — Replacing sensitive data elements with nonsensitive equivalents.

Transaction — A sequence of database operations treated as a single logical unit.

Transactional Database — Database optimized for transaction processing.

Transformation — Modifying or changing data as part of a pipeline.

Trigger — A database object that automatically executes a procedure in response to events.

TTL (Time To Live) — The lifespan of data before it is discarded.

UDF (User-Defined Function) — Custom function written by users for specialized computations.

UI (User Interface) — The means through which a user interacts with a system.

Unstructured Data — Data without a predefined model (e.g., text, video).

Upsert — Database operation that updates a record if it exists or inserts if it does not.

URI — Uniform Resource Identifier; a string that identifies a resource.

UUID — Universally Unique Identifier; unique ID used in databases.

Validation — Checking data for correctness.

Version Control — Managing changes to code or data.

Vertical Scaling — Increasing the capacity of a single machine.

Virtual Machine (VM) — Software emulation of a physical computer.

Visualization — Graphical representation of data.

VPC (Virtual Private Cloud) — Isolated network within a cloud provider.

Warehouse Schema — Organizational structure of a data warehouse.

Watermarking — Keeping track of the latest record processed in streaming data.

Workflow — Sequence of processes involved in completing a task.

Write-Ahead Log (WAL) — Log that records changes before they are committed to the database. It is commonly used in PostgreSQL and other databases to ensure durability during crashes.

YAML — Human-readable data serialization standard often used for configuration files.

YARN — Yet Another Resource Negotiator; resource management layer in Hadoop.

Zero Downtime Deployment — Deploying updates without interrupting service.

Index

NUMERICS

1NF. *See* first normal form
2NF. *See* second normal form
3NF. *See* third normal form
4NF. *See* fourth normal form
5NF. *See* fifth normal form

A

ABAC. *See* attribute-based access control
abacus, 2
access audits, 223
access control, 207, 216–217, 236
  access levels, 224–226
  authentication, 217–219
  authorization, 219–222
  models, 220
  principle of least privilege, 222–224
access control lists (ACLs), 221–222
access logs, 224
access tiers, 18
accessibility, data, 198, 199
ACID. *See* Atomicity, Consistency, Isolation, and
  Durability Compliance
ACLs. *See* access control lists
ad hoc requests, 23
administrator (access level), 224
aggregate functions, SQL, 68–71, 83–84
Agile methodology, 48, 49
AI. *See* artificial intelligence
AI/ML data engineers, 310–311
alerts
  access control, 224
  and cloud cost optimization, 305
  in data orchestration, 172–173

  data volume threshold, 194
ALTER command, 40
Amazon, 189, 261
Amazon EFS (Elastic File System), 284
Amazon Relational Database Service
  (RDS), 215–216
Amazon S3, 221, 285
Amazon Web Services (AWS), 280, 284
  availability of, 261
  Glue Data Catalog, 243
analytics data engineer, 310
AND statement, 65
Apache Airflow, 150, 287, 293
  DAGs in, 168, 284
  scheduling ETL pipeline with, 182–185
Apache Atlas, 243
Apache Cassandra, 260
Apache Flink, 163
Apache Hadoop, 257, 262–263, 301
  Hadoop Distributed File System, 263–265
  MapReduce, 263, 265–267, 271–272
  YARN, 266
Apache Iceberg, 29
Apache Spark, 150, 257, 259, 261, 267, 301
  architecture, 268
  Cluster Manager, 270
  DAG Scheduler and task execution, 271
  Driver Program, 269–270
  executors, 270–271
  and MapReduce, comparison, 271–272
  resilient distributed dataset, 267–268
  sample interview questions, 331–332
  Structured Streaming, 163
APIs, 6, 21, 216, 290
application monitoring system, 54

Printed and bound by CPI Group (UK) Ltd, Croydon, CR0 4YY

26/09/2025

14742287-0001